Kenmore

Micro/Convection Cooking

BENJAMIN

Home Economics Coordinator: LuAnne Dugan
Consulting Home Economists: Tammy Saxton, Betty Sullivan
Photography: Teri Sandison, Los Angeles

USER INSTRUCTIONS
PRECAUTIONS TO AVOID POSSIBLE EXPOSURE TO EXCESSIVE MICROWAVE ENERGY

(a) DO NOT ATTEMPT to operate this oven with the door open since open-door operation can result in harmful exposure to microwave energy. It is important not to defeat or tamper with the safety interlocks.

(b) DO NOT PLACE any object between the oven front face and the door or allow soil or cleaner residue to accumulate on sealing surfaces.

(c) DO NOT OPERATE the oven if it is damaged. It is particularly important that the oven door close properly and that there is no damage to the:
  (1) DOOR (bent)
  (2) HINGES AND LATCHES (Broken or loosened)
  (3) DOOR SEALS AND SEALING SURFACES

(d) THE OVEN SHOULD NOT BE ADJUSTED OR REPAIRED BY ANYONE EXCEPT PROPERLY QUALIFIED SERVICE PERSONNEL.

ISBN: 0-87502-205-7

Published by The Benjamin Company, Inc.
One Westchester Plaza
Elmsford, New York 10523

10 9 8 7 6 5 4 3 2

Printed in Japan

Part No. 14607

CONTENTS

Your Kenmore Micro/Convection oven provides a complete and exciting new world of cooking. You can now cook using the speed and efficiency of microwaves, the browning capabilities of convection, or a combination of both methods with micro/convection — all in a single cavity unit. Your kitchen now has the very latest technology that enables you to prepare simple or sophisticated recipes in a minimum amount of time and with the freedom and flexibility of a multi-purpose oven. We at Sears are confident that your new Kenmore oven will quickly become your favorite and most frequently used kitchen appliance.

There is nothing complicated about using this oven. All you need is a little understanding of the special possibilities it offers. Please take a few minutes to read the instructions here and in your Use & Care Manual to acquaint yourself with the principles and techniques involved in micro/convection cooking.

Beef Roast (page 58)

HOW YOUR OVEN WORKS

Convection ovens are very similar to the conventional ovens found in nearly everyone's home. The only difference is that convection ovens have a fan that assists in circulating heated air, thus bringing it more quickly and directly to the food being cooked. Because convection ovens and conventional ovens are so similar, very few changes are needed to adapt your conventional recipes for convection cooking. Perhaps the only adjustment will be how you attend to a food. The convection fan and concentrated heat require food to be turned or rotated more frequently. This helps to distribute heat evenly and provides better cooking results. For your information, heat-proof cookware may be used in convection cooking. **Also, throughout this book, the phrase "cook (convec)" refers only to convection cooking.**

In microwave cooking, ordinary electrical current is converted into high frequency microwaves, very much like the electromagnetic waves which bring us radio and television. Once these waves come in contact with moisture molecules, they cause these molecules to vibrate vigorously, thus producing friction heat similar to the heat generated by rubbing your hands together rapidly. It is this friction induced heat which actually cooks your food. A common misunderstanding about microwave energy is that it cooks the center of a food first. Actually the opposite is true. Microwaves first come in contact with moisture molecules on the outer surfaces of a food. The heat produced there is then conducted inward, which is why in a microwave oven you can cook a roast with a rare center, just as you would in a conventional oven. In short, in microwave cooking, just as in conventional cooking, food is cooked from the outside inward. As a word of assurance, the specially designed panel in the door of your oven prevents any and all microwave energy from escaping when your oven is operating in the microwave or micro/convection modes. Moreover, the oven shuts itself off automatically when the door is opened, thus preventing any accidental emission. **Throughout this book the phrase "cook (micro)" refers only to microwave cooking.**

In combination cooking, the best features of convection and microwave systems are brought together in a single, easy cooking method. The convection system heats, browns, and dries the surface of a food for crisping, while the microwave system adds speed and efficiency and prevents internal dehydration. For cooking poultry, many types of meat, pies, and other food, combination cooking will undoubtedly be your method of choice. **Throughout this book the phrase "cook (micro/convec)" refers to combination cooking.**

Microwave cooking calls for new techniques in arranging food, many of which create attractive cook-and-serve dishes.

A large beef roast takes longer to cook than the small portion of ground meat. If they were of equal weight, the roast would still take longer because of its greater density.

In this chapter you will be introduced to the basic principles of microwave, convection, and micro/convection cooking. Once you grasp these principles, using your new multi-mode oven will be easy and pleasurable. For example, as you will soon see, using the microwave method requires a knowledge that some food items cook faster than others because of their high moisture content or low density. By the same token, microwave cooking uses certain terms and methods that are different from those you may be familiar with in conventional cooking. Many foods cooked by the microwave method, for instance, actually complete their cooking time during *standing time*, after being removed from the oven. Moreover, how food is arranged in the cooking dish is important to how evenly it cooks. These and similar types of information found in this chapter will give you the foundation for gaining self-confidence with your new oven, allowing you to apply what you know to all sorts of recipes and cooking situations, whether microwave, convection, or micro/convection, from this cookbook and elsewhere.

ABOUT TIMING

Temperature settings and timings given for conventionally cooked recipes are meant to be guides to good cooking. This is also true for microwave, convection, or micro/convection cooking. You, the cook, have to be the judge as you consider your family's preferences and use your own instincts. Chances are, you can tell if a chicken is done simply by looking at it.

You might even scoff at the timing chart given on a package because you know that a particular food always seems to need more or less time. It is important to know that even though this oven is a marvel of computer technology, it is no more or less precise than any other cooking device.

Nevertheless, because of the speed with which it cooks, timing is more crucial in microwave cooking than in conventional cooking. When you consider that a cooking task requiring one hour in a conventional oven generally needs only one-quarter of that time with the microwave method, you can understand why microwave cooking requires a somewhat different approach to timing. Where an extra minute in conventional cooking is seldom critical, that same minute in microwave cooking can spell the difference between overcooked and undercooked food.

The same precautions about timing apply to micro/convection cooking. However, when combination cooking is used, the microwave mode cycles on and off, which makes timing somewhat less critical.

Convection cooking does not call for any more attention to timing than conventional cooking.

As you become familiar with your oven, you will recognize when to begin to check for doneness. **Remember that it is better to undercook and add more cooking time than to risk overcooking — then it's too late.**

Cooking times for the recipes in this book have been determined for you, of course. They are precise, but they can vary according to the quantity of food being cooked, its temperature prior to cooking, and other factors.

Cooking times would always be precise if a way could be found to guarantee that all foods would be exactly the same each time we cooked them, and if the electric company would maintain a constant power output (there are frequent changes in the voltage levels reaching our homes). The fact is that one potato or one steak differs from another in density, moisture or fat content, shape, weight, and temperature. This is true for all food. Consequently, the cook must be ready to adjust to these changes, to be flexible and observant. After all, you, and not the oven, are the cook.

While your oven can measure the internal temperature of a food when the temperature probe is used, it can't make judgments. You must do that. All of the recipes have been thoroughly kitchen tested by expert home economists. As in all fine cooking, however, cooking with this oven is enhanced by the personal touch you bring to it. As you cook, feel free to alter the timing.

Quantity

In conventional cooking, it is not always necessary to alter cooking time when increasing the quantity. It takes no longer to bake 4 potatoes than 2 in the conventional oven. In microwave cooking, more food requires more cooking time. One potato cooks in about 5 minutes; 3 potatoes may cook in 11 minutes; and 5 potatoes in about 18 minutes. Therefore, if the quantity in a recipe is changed, an adjustment in the timing is necessary.

When changing the quantity of a microwave or micro/convection recipe on your own, follow this general rule: When doubling, increase the cooking time by approximately 50 percent. When cutting a recipe in half, reduce the time by approximately 40 percent. Treat timing adjustments for quantity in convection cooking just as you would for conventional cooking.

Density

Dense food, such as potatoes, roast beef, and carrots take longer to cook than porous food, such as cakes, ground beef, or broccoli. Another characteristic of microwave energy is that it takes longer to penetrate denser substances. For that reason, more cooking time is needed to cook a 2-pound beef roast by the microwave method than is needed to cook a 2-pound meat loaf.

Shape and Size

In microwave cooking, thin cuts of food cook faster than thick cuts; small pieces cook faster than large. Because it is the unique nature of microwave energy to cook from the outside inward, this suggests how food of differing shapes and sizes should be arranged in order to get optimum cooking results. Thick or large pieces should be placed toward the outer edge of the cooking dish, while thin or small pieces should be placed toward the center. Where a single food item varies in shape, once again the thick portion should be toward the outer edge of the dish, with the thinner portion toward the center. A chicken drumstick, for instance, would have the bony end pointing inward. For best results, try to cook pieces of similar size and shape together.

Irregularly-shaped food is a special microwave cooking challenge. It should be placed in the dish with the thickest portions toward the outer edge of the dish. The center of the dish receives less microwave energy.

Moisture Content

In microwave and micro/convection cooking, food with a high moisture content cooks faster than dry food because the microwave energy is more easily absorbed by the moisture in the food. One cup of sliced zucchini, for instance, will cook faster than one cup of carrots because of the higher water content of the zucchini. In short, the amount of moisture within a food affects how rapidly it cooks.

Delicate Ingredients

The term "delicate" refers to food that cooks so quickly by the microwave method that it can easily overcook, toughen, curdle, or separate. Mayonnaise, cheese, eggs, cream, and dairy sour cream are a few of the most common items that fall into this category. Other food, such as snails, oysters, and chicken livers may actually "pop" or burst as a result of steam trapped beneath an outer membrane. **For this reason, a lower power setting is often recommended for cooking "delicate" items properly. When delicate ingredients are used in combination with other food, as in casseroles, stews, or soups, you may use a higher power setting, as the increased volume automatically slows down the cooking process.**

The amount of moisture within a food will determine how fast it cooks. With less moisture than zucchini, carrots take a bit longer to cook by the microwave method.

Starting Temperature

As in conventional cooking, the temperature at which food is placed in the microwave oven affects its cooking time. More time is needed to cook food just out of the refrigerator than food at room temperature. It takes longer, for example, to heat frozen green beans than canned green beans. By the same token, hot tap water comes to a boil sooner than cold water. **Recipes in this book assume that food is at its normal storage temperature.**

Sugar and Fat Content

Because microwave energy is drawn to sugar and fat, food which is high in these substances cooks more quickly than food that is low. This principle also applies to single food items with varying amounts of sugar and fat. For instance, the fruit or cheese filling of a sweet roll contains more sugar and therefore will heat faster than the roll itself. The roll may be warm to the touch upon coming from the oven while its center may be hot enough to burn your mouth. It is important to keep this in mind when using the microwave or micro/convection methods to cook items of a similar nature.

The high sugar content in the filling of a sweet roll will cause it to become very hot in an extremely short time. A plain roll reheats less quickly.

ABOUT COOKWARE

A wide variety of cookware and cooking utensils can be used in this oven. To show that an item is safe and recommended for microwave cooking, we have created a new term, *microproof*. The *Materials Checklist* and *Guide to Cookware* on the following pages will assist you in selecting the appropriate utensil for each cooking method. With the exception of metal, most materials are microproof for at least a limited amount of cooking time. Unless specifically approved, however, items made of metal, even partially, are never to be used with the microwave method, because they reflect microwaves and prevent them from passing into the food. In addition, metal that touches the oven walls will create a static charge and cause sparks, a condition known as arcing. Though arcing is not harmful to you, it will deface your oven. That is why we advise that, when used, all metal should be kept at least 1 inch from the oven walls when your oven is operating in either the microwave mode or micro/convection mode.

When selecting a new piece of cookware for microwave or micro/convection cooking, first check the manufacturer's directions. Also review the *Materials Checklist* and the *Guide to Cookware*. If you are still in doubt, try this test: Pour a cup of water into a glass measure and place in the oven next to the container or dish to be tested. Cook (micro) on HI for 1 minute. If the new dish feels hot, don't use it — it is absorbing microwave energy. If it feels warm, the dish may be used only for warming food. If it remains at room temperature, it is *microproof*.

Micro/Convection Cookware

The rules governing use of cookware for micro/convection cooking are easy to learn. **Simply remember that a piece of cookware must be suitable for both microwave use and convection use whenever it is to be placed on the wire rack.** The key here, of course, is the wire rack. Because of heat generated during the convection cycle of the micro/convection mode, the rack becomes very hot, just as it does in a conventional oven. Items such as plastic or paper that may have been perfectly safe for microwave use are now unsafe on the hot rack. As we all know, hot metal can melt plastic and even cause paper to ignite. **However, when a recipe calls for use of the ceramic tray rather than the wire rack, an item of cookware need only be heatproof.** Metal is acceptable for use on the ceramic tray during the micro/convection mode as long as it is kept at least 1 inch from the oven walls to prevent arcing.

Selecting Containers

Containers should accommodate the food being cooked. Whenever possible use round or oval dishes for the microwave method, as square corners in cookware attract higher concentrations of microwave energy, which overcooks food in those areas. Some cake and loaf recipes call for ring molds or bundt pans to help food cook more evenly as the center of a round or oval dish generally cooks more slowly than the outside. When a particular size or shape of container is specified in a recipe, it should be used. Varying the container size or shape may change the results. A casserole in a recipe refers for instance to a bowl-shaped cooking dish with its own lid. An 11 x 7-inch baking dish refers to a shallow cooking dish. For liquids, large containers are specified to prevent them from boiling over. **For best results, always try to use the dish cited in the recipe rather than substituting a different dish.**

Heatproof glass and ceramic cookware can be used for the microwave, micro/convection, and convection methods. Metal cookware can be used only for convection cooking.

Many plastic items are safe for microwave cooking use. Always check the manufacturer's recommendations.

GUIDE TO COOKWARE

ITEM	USE	MICRO	MICRO/CONVEC	CONVEC
Aluminum foil products	Shielding, broiling, many cooking functions	ltd.	ltd.	ok
Boilable pouches	Heating frozen food	ok	no	no
Candy thermometers	Making candy	*	*	*
Cast aluminum, stainless steel, cast iron	Most cooking functions	no	ltd.	ok
China plates, cups	Heating	ok	no	no
Corelle ®	Heating, cooking vegetables	ok	*	*
Corning Ware ®	Most cooking functions	ok	ok	ok
Metal pans	Most cooking functions	no	ltd.	ok
Metal-trimmed or glazed pottery	Cooking casseroles, soup, many cooking functions	no	no	ok
Oven cooking bags	Cooking roasts, poultry	ok	ok	ok
Paper towels, plates, liners, cups, etc.	Covering, heating, or cooking (as specified)	ok	no	no
Plastic wrap	Covering	ok	no	no
Plastic cookware, dishes, roasting racks	Heating, cooking, elevating food	ok	*	*
Pottery, earthenware, clay cookers	Most cooking functions	ok	ok	ok
Pyrex ®, and heatproof glass	Most cooking functions	ok	ok	ok
Soft plastics, sherbet cartons	Reheating for very short periods	ok	no	no
Microproof meat thermometers	Determining internal temperature of food	ok	ok	ok
Waxed paper	Covering	ok	no	no
Wood products	Spoons for stirring, skewers for kabobs	ok	no	no
Straw baskets (no metal trim)	Warming bread	ok	no	no

*Check manufacturer's recommendations. Must be microproof for microwave or micro/convection use and heatproof for convection use.
ltd. = limited use approved. See "About Cookware" and "Materials Checklist."

Materials Checklist

CHINA, POTTERY: Ideal for microwave use. However, if trimmed or glazed with metal, these items are not microproof and should be used only for convection cooking.

GLASS: Excellent cooking material for microwave, micro/convection, and convection cooking. Since ovenproof glass is always safe, "microproof" is not mentioned in any recipe where a glass item is specified.

METALS: Excellent for convection. Limited use *on the ceramic tray only* for micro/convection cooking. Not suitable for microwave cooking, except as follows:

Small strips of aluminum foil can be used to cover areas on large pieces of meat or poultry that defrost or cook more rapidly than other areas, for example, exposed bones or thin ends of a roast, or the wings or breastbone of poultry. In microwave cooking, this method is known as *shielding.*

Shallow aluminum frozen TV *dinner trays* with foil covers removed can be heated using the microwave method, provided the trays are not more than ¾-inch deep. Many convenience dinners come packaged, however, in containers ready for microwave use. As always, read the manufacturer's instructions.

Frozen poultry containing metal clamps may be defrosted in your microwave oven until the clamps can be comfortably removed.

Any item made of foil or metal must be kept at least 1 inch from oven walls.

WICKER AND WOOD: Can be used for microwave method only. No metal may be present in the utensil, as when what appears to be wicker is really plastic coated wire.

PAPER: Can be used for microwave method only. Not recommended for prolonged cooking or extended use, as paper is flammable. Paper plates may be used for cooking and reheating as long as they are not foil-lined. Waxed paper is a suitable covering.

PLASTICS: When using the microwave mode, use plastic utensils marked for microwave cooking and follow manufacturer's instructions. Plastics should not be used when operating your oven in the micro/convection or convection modes. Plastic wrap is a suitable covering when recommended for microwave use.

PLASTIC COOKING POUCHES: Can be used when marked for microwave cooking. Slit pouch to relieve steam.

Wire Rack

Your oven's wire rack has been designed to provide two different rack positions by simply inverting it. When placed in the guides located on the side walls of the oven in such a way that its wire platform is higher than the guides themselves, the rack is said to be in its UPPER POSITION. When inverted, it is in its LOWER POSITION (see accompanying photographs). Every recipe in this book calling for use of the wire rack will specify which position is needed.

The wire rack is used in the micro/convection and convection modes only, its various positions actually assisting in the cooking process by helping to distribute heat most effectively. When the oven is operating only in the microwave mode, the wire rack has limited uses. See Whole Meal Cooking, pages 136-138.

For quick reference on proper use of the wire rack, see the Accessories Guide (page 12).

Ceramic Tray

Because the ceramic tray is used for all microwave cooking, you will likely find it to be your most frequently used cooking surface. Moreover, the tray remains in the oven during micro/convection cooking, even when a recipe calls for the wire rack as the primary cooking surface. As a rule of thumb, we feel it best to handle the tray as little as possible, especially when its presence does not hamper the effectiveness of your oven when operating in the micro/convection mode.

When your oven is operating solely in the convection mode, the ceramic tray should be removed. Not only does it absorb heat that otherwise should be absorbed by the food being cooked, thereby lessening the cooking results, but it also becomes very hot from convection heat and must be handled with extreme care. As is often the case, where a recipe calls for use of the microwave mode as a preparatory cooking stage, the ceramic tray should be removed before completing the recipe in the convection mode. As the tray will not become hot from microwave energy, less care is needed when handling it.

In all there are only two general rules to remember for use of the ceramic tray:
(1) The tray should be in the oven whenever the microwave mode or micro/convection mode is used.
(2) The tray should be removed from the oven when the convection mode is used.

For quick reference on proper use of the ceramic tray, see the Accessories Guide (page 12).

The wire rack is shown here placed correctly in the UPPER POSITION of the oven.

The wire rack is shown here placed correctly in the LOWER POSITION of the oven.

ACCESSORIES GUIDE

METHOD	WIRE RACK	CERAMIC TRAY
Microwave	Remove from oven (Exception, Whole Meal Cooking).	Always use for microwave method.
Micro/Convection	Rack position specified by recipe. Never use metal containers on wire rack when in the micro/convection mode.	Remains in oven for micro/convection method.
Convection	Rack position specified by recipe.	Remove from oven.

Metal Pans for Micro/Convection Cooking

As noted earlier, metal acts as a barrier to microwaves. For that reason, the use of metal pans with the micro/convection method is generally not advised. Occasionally, however, metal pans can be used in micro/convection cooking if they are placed only on the ceramic tray. **(Never use metal pans when cooking on the wire rack during the micro/convection mode, as metal touching metal during the microwave cycle will cause severe arcing and will most certainly damage your oven.)** When metal pans are used for micro/convection cooking, food cooks only from the top down during the microwave cycle, as the top is the only area not shielded by metal from the microwaves. Except for a minimum of recipes that call for them, we recommend using metal pans in micro/convection cooking as little as possible. Of course, they are never to be used when your oven is operating only in the microwave mode.

ABOUT TECHNIQUES

The speed and effectiveness of microwave and micro/convection cooking are not only determined by the characteristics of food, but also by certain cooking techniques. You likely have used many of these techniques before in conventional cooking, but they do have particular applications with this oven due to the special qualities of microwave energy. Techniques used regularly in conventional cooking will continue to be important when cooking with the convection method.

Read the following discussions of terms and techniques with care. With a thorough understanding of their significance, you will be well on your way to becoming a self-confident cook with your new micro/convection oven.

Rotating

Because the circulation fan in a convection oven actually forces heated air into the oven cavity, food directly in the path of the concentrated heat tends to cook more quickly than food farther from the heat source. This is particularly true for smaller size ovens created for home use, such as your own. To lessen the effect of concentrated heat, food cooked by the convection and micro/convection methods should be rotated periodically, actually turned a quarter or half turn. Pies, cakes, and other baked goods in particular would rise or cook unevenly if not rotated at some point during the cooking process. For that reason, recipes in this book specify when to rotate a food in order to achieve maximum cooking results. When adapting your own recipes to the convection or micro/convection methods, remember the nature of convection heat, and don't forget to rotate, especially when a food must cook for an extended period of time.

Turning Over

As in conventional cooking, large roasts, whole poultry, hams, or hamburgers may have to be turned over to brown each side and heat evenly. Microwave defrosting also frequently calls for food to be turned over.

Stirring

Less stirring is required when cooking by the microwave method than when cooking conventionally. When a recipe does ask you to stir, however, stir from the outer edge of a dish toward its center, as food on the outside cooks faster. In addition to helping food heat more easily, stirring blends flavors.

Arrangement

How food is arranged in the oven and in the dish is directly related to how evenly and quickly your oven will defrost, heat, and cook when the microwave and micro/convection methods are used. Since microwaves penetrate the outer portions first, food should be arranged so that the denser, thicker areas are near the edge of the dish, with the thinner, more porous areas near the center. When cooking broccoli, for example, split the heavy stalks to expose more area to the microwaves and then overlap with florets. Or you can alternate florets of cauliflower with broccoli. This not only distributes the density of the food, which allows it to cook more evenly, but it creates an attractive dish as well. Similarly, place shrimp in a ring with the tails toward the center. Arrange chicken legs in a spoke-like fashion with the bony ends toward the center.

In microwave cooking, most items are arranged in a circle, rather than in rows. Muffins and potatoes are good examples of this principle.

Rearranging

Sometimes food that can't be stirred must be rearranged in the dish to allow it to heat evenly. Move the center food to the outer edge of the dish and outer food toward the center. Some poultry and beef recipes profit when the food is rearranged halfway through the cooking time. Be sure to use tongs and pot holders when cooking with the micro/convection or convection method because the dishes and oven will be hot.

Rolled fish fillets and chicken legs are shown properly arranged for microwave-method cooking.

Arrange potatoes end to end in a ring when cooking with the microwave or micro/convection methods.

Food that cannot be stirred, such as Swiss steak, may need to be rearranged in the dish to achieve the most uniform cooking results.

Shielding

When prepared by the microwave method, certain thin or bony areas of food may cook more quickly than thicker areas. Using aluminum foil to cover these more delicate areas, such as the wing tips of poultry, the head or tail of fish, or the breastbone of a turkey helps to shield them from overcooking, as microwaves are reflected by the foil. Shielding may also be used during defrosting to cover those portions that defrost more quickly. Whether cooking or defrosting, however, always keep the foil at least 1 inch from the oven walls, as foil, like any other metal, can cause arcing when your oven is operating in the microwave or micro/convection modes.

When a casserole lid is not available, plastic wrap approved for microwave use by the manufacturer makes an excellent substitute.

Covering

Covers suitable for microwave cooking may differ from those used for micro/convection and convection cooking. As microwaves do not produce heat in the oven cavity, paper towels, waxed paper, and plastic wrap make excellent covers, whereas to use these items when your oven is operating in its micro/convection or convection modes might signal disaster. The convection heat would likely melt the plastic wrap or cause the paper to ignite.

Here are some handy rules for choosing covers when cooking by the microwave method:

(1) Because it creates a very tight seal, plastic wrap traps steam and retains maximum moisture. It makes an excellent substitute for a casserole lid and often is the covering of choice for cooking vegetables.

(2) Waxed paper has dual properties. It retains heat while allowing steam to escape. It is best for covering meat, poultry, and fish.

(3) Paper toweling allows steam to escape and prevents splattering. It is especially useful for cooking and crisping bacon.

A word of caution: plastic wrap, waxed paper, and paper toweling may only be used for cooking by the microwave method. Casseroles which usually have their own lids are the best choice when covers are needed in micro/convection and convection cooking.

Browning

Microwave cooking is not known for its browning capabilities, though it is famous for its speed and efficiency. Convection cooking, on the other hand, produces excellent browning. For this reason, when browning or crisping are desirable, we recommend using the convection or micro/convection methods.

Standing Time

During standing time, heat continues to be conducted from the outside of the food to the center. After the oven is turned off, food may remain in the oven or be placed on a heatproof surface for standing time.

This procedure is an essential part of food preparation with the microwave method. Some foods, such as roasts, require standing time to allow the heat to spread evenly and to complete reheating or cooking. With cakes, pies, and quiches, standing time permits the center to finish cooking. During standing time outside the oven, place food on a flat surface, such as a heat-resistant breadboard or countertop, when using the microwave or micro/convection methods.

Beef roasts of the same weight illustrate the effect of standing time. The roast on the left was sliced immediately after the cooking time ended. The roast on the right was given its recommended 10-minute standing time and continued to cook to medium doneness.

Piercing allows steam to escape and prevents bursting in items such as squash, potatoes, and egg yolks.

Piercing

Because the skins and membranes of such foods as egg yolks, potatoes, liver, chicken giblets, eggplant, and squash retain moisture, it is necessary to pierce them before cooking. This allows steam to escape and prevents bursting during cooking time. For example, pierce sausage casing in several places before cooking. A toothpick may be used for egg yolks; a fork is best for potatoes. Pierce squash deeply several times with a long-tined fork.

Adjusting for High Altitudes

As in conventional cooking, microwave cooking at high altitudes requires adjustments in cooking time for leavened products like breads and cakes. Other food may require a slightly longer cooking time to become tender, since liquids boil at lower temperatures at higher altitudes. Usually, for every 3 minutes of microwave cooking time you must add 1 minute to compensate for the higher altitude. Therefore, a recipe calling for 3 minutes needs 4 minutes, and a recipe requiring 6 minutes needs 8 minutes. The wisest way to proceed is to start with the time given in the recipe and then check for doneness before cooking further. Remember: You can always add time, but you can't subtract it once a food is overcooked.

It may be advisable to consult your local utility for specific information about your area.

About Safety

As with any appliance, from food processors to refrigerators, you must exercise reasonable caution when using your oven in the microwave mode. Do not, for instance, heat baby bottles or baby food. Microwaves can cause pressure to build up inside the closed bottle, thereby possibly making the rubber nipple blow off and causing injury to yourself or to your child. Moreover, when boiling water, take special care when removing it from the oven. This is particularly true when reheating water that has already been heated and also when adding ingredients to hot water, for example when preparing instant soup. The rapid reoxygenation of the water, when adding instant coffee or soup granules, can cause it to erupt and possibly scald you.

For various reasons, we also recommend that you avoid using the microwave method for:

1. Cooking eggs *in* the shell. The steam build-up inside the membrane can cause the egg to explode and create a considerable mess in your oven. When cooking eggs out of the shell, remember to pierce the membrane with a toothpick so as to prevent a similar explosion.

2. Deep-fat frying. Cooking food in hot oil in the microwave oven is difficult and hazardous.

3. Popping corn. Do not attempt to pop corn in a paper bag. The corn can dehydrate and overheat, possibly causing the bag to catch fire. Many microwave popcorn products are on the market today which are safe for microwave use. Always read manufacturer's instructions.

Follow these precautions, use the microwave feature of your oven with common sense and safety in mind, and you will be assured of years of enjoyable and trouble-free cooking.

Your micro/convection oven is a multi-mode cooking appliance that gives you a great deal of cooking flexibility. Where speed and efficiency are high priorities, you have the microwave mode at your disposal. Where browning and crisping are desired, you have the convection mode. Or you may have the best of both methods with the micro/convection mode. As each of these three methods has its own particular strengths and virtues, your oven allows you to achieve maximum results from the greatest number of cooking situations. The microwave method is far superior to any other method for retaining moisture and freshness of cooked vegetables. Moreover, it has no equal in the field of defrosting. Its only drawback is its inability to brown food well. But then, when browning is a priority, you have the convection method for preparing meat and baked goods. All in all, you will find very few cooking needs your micro/convection oven won't satisfy.

Before looking at the unique features of your oven, we'd like to direct your attention to the Use and Care Manual which accompanies this cookbook. In addition to giving directions for the correct installation of your oven, the Use and Care Manual provides everything you need to know to operate your oven properly. It contains additional information about your oven's features, detailed step-by-step instructions for programming the oven, and much more. Please give it careful review.

The temperature probe is one of many special features designed into your oven. Here the probe is shown inserted properly in a beef roast. Similar placement of the probe is used for hams.

The probe is always inserted into the densest area of a food. Here it is placed properly in the inside thigh muscle of a chicken.

WHAT TO USE WHEN

Though each recipe in this book specifies which cooking mode to use, there undoubtedly will be times when you wish to use your own recipes or adapt recipes from other cookbooks. The GUIDE TO COOKING METHODS (page 17) was designed for just such occasions. "Best" refers to the cooking method that produces the most satisfactory results when cooking a particular food type. Equal and alternate methods are listed as "Good." If a method is not recommended, "No" appears. For recipes that require multistage preparation, you will soon acquire a feel for which cooking method serves the recipe's needs best.

TOUCH PADS

The touch pads on your oven's control panel need only be touched to be activated. A beep will sound to show a setting has been entered. Moreover, indicator lights will appear in your oven's display window to confirm what setting has been received.

As you can see from its control panel, your oven has touch pads for many unique features, ranging from QUICK-ON to PAUSE. Descriptions of these features, as well as detailed discussions of how they are properly programmed, are presented thoroughly in your Use and Care Manual.

GUIDE TO COOKING METHODS

FOOD	MICRO	MICRO/CONVEC	CONVEC
Appetizers	Good	Good	Good
Bread, baking rising	No Best	Good No	Best No
Cakes, batter angel food	Good No	Good No	Best Best
Candies	Best	No	No
Casseroles	Good	Best	Good
Cookies, drop bar	No Good	Good Best	Best Good
Defrosting	Best	No	No
Eggs	Best	Good	Good
Fruit	Best	Good	Good
Hot drinks	Best	No	No
Meat, roasting	Good	Best	Good
Pies, 1-crust 2-crust	Good No	Best Best	Good Good
Poultry	Good	Best	Good
Quiches	Good	Best	Good
Reheating	Best	Good	Good
Sauces	Best	No	No
Seafood, poaching broiling	Best No	Good Good	No Best
Soup	Best	Good	No
Vegetables	Best	Good	No

MICROWAVE "MULTI-POWER"

The "multi-power" feature of your oven's microwave mode allows you to select any setting from 0 (0% power) to 100 (100% power, or HI). This enables you to cook with more control and accuracy, as your oven can be set to suit the food being cooked.

While a majority of recipes in this book using the microwave mode call for cooking on HI, some food needs to be cooked more slowly. To simplify things for you, the **GUIDE TO "MULTI-POWER" SETTINGS** (right) lists the main microwave power settings recommended for a variety of cooking situations. You will find it especially useful when adapting your own recipes to the microwave method.

GUIDE TO "MULTI-POWER" SETTINGS

POWER LEVEL	POWER SETTINGS	SUGGESTED COOKING USES
10	WARM	· Softening cream cheese · Keeping casseroles and main dishes warm
20	LOW	· Softening chocolate · Heating breads, rolls, pancakes, tacos, tortillas and french toast · Clarifying butter · Taking the chill out of fruit · Heating small amounts of food
30	DEFROST	· Thawing meat, poultry, and seafood · Completing the cooking cycle of casseroles, stews, and some sauces · Cooking small quantities of most food
40	BRAISE	· Cooking less tender cuts of meat in liquid or slow cooking dishes · Completing the cooking cycle of less tender roasts
50	SIMMER	· Cooking stews and soups after bringing to a boil · Cooking baked custards and pasta
60	BAKE	· Cooking scrambled eggs · Cooking cakes
70	ROAST	· Cooking rump roast, ham, veal, and lamb · Cooking cheese dishes · Cooking quick breads and cereal products
80	REHEAT	· Reheating precooked or prepared food quickly · Heating sandwiches
90	SAUTE	· Cooking onions, celery, and green peppers quickly · Reheating meat slices quickly
100 (HI)	MAX POWER	· Cooking tender cuts of meat · Cooking poultry, fish, vegetables, and most casseroles · Preheating the browning dish · Boiling water · Thickening some sauces

TEMPERATURE PROBE

When properly inserted, the temperature probe enables you to cook food to a preselected internal temperature. In addition, your oven is designed with a HOLD WARM feature which allows food to maintain its desired temperature for up to 1½ hours once its actual cooking time has ended.

When using the probe, rather than programming the oven to cook a certain number of minutes, you instead program the temperature a food is to reach prior to standing time. (Standing time is, as we noted earlier, that period of time needed to raise a food to its final desired temperature once the oven has stopped.) In the microwave mode, if a power level other than 100% or HI is required (see GUIDE TO "MULTI-POWER" SETTINGS), the lower power level must be set by using your oven's MICRO POWER feature. In the convection mode, the actual temperature of the oven's interior must be programmed by using the OVEN TEMP/PREHEAT feature. As you will remember, microwaves do not heat the oven cavity itself, but rather go directly to the food. With convection cooking, on the other hand, the heat of the oven's interior is what does the cooking.

For the probe to read the internal temperature of a food accurately, it must be inserted properly. An easy guideline to remember is this: **the probe tip must be inserted into the densest portion of a food, that part which cooks most slowly.** For proper placement in a casserole, the probe should stand vertically in the center of the dish. For a roast or ham, it should be inserted horizontally into the thickest part of the meat. For poultry, it should enter the thigh, between the breast and thigh muscle. Another important rule to remember when using the temperature probe is: **the probe must never be inserted in such a way that it touches fat, bone, or metal foil being used for shielding, as these substances cause the probe to give misleading readings of the doneness of a food.** Fat, for instance, is very high in moisture and cooks more quickly than meat, as you'll remember from our discussion of "Sugar and Fat Content" in the preceding chapter. Therefore, were the probe to base the internal temperature of an entire roast on the temperature of cooking fat, the meat itself would turn out considerably underdone.

Care of the probe is quite simple. After using it, wash the metal probe tip in warm, soapy water, that part, in other words, which was inserted into the food. Then rinse and dry. Do not immerse the entire probe in water or wash it in a dish washer.

Suggested Temperature Probe Settings

As standing time is an essential part of the total cooking process when using the microwave method, an allowance must be made for cooking that occurs

Soups, casseroles, and similar dishes can be cooked using the temperature probe. Cover with plastic wrap and tuck wrap around the probe, as shown here.

once your oven has stopped. Therefore, the temperature at which you program the probe will not be the final temperature a food reaches before serving.

For example, a roast beef cooked to 120°F will rise to 135°F after 10 minutes of standing time, which is the proper serving temperature for rare beef. When taken out of the oven at 165°F, lamb will rise to its proper serving temperature of 170°F to 180°F. In general, you can assume the temperature of most food will increase 5° to 15° during standing time, the primary exception being liquids. Coffee and other heated beverages actually drop from 150°F to 135°F during 10 minutes of standing time.

While the recipes and cooking guides in this book give you precise information regarding temperature probe settings and standing times, you will undoubtedly want to prepare your own recipes using the probe. As a general guide, you will find the following chart helpful.

Suggested Temperature Probe Settings
120°F Rare Beef
130°F Medium Beef, Fully Cooked Ham
140°F Fish Steaks and Fillets, Well Done Beef
150°F Vegetables, Hot Drinks, Soups, Casseroles
155°F Veal
165°F Well Done Lamb, Well Done Pork
170°F Poultry Parts
180°F Well Done Whole Poultry
Refer to individual Cooking Guides (see index) for specific instructions.

Programming the Temperature Probe

To prepare food for probe cooking, place food in the container called for by specific recipe. Insert the probe in such a way that the first inch of the probe tip is fastened securely in the center of the food. As we have said, the probe should not touch fat, bone, or aluminum foil used for shielding. Except when cooking casseroles or heating liquids, insert the probe as horizontally as possible. Plug probe into the receptacle on the side wall of oven cavity. The probe should not touch the cooking container or any part of the oven's interior.

For cooking by the **Convection** method, touch OVEN TEMP/PREHEAT. Then touch the number pads representing the desired preheat temperature. A temperature of 400°F is programmed, for example, by touching 4-0-0. **(Since your oven is designed to preheat automatically to 350°F in the convection mode, you need not program the oven with a preheat temperature anytime 350°F is desired.)** Then touch PAUSE. Once you have programmed the preheat stage, then touch CONVEC TEMP, followed by the number pads representing the internal temperature desired. Then press START. At this point your oven will begin preheating. Once it reaches its preheat temperature, it will flash PROBE in the display window of the control panel. At this point, place the food in the oven and plug the probe into the oven wall. Close the door and press START once again. When the food reaches its programmed internal temperature, your oven will signal with a beep.

For **Micro/Convection** cooking with the probe, follow the same steps used for the convection method. In place of touching CONVEC TEMP, touch MICRO/CONVEC TEMP. While the preheat stage is possible with the micro/convection method, it is often unnecessary.

For cooking by the **Microwave** method, touch MICRO/POWER to program the power level at which the food is to cook. Then touch the number pads representing this level. If 80% power is desired, you would touch 8-0. However, remember that this step is needed only when cooking on a power level other than 100%, or HI. As we pointed out earlier, your oven is designed to cook automatically on HI unless another power level is programmed. After setting the power level, then touch MICRO/TEMP, followed by the number pads representing the microwave probe temperature desired. Place the food in the oven. Plug in the probe. Touch START. It's as simple as that. Once again, your oven will beep when a food reaches its programmed probe temperature.

A few final words of caution regarding use of the probe: (1) Never operate the oven with the temperature probe in the cavity unless the probe is properly inserted in a food and also plugged in the oven's side wall; (2) Handle cooking containers with care when cooking by the probe method in the **convection and micro/convection modes, as they (and the oven) will be hot. Kitchen mittens or hot pads may be appropriate.**

DEFROSTING

The microwave method is the last word in defrosting. It's efficient. It's wonderfully fast, defrosting food in a fraction of the time required by conventional means. And now, due to the unique technology of your new Micro/Convection oven, it's more convenient than ever.

In addition to the Defrost Feature applicable to the particular oven model you have purchased, as described in detail by this chapter and by your Use and Care Manual, your Micro/Convection appliance gives you the option of defrosting manually. As you will see, the defrost information presented by defrosting guides in the meat, poultry, and seafood chapters of this book apply strictly to manual defrosting techniques. Some people like their oven essentially to do the defrosting on its own, with a minimal amount of attention. Others, however, enjoy taking a greater hand in the process, and in fact sometimes achieve even quicker results by attending manually to thawing food. At least by providing you with information for defrosting manually as well as for using a special microwave defrost mode, we have given you a greater range of choices as a cook.

Despite whatever method you choose, defrost mode or manual, many of the same principles and techniques that apply to cooking by the microwave method also apply to defrosting with microwaves. Microwaves are attracted to water or moisture molecules. As soon as they begin to thaw a food, they tend to be drawn to the increased moisture of the thawed portion. For this reason, special techniques can be indispensible for preventing the thawed portion from starting to cook before the rest is defrosted. When thawing ground beef, for example, you are asked to scrape away the thawed portions with a fork and return the remainder to the oven for further defrosting. Shielding is used to protect more delicate areas of food, such as the head and tail of fish or wing tips of whole poultry. Turning over and rotating are two techniques that help to distribute heat more evenly. In fact, you should be familiar with all of these terms, having been introduced to them in the section on TECHNIQUES in the last chapter.

General Defrosting Instructions

● Because of the unknown differences in such things as the fat content, density, and percentage of bone in food, defrosting times given in the DEFROST GUIDES in the meat, poultry, and seafood chapters are conservative. A general rule of thumb is that food should be "workable," though it may be somewhat icy when removed from the oven. Standing time will quickly complete the defrosting process.

● Two things must always be done when defrosting food in foil trays: (1) remove the top so that microwaves can reach the food; (2) even more importantly, keep the foil tray *at least 1 inch away* from the walls of the oven. Otherwise arcing may occur.

● Metal clips should be removed as soon as possible during the defrosting process. Metal twist-ties on bags should be replaced with rubber bands.

● All meat, poultry, and seafood wrappers should be removed before defrosting. Otherwise, steam can develop inside the closed package and cause portions to begin cooking.

● Plastic packaging for microwave-ready vegetables should be pierced to relieve steam. Precooked frozen vegetables defrost, as well as reheat, well on HI. (The normal power setting for defrosting is 30.)

● Thin or bony ends of poultry or fish may need to be "shielded" (covered with small strips of aluminum foil) to prevent these areas from beginning to cook while the rest defrosts.

● To help them thaw more evenly, larger items should be turned over and rotated halfway through defrost time. You may find that more frequent rotation and turning over produces even better results.

● Standing time is essential to defrosting anything that cooks very quickly, such as fish and seafood. Such items should be icy in the center when taken from the oven. Otherwise their edges may begin to cook while the rest is still defrosting.

● Food texture has a large effect upon the defrosting process, just as it does the cooking process. Relatively porous food such as cake and bread defrost very quickly and must be checked frequently.

● When thawing ground meat, defrost in stages, removing thawed portions with a fork and then returning the unthawed portion to the oven.

● Thin or sliced items, such as fish fillets and meat patties, should also be defrosted in stages. Thawed portions should be separated and removed and unthawed portions returned to the oven for further defrosting.

● Frequent stirring is recommended for thawing casseroles, sauced foods, and soups, as stirring distributes heat more evenly. For broth-based soup, begin defrosting on HI and reduce power to 50 halfway through defrosting time. For casseroles and cream-based soup, begin defrosting at 70 and reduce power to 30 halfway through defrosting time.

Programmed Defrost

If your oven is equipped with a Programmed Defrost feature (see Use and Care Manual or look for the touch pad on your oven's control panel displaying PROGRAMMED DEFROST), the following information applies to you.

To help familiarize you with the Programmed Defrost method, we have provided the following lesson plan to walk you through a typical defrosting situation. Let's begin by defrosting 2 pounds of ground beef.

1. As you will see from the PROGRAMMED DEFROST GUIDE — MEAT on page 21, the total defrost time for 2 pounds of ground beef is 8 to 9 minutes. The directions also call for removing thawed portions with a fork (top and bottom) halfway through defrost time, which means that we will divide the total defrosting process into two equal parts.

2. Unwrap beef and place in a microproof dish, to catch any drippings. Set dish on ceramic tray. (Remember that the ceramic tray must be in the oven when the microwave mode is in operation.) Close oven door.

3. Touch CLEAR. This erases any previous programming.

4. To program the first defrosting stage, touch PROGRAMMED DEFROST. Then touch 4-3-0, or 4 minutes 30 seconds, which is the first half of the total defrost time.

5. Touch START. After 4½ minutes of defrost time have elapsed, your oven will signal with a beep that it's time to attend to the food. Open door. Remove any thawed portions from ground beef and return remainder to oven. Close oven door.

6. Touch PROGRAMMED DEFROST. Then touch 4-3-0 for the second half of total defrost time.

START

7. Touch START. When the oven is finished, it will beep once again and turn off automatically. At this point, remove beef from oven and let stand 5 minutes, as called for in the DEFROST GUIDE. Standing time will complete the defrosting process.

While the foregoing program for defrosting ground beef gives you the essence of how to operate the Programmed Defrost feature, as well as how to use the PROGRAMMED DEFROST GUIDE, we have prepared additional sequences (in recipe form) for some of the most commonly defrosted foods. See page 23.

PROGRAMMED DEFROST GUIDE — MEAT

CUT AND WEIGHT	PROGRAMMED DEFROST TIME	STANDING TIME	DIRECTIONS
BEEF			
Flank steak	3 to 4 min. per lb.	5 - 10 min.	Turn over halfway through defrost time.
Ground beef 1 lb 2 lbs.	4 to 4½ min. 8 to 9 min.	5 min. 5 min.	Turn over once. Remove thawed portions with fork (top and bottom). Return remainder to oven to finish defrosting. The best way to freeze ground beef is in a doughnut shape.
Pot roast, chuck Under 4 lbs.	3 to 4 min. per lb.	10 min.	Turn over halfway through defrost time.
Rib roast, rolled 3 to 4 lbs.	5 to 7 min. per lb.	30 - 45 min.	Turn over halfway through defrost time.
Round steak	3 to 4 min. per lb.	5 - 10 min.	Turn over halfway through defrost time.
Rump roast 3 to 4 lbs.	3 to 5 min. per lb.	30 min.	Turn over halfway through defrost time.
Sirloin steak ½ inch thick	3 to 4 min. per lb.	5 - 10 min.	Turn over halfway through defrost time.
Stew beef 2 lbs.	3 to 4 min. per lb.	8 - 10 min.	Turn over halfway through defrost time.
Tenderloin steak	4 to 5 min. per lb.	10 min.	Turn over halfway through defrost time.
LAMB			
Cubed for stew	6 to 7 min. per lb.	5 min.	Turn over halfway through defrost time. Separate.
Ground lamb Under 4 lbs.	3 to 4 min. per lb.	5 - 10 min.	Turn over halfway through defrost time. Remove thawed portions with fork (top and bottom). Return remainder to oven to finish defrosting.
Chops 1 inch thick	4 to 6 min. per lb.	15 min.	Turn over twice (dividing defrost time into 3 periods).
Leg 5 to 8 lbs.	3 to 4 min. per lb.	15 - 20 min.	Turn over twice (dividing defrost time into 3 periods).
PORK			
Bacon 1 lb.	1½ to 2½ min.	3 - 5 min.	Defrost until strips separate.
Chops ½ inch thick 1 inch thick	4 to 5 min. per lb. 5 to 6 min. per lb.	5 - 10 min. 10 min.	Separate and turn chops over halfway through defrost time.
Roast Under 4 lbs.	3 to 4 min. per lb.	30 - 45 min.	Turn over halfway through defrost time.
Spareribs, Country-style ribs 2 to 3 lbs.	4 to 6 min. per lb.	10 min.	Turn over halfway through defrost time.

PROGRAMMED DEFROST GUIDE — MEAT (cont'd)

CUT AND WEIGHT	PROGRAMMED DEFROST TIME	STANDING TIME	DIRECTIONS
PORK (Cont'd)			
Sausage, bulk 1 lb.	1½ to 2½ min.	3 - 5 min.	Turn over halfway through defrost time. Remove thawed portions with fork (top and bottom). Return remainder to oven to finish defrosting.
Sausage, links 1 lb.	2 to 4 min.	4 - 6 min.	Turn over halfway through defrost time. Defrost until pieces can be separated.
VEAL			
Roast 3 to 4 lbs.	4 to 6 min. per lb.	30 min.	Turn over halfway through defrost time.
Chops ½ inch thick	3 to 5 min. per lb.	20 min.	Turn over halfway through defrost time. Separate chops and continue defrosting.
VARIETY MEAT			
Hot dogs 1 lb.	4 to 5 min.	5 min.	
Liver 1 lb.	4 to 5 min.	10 min.	Turn over halfway through defrost time.
Tongue 1 lb.	6 to 7 min.	10 min.	Turn over halfway through defrost time.

PROGRAMMED DEFROST GUIDE — POULTRY

ITEM AND WEIGHT	PROGRAMMED DEFROST TIME	STANDING TIME	DIRECTIONS
CHICKEN			
Whole 2 to 3 lbs.	5 to 7 min. per lb.	25 - 30 min.	Turn over halfway through defrost time. Immerse in cold water for standing time.
Cut up 2 to 3 lbs.	4 to 5 min. per lb.	10 - 15 min.	Turn over halfway through defrost time. Separate pieces when partially thawed. Shield if necessary. Rinse in cold water.
TURKEY			
Whole Under 8 lbs.	3 to 4 min. per lb.	60 min.	Turn over halfway through defrost time. Immerse in cold water for standing time.
Breast Under 4 lbs.	3 to 4 min. per lb.	20 min.	Turn over halfway through defrost time.
Drumsticks 1 to 1½ lbs.	4 to 5 min. per lb.	15 - 20 min.	Turn over halfway through defrost time. Separate pieces when partially thawed.
Roast, boneless 2 to 4 lbs.	2½ to 3 min. per lb.	10 min.	Remove from foil pan. Cover with waxed paper.
CORNISH HENS			
Whole 1 - 1 to 1½ lbs.	6 to 8 min. per lb.	20 min.	Turn over halfway through defrost time.

PROGRAMMED DEFROST GUIDE — FISH AND SEAFOOD

ITEM AND WEIGHT	PROGRAMMED DEFROST TIME	STANDING TIME	DIRECTIONS
FISH			
Fish fillets 1 lb. 2 lbs.	4 to 5 min. 5 to 6 min.	5 min. 5 min.	Remove from package and place in shallow microproof dish. Turn over halfway through defrost time. Carefully separate fillets under cold running water.
Fish steaks 1 lb.	4 to 5 min.	5 min.	Defrost in package on microproof dish. Turn over halfway thorugh defrost time. Carefully separate steaks under cold running water.
Whole fish 8 to 10 oz. 1½ lb. to 2 lbs.	3 to 5 min. 4 to 6 min.	5 min. 5 min.	Use shallow microproof dish that will hold whole fish. Cover head of fish with aluminum foil. Fish should be icy when removed. Standing time will complete defrosting.

PROGRAMMED DEFROST GUIDE — FISH AND SEAFOOD (cont'd.)

ITEM AND WEIGHT	PROGRAMMED DEFROST TIME	STANDING TIME	DIRECTIONS
Lobster tails 8 oz. pkg.	4 to 6 min.	5 min.	Remove from package to microproof dish.
Crab legs 8 to 10 oz.	4 to 6 min.	5 min.	Place in microproof dish. Break the legs apart. Turn over halfway through defrost time.
Crabmeat 6 oz.	3 to 4 min.	5 min.	Defrost in package on microproof dish. Break apart. Turn over halfway through defrost time.
Shrimp 1 lb.	2 to 3 min.	5 min.	Remove from package to microproof dish. Spread loosely and rearrange during thawing, as necessary.
Scallops 1 lb.	4 to 6 min.	5 min.	Defrost in package, if in block; spread out on microproof dish if in pieces. Turn over and rearrange during thawing, as necessary.
Oysters 12 oz.	2 to 3 min.	5 min.	Remove from package to microproof dish. Turn over and rearrange during thawing, as necessary.

CUT-UP CHICKEN

Defrost Time: 9 minutes

2 pounds frozen chicken parts

Remove chicken from package and place in microproof baking dish. Place in oven. Touch PROGRAMMED DEFROST. Touch 4-3-0. Touch START.

Turn parts over and separate. Cover any warm areas with small strips of aluminum foil, keeping foil at least 1 inch away from oven wall. Touch PROGRAMMED DEFROST. Touch 4-3-0. Touch START.

Rinse chicken parts in cold water. Let stand 10 to 15 minutes to complete thawing.

STEW BEEF

Defrost Time: 7 minutes

2 pounds frozen beef for stew

Remove beef from package and place in shallow microproof baking dish. Place in oven. Touch PROGRAMMED DEFROST. Touch 3-3-0. Touch START.

Turn beef over. Touch PROGRAMMED DEFROST. Touch 3-3-0. Touch START.

Let stand 8 to 10 minutes to complete thawing.

FISH FILLETS

Defrost Time: 5 minutes

1 pound frozen fish fillets

Remove fish from package. Place in shallow microproof baking dish. Place in oven. Touch PROGRAMMED DEFROST. Touch 2-3-0. Touch START.

Turn fillets over. Touch PROGRAMMED DEFROST. Touch 2-3-0. Touch START.

Carefully separate fillets under cold running water. Let stand 5 minutes to complete thawing.

PORK CHOPS

Defrost Time: 9 minutes

2 pounds frozen pork chops, 1/2 inch thick

Remove chops from package and place in microproof baking dish. Place in oven. Touch PROGRAMMED DEFROST. Touch 4-3-0. Touch START.

Separate and turn chops over. Touch PROGRAMMED DEFROST. Touch 4-3-0. Touch START.

Let stand 5 to 10 minutes to complete thawing.

Auto Defrost

If your oven is equipped with an Auto Defrost feature (See Use and Care Manual or look for touch pads on your oven's control panel displaying DEF1, DEF2, and DEF3), the following information applies to you.

To familiarize you with the Auto Defrost method, we have provided the following lesson plan. Additional information is given in your Use and Care Manual, but the essence of Auto Defrost is automatic preprogramming. Your oven only needs to know the type and weight of a food before it can begin defrosting on its own. It is designed, in other words, to interpret how long it will take to defrost a particular food at a particular weight, to pause when food needs attending to, and more.

Let's begin by defrosting 1 pound 8 ounces of ground beef:

1. Unwrap beef and place in a microproof dish, to catch any drippings. Set dish on ceramic tray. (Remember that the ceramic tray is always in the oven when the microwave mode is in operation.) Close oven door.

2. Touch CLEAR. This erases any previous programming.

3. As you will see from the AUTO DEFROST GUIDE— MEAT (page 25), ground beef defrosts on DEF1. Touch DEF1.

4. As the weight of a food is programmed by converting ounces into tenths of a pound, 1 pound 8 ounces of ground beef becomes 1.5 pounds. (Food may be entered in decimal increments from .1 to 9.9 pounds.)

    Touch 1-5. The amount entered will appear in your oven's display window.

START   `PAUS`

5. Touch START. The oven will begin defrosting automatically. Once the first stage of the defrosting sequence is complete, PAUS will appear in the display window and a beep will signal that it's time to attend to the food. As you will see from the "At Pause" column in the AUTO DEFROST GUIDE—MEAT, you must now remove any thawed portions of the ground beef with a fork (top and bottom) and return the remainder to the oven for the final defrosting sequence. Close oven door.

    NOTE: If the oven door is not opened during the pause time segment, the oven will restart automatically after 5 minutes. Because turning over, rotating, and separating are essential for achieving best defrosting results, follow the directions provided in the "At Pause" columns of the Auto Defrost Guides.

START

6. Touch START. The oven resumes defrosting and indicates in the display window how much defrost time remains. When it's done, it will once again signal with a beep and shut off automatically.

MEMORY/RECALL

7. NOTE: As explained thoroughly in your Use and Care Manual, your oven can be programmed to begin cooking automatically following the AUTO DEFROST sequence. After entering AUTO DEFROST information as described above, touch MEMORY/RECALL. Then set the time, power levels, and pauses necessary for up to 2 to 3 more cooking cycles.

Though your oven defrosts automatically by food type and weight, as we've said, we thought it helpful to present additional defrosting plans (in recipe format) for some of the most commonly defrosted foods. See pages 25 and 26.

AUTO DEFROST GUIDE — MEAT
Use **DEF 1** Setting

Food	At Pause	Special Notes
Beef		Meat of irregular shape and large, fatty cuts of meat should have the narrow or fatty areas shielded at the beginning of a defrost sequence.
Ground beef (bulk)	Remove thawed portions with fork (top and bottom). Return remainder to oven.	We do not recommend defrosting less than 1/1 pound ground beef.
Ground beef (patties)	Separate and rearrange.	Do not defrost less than 2 four-ounce patties.
Round steak	Turn over. Cover warm areas with aluminum foil.	Use a microwave roasting rack.
Flank steak	Turn over. Cover warm areas with aluminum foil.	Use a microwave roasting rack.
Tenderloin steak	Turn over. Cover warm areas with aluminum foil.	Use a microwave roasting rack.
Chuck roast	Turn over. Cover warm areas with aluminum foil.	Use a microwave roasting rack.
Stew beef	Remove thawed portions with fork. Separate remainder. Return remainder to oven.	
Pot roast, Rib roast, rolled Rump roast	Turn over. Cover warm areas with aluminum foil.	Use a microwave roasting rack.
Lamb		
Cubed for stew	Remove thawed portions with fork. Separate remainder. Return remainder to oven.	
Ground lamb	Removed thawed portions with fork (top and bottom). Return remainder to oven.	
Chops (1 inch thick)	Separate and rearrange.	Use a microwave roasting rack.
Leg	Turn over. Cover warm areas with aluminum foil.	Use a microwave roasting rack.
Pork		
Chops (1/2 inch thick)	Separate and rearrange.	Use a microwave roasting rack.
Spareribs Country-style ribs	Turn over. Cover warm areas with aluminum foil.	Use a microwave roasting rack.
Sausage, bulk	Remove thawed portions with fork (top and bottom). Return remainder to oven.	
Sausage, links	Separate and rearrange.	
Roast	Turn over. Cover warm areas with aluminum foil.	Use a microwave roasting rack.
Veal		
Chops (1/2 inch thick)	Separate and rearrange.	Use a microwave roasting rack.
Roast	Turn over. Cover warm areas with aluminum foil.	Use a microwave roasting rack.
Variety Meat		
Liver, sliced	Separate pieces and rearrange.	
Hot Dogs (8 jumbo)	Separate and rearrange.	Use a microwave roasting rack.

GROUND BEEF

Defrost Time: 9¼ minutes

1 pound frozen lean ground beef

Remove beef from package and place in shallow microproof baking dish. Place in oven. Touch DEF 1. Touch 1-0. Touch START. (*Oven defrosts: 70, 2 minutes.*)

At Pause, remove thawed portions with fork (top and bottom). Return remainder to oven. Touch START. (*Oven defrosts: 30, 2 minutes, 15 seconds; 0.4, 5 minutes.*)

STEAKS

Defrost Time: 16½ minutes

1 frozen steak (2 pounds)

Remove beef from package and place on microproof roasting rack. Place in oven. Touch DEF 1. Touch 2-0. Touch START. (*Oven defrosts: 70, 3½ minutes.*)

At Pause, turn steak over. Cover any warm areas with small strips of aluminum foil, keeping foil at least 1 inch away from oven wall. Touch START. (*Oven defrosts: 30, 4 minutes; 0.4, 9 minutes.*)

STEW BEEF

Defrost Time: 16½ minutes

2 pounds frozen beef for stew

Remove beef from package and place in shallow microproof baking dish. Place in oven. Touch DEF 1. Touch 2-0. Touch START. (*Oven defrosts: 70, 3½ minutes.*)

At Pause, separate beef into pieces. Touch START. (*Oven defrosts: 30, 4 minutes; 0.4, 9 minutes.*)

PORK CHOPS

Defrost Time: 16½ minutes

2 pounds frozen pork chops, ½ inch thick

Remove chops from package and place in microproof baking dish. Place in oven. Touch DEF 1. Touch 2-0. Touch START. (*Oven defrosts: 70, 3½ minutes.*)

At Pause, turn chops over and separate. Touch START. (*Oven defrosts: 30, 4 minutes; 0.4, 9 minutes.*)

QUARTERED CHICKEN

Defrost Time: 27 minutes

2 pounds frozen chicken parts

Remove chicken from package and place in microproof baking dish. Place in oven. Touch DEF 2. Touch 2-0. Touch START. (*Oven defrosts: 70, 4½ minutes.*)

At Pause, turn parts over and separate. Cover any warm areas with small strips of aluminum foil, keeping foil at least 1 inch away from oven wall. Touch START. (*Oven defrosts: 30, 4½ minutes; 0.4 18 minutes.*)

Rinse chicken parts in cold water.

WHOLE CHICKEN

Defrost Time: 40½ minutes

1 frozen broiler-fryer chicken (3 pounds)

Remove chicken from package. Place chicken, breast-side up, in microproof baking dish. Place in oven. Touch DEF 2. Touch 3-0. Touch START. (*Oven defrosts: 70, 6 minutes, 45 seconds.*)

At Pause, turn chicken over. Cover any warm areas with small strips of aluminum foil, keeping foil at least 1 inch away from oven wall. Touch START. (*Oven defrosts: 30, 6 minutes, 45 seconds; 0.4, 27 minutes.*)

Immerse in cold water 30 minutes.

FISH FILLETS

Defrost Time: 18 minutes

1½ pounds frozen fish fillets

Remove fillets from package and place in shallow microproof baking dish. Place in oven. Touch DEF 3. Touch 1-5. Touch START. (*Oven defrosts: 30, 5 minutes, 45 seconds.*)

At Pause, separate fillets and rearrange. Touch START. (*Oven defrosts: 10, 5 minutes, 45 seconds; 0, 6½ minutes.*)

Separate fillets and rinse in cold water.

SHRIMP

Defrost Time: 14 minutes

1 package (1 pound) frozen shrimp

Remove shrimp from package and arrange in round shallow microproof baking dish with tails toward center of dish. Place in oven. Touch DEF 3. Touch 1-0. Touch START. (*Oven defrosts: 30, 4½ minutes.*)

At Pause, rearrange. Touch START. (*Oven defrosts: 10, 4½ minutes; 0, 5 minutes.*)

AUTO DEFROST GUIDE — POULTRY
Use **DEF 2** Setting

Food	At Pause	Special Notes
Capon	Turn over (finish defrosting breast-side down). Cover warm areas with aluminum foil.	Place capon breast-side up on microwave roasting rack.
Chicken		
Whole (4 pounds & under)	Turn over (finish defrosting breast-side down). Cover warm areas with aluminum foil.	Place chicken breast-side up on microwave roasting rack. Remove giblets when chicken is only partially defrosted. Finish defrosting by immersing in cold water.
Cut-up	Separate pieces and rearrange. Turn over. Cover warm areas with aluminum foil.	Use a microwave roasting rack.
Breasts (boneless)	Separate and turn over. Cover with waxed paper.	Use a microwave roasting rack.
Cornish Hens Whole	Turn over. Cover warm areas with aluminum foil.	Place hens breast-side up on microwave roasting rack.
Duckling Whole	Turn over (finish defrosting breast-side down). Cover warm areas with aluminum foil.	Place duckling breast-side up on microwave roasting rack.
Turkey Whole	Turn over (finish defrosting breast-side down). Cover warm areas with aluminum foil.	Place turkey breast-side up on microwave roasting rack.
Roast (boneless)	Turn over. Separate pieces and rearrange.	Remove from foil pan. Cover with waxed paper. Use a microwave roasting rack.
Breast	Turn over. Cover warm areas with aluminum foil.	Use a microwave roasting rack.
Legs and thighs	Turn over. Cover warm areas with aluminum foil.	Use a microwave roasting rack.
Fillets	Separate and rearrange.	Cover with waxed paper.

*To ensure proper defrosting of large whole poultry, remove gravy pack/giblets as soon as possible.

AUTO DEFROST GUIDE — FISH AND SHELLFISH
Use **DEF 3** Setting

Food	At Pause	Special Notes
Fish Fish Fillets	Turn over. Separate fillets when partially thawed.	Use a microwave roasting rack. Carefully separate fillets under cold water.
Fish steak	Separate and rearrange.	Use a microwave roasting rack.
Whole fish	Turn over.	Use a microwave roasting rack. Cover head and tail with aluminum foil.
Shellfish Crab legs	Turn over and rearrange.	Use a microproof baking dish.
Crabmeat	Break apart. Turn over.	Use a microproof baking dish.
Lobster tails	Turn over and rearrange.	Use a microproof baking dish.
Oysters (shucked)	Break apart and rearrange.	Use a microproof baking dish.
Shrimp	Break apart and rearrange.	Use a microproof baking dish.
Scallops	Break apart and rearrange.	Use a microproof baking dish.

Note: Many small pieces of fish, or shellfish may be completely defrosted at the Pause. If so, remove from oven.

You can automatically defrost/reheat frozen vegetables (Recipe No. 8) with this oven. The quantity can be increased by using the "Quantity" touch pad.

Most microwave ovens require you to select the power level and to set the timing, or temperature probe setting, for all cooking. Your new Kenmore oven takes cooking convenience one step further and enables you to cook foods or recipes automatically. The power level and timing, or probe temperature (when the temperature probe is used), are stored in the oven's microcomputer, waiting for you to cook simply by selecting the recipe number you want to prepare.

Recipe numbers 1 through 25 cover some of our most frequent reheating, defrosting, or cooking needs, and have been permanently stored in your oven's memory. Moreover, each recipe has been programmed in such a way that the quantity for which it was designed can be increased by following a very simple procedure. For example, the base quantity (the amount for which the recipe was programmed) of a baked potato is a single 6-ounce potato. Depending upon the weight of additional potatoes, you can cook up to 5.9 times the base amount, or 5 to 6 potatoes totaling 35.4 ounces, simply by using the QUANTITY touch pad.

In addition to the 25 permanently-stored recipes, you can store additional recipes by programming the cooking information yourself. Once programmed, a recipe remains in your oven's memory until you decide to change it or until a loss of power occurs — and you can change recipes as often as you like. For information on the number of "programmable" recipes your oven's memory can hold, consult your Use and Care Manual. Also use the Manual as a supplement to the information you will find in this chapter regarding the 25 permanently-stored recipes and their use, instructions on programming your own recipes, and tips to help assure that automatic cooking will become one of your oven's most appreciated features.

Using the QUANTITY Touch Pad

Learning to use the QUANTITY touch pad is essential for successful automatic cooking with this oven, as the QUANTITY pad allows you to vary the amounts for which the automatic recipes have been programmed. The guide on pages 29 and 30 lists each of the 25 foods or recipes and their basic quantities. Look at recipe No. 2 (Bacon) for example. To the right of the recipe name is a column labeled Basic Quantity, which shows you the actual amount your oven is programmed to cook automatically. If you would like to cook only 2 slices, all that is needed is to select Recipe #2. If, on the other hand, you would like to prepare 4 slices, you must then make adjustments in the programmed recipe by using the QUANTITY pad. As the Quantity Multiplier column indicates, you can cook up to 5.9 times the programmed amount, or a total of 12 slices at one time.

Recipes 1 through 17 can be increased by 1.1 up to 5.9 times their basic quantities. Recipes 18 and 19 can be increased by 1.1 up to 2.9 times their basic quantities. Recipe 20 for Muffins cannot be increased, as only one microproof muffin ring will fit in the oven at any one time. (To bake more than six muffins, simply repeat the process by selecting Recipe 20 as many times as you need.) Recipes 21 through 25 are temperature probe recipes and need not be varied by means of the QUANTITY pad. When operating in the probe mode, your oven cooks or reheats food to the correct internal temperature regardless of weight or size. Basic quantities for the probe recipes are listed in the guide simply for convenient reference.

When using the QUANTITY feature of your oven, it is vital to understand that all quantities for Recipes 1 through 19 are calculated on the basis of weight rather than the number of items being prepared. While it might appear at first glance, for example, that 2 potatoes of differing size might be cooked automatically by multiplying the Basic Quantity by 2, in actuality their total weight may be 2.5 times greater than the base quantity of one 6-ounce potato, in which case a quantity multiplier of 2.5 would be used. With similar items, such as corn on the cob and hamburger patties, it is a good practice to estimate their weight and then enter how many times the estimated total weight exceeds the basic quantity weight. With package sizes of various convenience mixes or frozen products, the weight of the package must be compared to the basic quantity and then adjusted accordingly by means of the QUANTITY feature.

A brownie mix is baked automatically with Recipe No. 19. You can adjust for package sizes by using the QUANTITY touch pad.

As noted earlier in this book, food can vary greatly in density, texture, fat content, and other factors. Automatic cooking is based on repeated testing to determine average cooking times. You may occasionally need to add a bit more time manually to adjust for personal preferences and the characteristics of the food being cooked.

You can always interrupt automatic cooking to check on the food simply by opening the door. If the food is done to your preference prior to the end of the automatic sequence, simply touch CLEAR. If you wish to continue the automatic cooking sequence, simply close the door and touch START.

For your convenience, on pages 30-33 we have presented all 25 Automatic Recipes in actual recipe form. Each is written for the Basic Quantity of that recipe. Though the quantity may vary, depending on the amount of any item you would like to prepare, the method of preparation for each recipe will remain essentially the same.

PROGRAMMABLE RECIPES

In addition to its 25 Automatic Recipes, your oven has the memory capacity for retaining a number of recipes that you may program yourself. By using the NEW RECIPE feature and RECIPE # feature, you can enter your own favorite recipes, assign them numbers, and recall them whenever you like. Moreover, the multi-stage memory of your oven enables you to program recipes which require a series of steps in their preparation. For example, you may want your oven to pause at some point in a recipe to allow you to stir, turn over, or rotate a food. Or you may want your oven to change power levels midway through a cooking sequence. These and other functions can all be programmed as you enter your own recipes into the oven's memory. For additional information regarding the use of this very convenient feature, consult your Use and Care Manual.

COOKING AUTOMATICALLY

To introduce you to the simplicity of Automatic Cooking, we've prepared a step-by-step plan for reheating a cup of coffee. What is unique is that the steps followed by this plan are essentially the same for all automatic recipes. First you recall a particular recipe from your oven's memory bank. Then you program the quantity of food being cooked, if different from the basic quantity called for by an automatic recipe. Then you touch START. Could anything be more simple?

Let's see how it works.

Reheating Coffee

Experienced microwave cooks refrigerate leftover coffee and reheat it throughout the day in the oven. Here is a situation where we would like to reheat two cups, using the QUANTITY feature.

2 cups (8 ounces each) coffee

1. Fill two of your favorite coffee cups or mugs with coffee from the refrigerator, or at room temperature. As always, be sure your cups are *microproof.* Place cups in oven.

2. Close oven door and touch CLEAR. (*This step assures that the oven is ready to accept new settings. It is usually not necessary.*)

3. Touch the RECIPE # pad. Touch 1.

4. Touch QUANTITY. Touch 2. (*Note: If you are using large mugs instead of 8-ounce cups, you may want to touch 2 and 5. This will increase the basic quantity by 2½ times, or from 8 ounces to 20 ounces.*)

START

5. Touch START. (*Oven cooks: HI, 2 minutes 24 seconds.*)

6. At the beep, remove cups from oven freshly heated.

PROGRAMMING RECIPES

Programming recipes is really very simple. In essence, it involves little more than going through the same steps you would use to cook any recipe by the microwave method. The only difference is that you are entering those steps into the oven's memory and assigning them a number for future use. Store and record the recipe information by using the NEW RECIPE feature. Recall it by means of the RECIPE # feature. Once you have walked through a sample recipe, you should have a basic grasp of how your oven's Programmable Recipe feature works. Here is how you would go about programming Tomato Citrus Soup.

TOMATO CITRUS SOUP

Cooking Time: 5 to 5½ minutes

> 1 **can (10½ ounces) condensed**
> **tomato soup, undiluted**
> 1 **cup orange juice**
> ⅓ **cup chicken broth**
> 1 **teaspoon lemon juice**
> ½ **teaspoon sugar**

Combine tomato soup, orange juice, chicken broth, lemon juice, and sugar in 4-cup glass measure. Cook (micro) on HI, 5 to 5½ minutes or until hot.

Serve with croutons, Parmesan cheese, or a dollop of sour cream.

2 servings

1. Touch CLEAR. This erases any previous programming.

2. Touch NEW RECIPE. Touch RECIPE #.

3. Because this recipe is a one-step recipe, it must be programmed accordingly. Consult your Use and Care Manual for a listing of recipe numbers and stages which may be programmed into your oven. Here we will use number 26, which accommodates a one-step recipe. Touch 2-6.

4. Because automatic cooking does not allow for setting a range of times, such as 5 to 5½ minutes, we must decide on an exact cooking time. For the sake of demonstration, we'll use 5 minutes. Touch MICRO TIME. Touch 5-0-0. (It was not necessary to touch MICRO POWER because your oven automatically selects HI whenever a lower power is not entered.)

5. Touch NEW RECIPE. It's that simple. Tomato Citrus Soup is now programmed into your oven's memory.

AUTOMATIC RECIPES 1 TO 17

NO.	RECIPE NAME	BASIC QUANTITY	QUANTITY MULTIPLIER
1	Cup of Coffee	1 cup (8 ounces)	5.9
2	Bacon	2 slices	5.9
3	Baked Potato	1 potato (6 ounces)	5.9
4	Hot Dog	1 hot dog (3 ounces)	5.9
5	Scrambled Eggs	2 eggs (5½ ounces)	5.9
6	Fresh Corn-on-the-Cob	1 ear (7 ounces)	5.9
7	Basic White Rice	½ cup (uncooked)	5.9
8	Frozen Vegetables	10-ounce package	5.9
9	Defrosting Ground Beef	1 pound	5.9
10	Melted Butter	2 tablespoons	5.9
11	Hamburger Patty	1 patty (¼ pound)	5.9
12	Fish Steaks	2 steaks (8 ounces each)	5.9
13	Chicken Pieces	8 ounces	5.9
14	Pork Chop	1 chop (8 ounces, ¾ inch thick)	5.9
15	Scalloped Potatoes	5¼-ounce package	5.9
16	Basic White Sauce	1 cup	5.9
17	Pudding Mix	3¼-ounce package	5.9

AUTOMATIC RECIPES 18 TO 25

NO.	RECIPE NAME	BASIC QUANTITY	QUANTITY MULTIPLIER
18	Cake Mix	9-ounce package	2.9
19	Brownie Mix	16-ounce package	2.9
20	Muffins	6 muffins	Repeat
21	Canned Entrée	16 ounces	Probe
22	Canned Soup	1 can	Probe
23	Meat Loaf	1½ pounds	Probe
24	Precooked Ham	3 to 5 pounds	Probe
25	Reheating Casseroles	4 to 6 servings	Probe

Note: Probe recipes may be any quantity desired provided the dish will fit the oven.

RECIPE NO. 1

CUP OF COFFEE

Cooking Time: 1½ minutes

> **1 cup (8 ounces) brewed coffee, refrigerated or at room temperature**

Pour coffee into microproof cup or mug. Place in oven. Touch RECIPE #. Touch 1. Touch START. (*Oven cooks*: HI, 1½ *minutes.*)

1 *serving*

RECIPE NO. 2

BACON

Cooking Time: 2¾ minutes

> **2 slices bacon**

Place bacon on white paper towel on microproof plate. Cover with additional paper towel. Place in oven. Touch RECIPE #. Touch 2. Touch START. (*Oven cooks*: HI, 2¾ *minutes.*)

1 *serving*

RECIPE NO. 3

BAKED POTATO

Cooking Time: 8 minutes

> **1 baking potato (6 ounces)**

Scrub potato and rinse well. Pierce several times with a fork. Place on microwave roasting rack. Place in oven. Touch RECIPE #. Touch 3. Touch START. (*Oven cooks*: HI, 4 *minutes.*)

At Pause, turn potato over. Touch START. (*Oven cooks*: HI, 4 *minutes.*)

1 *serving*

RECIPE NO. 4

HOT DOG

Cooking Time: 1 minute 20 seconds

> **1 jumbo hot dog (3 ounces)**
> **1 hot dog bun, split**

Score hot dog in several places with a knife. Place on microproof plate. Place in oven. Touch RECIPE #. Touch 4. Touch START. (*Oven cooks*: 80, 50 *seconds.*)

At Pause, remove hot dog from oven and place in bun. Return to oven. Touch START. (*Oven cooks*: 80, 30 *seconds.*)

1 *serving*

RECIPE NO. 5

SCRAMBLED EGGS

Cooking Time: 3 minutes

> **2 eggs (5½ ounces)**
> **4 tablespoons milk**
> **2 teaspoons butter or margarine**

Break eggs into small microproof bowl. Add milk and beat well with a fork. Add butter and cover with waxed paper. Place in oven. Touch RECIPE #. Touch 5. Touch START. (*Oven cooks*: 60, 1½ *minutes.*)

At Pause, stir. Cover. Touch START. (*Oven cooks*: 60, 1½ *minutes.*)

Stir and let stand 1 minute before serving.

1 *serving*

RECIPE NO. 6

FRESH CORN-ON-THE-COB
Cooking Time: 5½ minutes

**1 unhusked ear of corn
(7 ounces)**

Discard any discolored outer husks. Soak corn in cold water 5 to 10 minutes. Drain well; do not dry. Place on microwave roasting rack. Place in oven. Touch RECIPE #. Touch 6. Touch START. (*Oven cooks: HI, 3½ minutes; stands, 0, 2 minutes.*)

1 serving

RECIPE NO. 7

BASIC WHITE RICE
Cooking Time: 20 minutes

**½ cup long grain white rice
1 cup water**

Place rice in 2-quart microproof casserole. Add water. Cover tightly with casserole lid. Place in oven. Touch RECIPE #. Touch 7. Touch START. (*Oven cooks: HI, 4 minutes; 50, 11 minutes; stands, 0, 5 minutes.*)

2 servings

RECIPE NO. 8

FROZEN VEGETABLES
Cooking Time: 6 minutes

**1 package (10 ounces) frozen
vegetables**

If vegetables are packaged in a plastic pouch, slit pouch and place, cut-side down, in microproof casserole or serving dish. Remove any foil wrapping from other vegetable cartons and place on microproof plate.

Place in oven. Touch RECIPE #. Touch 8. Touch START. (*Oven cooks: HI, 6 minutes.*)

2 to 4 servings

RECIPE NO. 9

DEFROSTING GROUND BEEF
Defrosting Time: 12 minutes

1 pound frozen ground beef

Remove frozen ground beef from packaging and place in microproof casserole or baking dish. Place in oven. Touch RECIPE #. Touch 9. Touch START. (*Oven defrosts: 30, 4 minutes.*)

At Pause, remove thawed portions with a fork (top and bottom). Return remainder to oven. Touch START. (*Oven defrosts: 30, 3 minutes; stands, 0, 5 minutes.*)

1 pound

RECIPE NO. 10

MELTED BUTTER
Cooking Time: 45 seconds

**2 tablespoons butter or margarine,
refrigerated**

Place butter in 1-cup glass measure. Place in oven. Touch RECIPE #. Touch 1-0. Touch START. (*Oven cooks: HI, 45 seconds.*)

2 tablespoons

RECIPE NO. 11

HAMBURGER PATTY
Cooking Time: 8 minutes

1 hamburger patty (¼ pound)

Remove ceramic tray. Place wire rack in upper position of oven. Touch RECIPE #. Touch 1-1. Touch START. (*Oven preheats to 450°F.*)

Place patty in broiling pan. At Pause, place in oven on wire rack. Touch START. (*Oven cooks: convec, 5 minutes.*)

At Pause, turn patty over. Touch START. (*Oven cooks: convec, 3 minutes.*)

1 serving

RECIPE NO. 12

FISH STEAKS
Cooking Time: 10 minutes

**2 halibut, salmon, or swordfish steaks
(8 ounces each)
2 tablespoons butter or margarine,
melted
2 teaspoons lemon juice
½ teaspoon dill weed**

Arrange fish in round or oval microproof baking dish. Combine butter and lemon juice. Brush over fish. Sprinkle with dill. Cover with waxed paper and place in oven. Touch RECIPE #. Touch 1-2. Touch START. (*Oven cooks: HI, 4 minutes.*)

At Pause, turn fish over. Spoon remaining melted butter mixture over fish. Cover. Touch START. (*Oven cooks: HI, 3 minutes; stands, 0, 3 minutes.*)

2 servings

CHICKEN PIECES

Cooking Time: 10 minutes

> **½ pound broiler-fryer chicken pieces**

Touch RECIPE #. Touch 1-3. Touch START. (*Oven pre-heats to 350°F.*)

Arrange chicken pieces in 8-inch round microproof and heatproof baking dish. Season to taste. At Pause, set on ceramic tray. Touch START. (*Oven cooks: micro/convec, 10 minutes.*)

1 *serving*

PORK CHOP

Cooking Time: 6 minutes

> **1 loin pork chop (8 ounces,**
> **¾ inch thick)**

Place chop on microwave roasting rack in microproof baking dish. Place in oven. Touch RECIPE #. Touch 1-4. Touch START. (*Oven cooks: HI, 3 minutes.*)

At Pause, turn chops over. Touch START. (*Oven cooks: HI, 3 minutes.*)

1 *serving*

SCALLOPED POTATOES

Cooking Time: 21 minutes

> **1 package (5¼ ounces) scalloped**
> **potato mix**

Prepare potato mix, as directed on package, in 2-quart microproof casserole. Cover with casserole lid and place in oven. Touch RECIPE #. Touch 1-5. Touch START. (*Oven cooks: HI, 10 minutes.*)

At Pause, add or stir according to package directions. Cover and return to oven. Touch START. (*Oven cooks: HI, 6 minutes; stands, 0, 5 minutes.*)

4 *servings*

BASIC WHITE SAUCE

Cooking Time: 5 minutes

> **2 tablespoons butter or margarine**
> **2 tablespoons all-purpose flour**
> **1 cup milk**
> **⅛ teaspoon white pepper**
> **⅛ teaspoon nutmeg**

Place butter in 4-cup glass measure. Place in oven. Touch RECIPE #. Touch 1-6. Touch START. (*Oven cooks: HI, 1 minute.*)

At Pause, stir flour into butter until smooth. Whisk in milk, pepper, and nutmeg, blending well. Place in oven. Touch START. (*Oven cooks: HI, 3 minutes.*)

At Pause, stir. Return to oven. Touch START. (*Oven cooks: HI, 1 minute.*)

Remove from oven and whisk briskly until smooth.

1 *cup*

PUDDING MIX

Cooking Time: 9 minutes

> **1 package (3¼ ounces) pudding and**
> **pie filling mix**
> **2 cups milk**

Place pudding mix in 2-quart microproof bowl. Stir in milk until well blended. Place in oven. Touch RECIPE #. Touch 1-7. Touch START. (*Oven cooks: HI, 5 minutes.*)

At Pause, stir. Return to oven. Touch START. (*Oven cooks: HI, 4 minutes.*)

Chill in individual dessert dishes.

4 *servings*

CAKE MIX (2 LAYERS)

Cooking Time: 9 minutes

> **1 package (18½ ounces) cake mix**

Line bottoms of two 9-inch round microproof cake dishes with waxed paper. Prepare cake batter according to package directions. Pour into prepared dishes and place one dish in oven. Touch RECIPE #. Touch 1-8. Touch START. (*Oven cooks: 50, 7 minutes.*)

At Pause, rotate dish one-quarter turn. Touch START. (*Oven cooks: HI, 2 minutes.*)

Let cool in pan 3 to 5 minutes before inverting onto serving plate.

Repeat with remaining dish.

2 *layers*

RECIPE NO. 19

BROWNIE MIX

Cooking Time: 7½ minutes

1 package (16 ounces) brownie mix

Butter 9-inch round microproof baking dish. Prepare brownie batter according to package directions. Pour into prepared baking dish. Place in oven. Touch RECIPE #. Touch 1-9. Touch START. (*Oven cooks: HI, 3½ minutes.*)

At Pause, rotate dish one-quarter turn. Touch START. (*Oven cooks: HI, 4 minutes.*)

Let stand in baking dish until cool.

16 brownies

RECIPE NO. 20

MUFFINS

Cooking Time: 2 minutes

1 package (14 ounces) muffin mix

Prepare batter according to package directions. Spoon batter into paper-lined microproof muffin ring, filling each compartment about half full. Place in oven. Touch RECIPE #. Touch 2-0. Touch START. (*Oven cooks: HI, 2 minutes.*)

Repeat twice with remaining batter.

18 muffins

RECIPE NO. 21

CANNED ENTREE

Approximate Cooking Time: 5 minutes

1 can (16 ounces) chili, stew, macaroni, etc.

Pour entrée into 1-quart microproof casserole. Position temperature probe in center of dish. Cover with plastic wrap, tucking wrap around probe. Place in oven. Plug in probe. Touch RECIPE #. Touch 2-1. Touch START. (*Oven cooks: 80, about 5 minutes to 160°F.*)

2 servings

RECIPE NO. 22

CANNED SOUP

Approximate Cooking Time: 7½ minutes

1 can (10¾ ounces) condensed soup

Prepare soup, according to directions on can, in 1-quart microproof casserole. Position temperature probe in center of dish. Cover with plastic wrap, tucking wrap around probe. Place in oven. Plug in probe. Touch RECIPE #. Touch 2-2. Touch START. (*Oven cooks: 80, about 7½ minutes to 160°F.*)

2 servings

RECIPE NO. 23

MEAT LOAF

Approximate Cooking Time: 19 minutes

1½ pounds of lean ground beef
3 slices fresh bread
2 eggs, lightly beaten
1 medium onion, minced
2 tablespoons chopped fresh parsley
½ teaspoon salt
¼ teaspoon freshly ground pepper

Place beef in bowl. Shred bread, combining with beef. Add remaining ingredients and mix well. Place beef mixture into 8-cup microproof ring mold. Position temperature probe in center of beef mixture. Cover with waxed paper. Place in oven. Plug in probe. Touch RECIPE #. Touch 2-3. Touch START. (*Oven cooks: HI, about 14 minutes to 160°F; stands, 0, 5 minutes.*)

4 servings

RECIPE NO. 24

PRECOOKED HAM

Approximate Cooking Time: 25 minutes

1 precooked canned ham (3 to 5 pounds)

Place ham on microwave roasting rack in 12 × 7-inch microproof baking dish. Cover lightly with waxed paper. Place in oven. Touch RECIPE #. Touch 2-4. Touch START. (*Oven cooks: 70, 15 minutes.*)

At Pause, turn ham over. Cover. Insert temperature probe horizontally into center of ham. Plug in probe. Touch START. (*Oven cooks: 70, about 10 minutes to 130°F.*)

6 servings

RECIPE NO. 25

REHEATING CASSEROLE

Approximate Cooking Time: 21 minutes

1 precooked casserole (about 2 quarts), refrigerated or at room temperature

Make certain casserole is in a microproof container. Position temperature probe in center of casserole. Cover with plastic wrap, tucking wrap around probe. Place in oven. Plug in probe. Touch RECIPE #. Touch 2-5. Touch START. (*Oven cooks: 80, about 21 minutes to 150°F.*)

4 to 6 servings

To give you hands-on experience cooking with your new Micro/Convection oven, as well as to demonstrate how easy it is to operate, we have designed three lesson plans. Each plan employs a different cooking method. First you'll use the MICROWAVE method to prepare a cup of hot tea. Next the CONVECTION method will provide the hot, dry environment needed for fixing Hot Dog Wrap-Ups. And finally, you'll use the speed and browning capabilities of your oven's MICRO/CONVECTION method to prepare a Baked Apple. In sum, these lessons aim to demonstrate how all three cooking methods can be combined to prepare an entire meal, in this case a pleasant lunch for one.

A CUP OF TEA (**MICROWAVE**)

| CLEAR |

1. Fill your favorite cup or mug with water. (**Since the microwave method will be used, remember: your cup must not contain gold or silver trim and it must be "microproof." If you're uncertain whether your cup is safe for microwave use, follow the test on page 9.**) Place cup in oven, close oven door, and touch CLEAR if any previous programming needs erasing.

| MICRO TIME | 2 | 0 | 0 |

2. Touch MICRO TIME, then 2-0-0. Your oven is now programmed to cook (micro) on HI for 2 minutes. It is not necessary to touch MICRO POWER, as your oven cooks automatically on HI when the microwave method is used unless programmed to another setting.

| START |

3. Touch START.

4. When your oven has completed its cooking time, it will turn itself off automatically and signal with a beep. At that point, remove cup from the oven, carefully testing its handle, which may be warm from the heated water.

5. Stir in instant coffee, tea, or soup. (**Sudden reoxygenation prompted by rapid stirring can cause the heated water to bubble over when instant coffee and soup granules are added. Stir in these ingredients slowly to avoid clean-up or injury.**)

HOT DOG WRAP-UPS (**CONVECTION**)

| CLEAR |

1. Remove ceramic tray. Place wire rack in upper position of oven. Touch CLEAR if any previous programming needs erasing.

2. Touch OVEN TEMP/PREHEAT, then 3-6-0. Your oven is now programmed to preheat to 360°F.

START

3. Touch START.

4. Prepare Hot Dog Wrap-Ups according to recipe on page 43, arranging 8 on a cookie sheet and 8 on a plate. Cover plate with plastic wrap and refrigerate for later use.

5. When oven beeps, it has reached its preheat temperature of 360°F. Place cookie sheet on wire rack and close oven door.

6. Touch OVEN TEMP/PREHEAT, then3-6-0. (Your oven is now programmed to cook at 360°F. Without this step, it will cook automatically at 350°F.)

7. Touch CONVEC TIME, then 1-5-0-0. This finishes programming your oven to cook by the convection method at 360°F for 15 minutes. **(It was necessary to enter 15 minutes as 1-5-0-0, as your oven always interprets the right two digits of a cooking time as seconds and the left two as minutes. Therefore, it will interpret 1-0-0 as 1 minute 00 seconds rather than 100 seconds.)**

BAKED APPLE
(MICRO/CONVECTION)

    1 **large apple**
    2 **teaspoons brown sugar**
    1 **teaspoon chopped walnuts**
    1 **teaspoon raisins**
  ¼ **teaspoon cinnamon**
    3 **tablespoons water**

CLEAR

1. Core apple, making criss-cross cuts around top. Remove small portion of inner pulp. Combine sugar, walnuts, and raisins and place in center of apple. Sprinkle with cinnamon. Place apple in small microproof and heatproof dish. Add water.
      Place wire rack in lower position of oven. Place dish on rack. Close oven door. Touch CLEAR if previous programming needs erasing.

2. Touch MICRO/CONVEC TIME, then 6-0-0. Your oven is now programmed to cook by the micro/convection method at 350°F for 6 minutes. As your oven is designed to cook automatically at 350°F by the micro/convection method, it is not necessary to set cooking temperature for this recipe.

START

3. Touch START. Upon completing its cooking time, your oven will turn off automatically and signal with a beep. At this point, remove from oven and enjoy with your Hot Dog Wrap-Ups and coffee or tea.

There is so much more that you can do in this oven than ever before in a single-cavity unit. Because you have such flexibility, you may be concerned about which method to choose for a particular cooking task — convection, micro/convection, or microwave — when cooking on your own. To help you decide, we have prepared the following chart. Also you have the recipes in this book to use as guides. When you are ready to convert one of your own, find a similar recipe from among the following pages for an idea of how to proceed.

SELECTING A COOKING METHOD

FOOD	CONVECTION	MICRO/CONVECTION	MICRO
Appetizers	Best for pastry or breaded items.	Very good when some surface browning with moist interior is desired.	Excellent when crispness is not needed. Best for reheating all types.
Bread	Slow heating and crisping of filled sandwiches.	Best for baking small loaves.	Thawing frozen baked rolls, bread. Quick warming.
Cakes	Best for muffins & cupcakes when a browned top is desired.	Best for layer cakes, brownies and coffeecakes.	Good for quickly cooking muffins & cupcakes when dark flour, spices, or frosting are used.
Candies	Not used.	Not used.	Excellent for most types.
Casseroles	Slow baking when crisp top is wanted.	Very good for most scalloped dishes.	Excellent when top browning is not important.
Cookies	Excellent for small batches of drop cookies.	Very good for crisp bar cookies.	Good for very quick cooking of bar cookies.
Eggs	Best for omelets when some browning is desired.	Good for egg and vegetable casseroles.	Excellent for all scrambled egg dishes.
Fruit	Very good for fruit-filled pies when fully-browned crust is desired.	Good for fruit pies.	Excellent for baked apples, poached pears, similar fruit.
Hot drinks	Not used.	Not used.	Excellent for reheating in microproof containers.

SELECTING A COOKING METHOD (Continued)

FOOD	CONVECTION	MICRO/CONVECTION	MICRO
Pies	Best for two-crust pies.	Best for one-crust or lattice-topped pies.	Reheating or defrosting fully-baked pies.
Poultry	Excellent for maximum browning. Inside will lose some moisture.	Very good for all small poultry. Slight browning. Little moisture loss.	Excellent for cooking poultry in casseroles, or to use in salads, etc. Very slight color, no moisture loss.
Reheating	Very good to retain crispness. Use for frozen french-fried foods, etc.	Acceptable when minimal added browning desired.	Excellent for most reheating needs.
Roasts	Very good for all small roasts. Good color.	Good for very tender small roasts. Some color.	Good for the quickest cooking of tender roasts. Very little color.
Sauces	Not used.	Not used.	Excellent for all sauces.
Seafood	Very good for most breaded items when maximum crispness desired.	Very good for steaks or fillets. Some crisping, little moisture loss.	Excellent for quick cooking of all seafood. Provides a poached texture.
Soup	Not used.	Not used.	Excellent for cooking small portions of homemade soup. Excellent for reheating canned and frozen soup.
Steaks, chops	Good for slow cooking of less tender cuts.	Good for quickly cooking tender chops.	Best for all defrosting and reheating needs.
Vegetables	Good for slow cooking casseroles. Provides top browning.	Very good for baked potatoes. Gives a crisp skin & moist inside.	Excellent for all vegetables with very little water required.

NOTES FOR ADAPTING RECIPES

Candies, always difficult to prepare by conventional cooking because of the need for double boilers, the mess of scorched pans, constant stirring, and other time-consuming techniques, are now easy to make. Ingredient adjustments are not needed and the microwave method is best.

Chicken recipes will benefit from micro/convection cooking when converted. If the exterior must be very crisp, preheating the oven will enable micro/convection cooking to provide superior results over any other method.

Prepare most casseroles and stews exactly as you would conventionally and use the micro/convection method. Cheese toppings for casseroles usually should be added just before the end of the cooking time.

As a general rule, you can assume that most microwave recipes are cooked in about one-quarter to one-third of the conventional recipe time. Check for doneness after one-quarter of the time before continuing to cook.

When you make your shopping list, note carefully the size and weight of items needed for a recipe. Large items — a turkey over 10 pounds, for example — won't fit in this oven. Also, cooking times given are based on amounts specified in the recipe.

A SAMPLE CONVERSION

To help acquaint you further with the art of recipe conversion, we have prepared two recipes for your comparison. The first is a conventional recipe for Chicken Cacciatore; the second is the same recipe, but converted for use with the micro/convection method. Our first step in making this conversion was to find a recipe in this book similar to Chicken Cacciatore in ingredients and preparation, in this case Chicken Marengo on page 77. Letting Chicken Marengo serve as our guide, compare the conventional and converted recipes carefully and study the differences.

First, the amount of butter needed in the traditional skillet is much greater than that needed when cooking by the micro/convection method. The skillet needs to be well lubricated so the food will not stick and burn from the direct heat essential in stove-top cooking. Also more wine is needed in the conventional version to compensate for evaporation during the longer cooking time. Because the oven operates in the microwave mode a percentage of time during micro/convection cooking, this takes us back to two principles of microwave energy we discussed earlier. First, microwave cooking is considerably faster than conventional cooking, allowing less time for evaporation to occur. And second, microwave energy itself actually causes less evaporation. Keeping these and similar principles in mind will help you immeasurably when converting conventional recipes.

CHICKEN CACCIATORE

Conventional Style
4 to 6 servings

¼ cup butter or margarine
1 medium onion, chopped
1 medium green pepper, thinly sliced
1 can (28 ounces) whole tomatoes
¼ cup all-purpose flour
1 bay leaf
1 tablespoon parsley flakes
½ teaspoon salt
1 clove garlic, minced
½ teaspoon oregano
1 teaspoon paprika
¼ teaspoon basil
1 cup dry red wine
1 frying chicken (about 3 pounds), cut up

Preheat oven to 350°F. Melt butter in medium skillet over medium heat. Add onion and green pepper and cook, stirring occasionally, until onion is transparent. Add tomatoes and flour and stir until smooth. Add all remaining ingredients, except chicken. Cover and cook until sauce is slightly thickened, about 5 minutes, stirring every minute. Arrange chicken in a baking dish and pour sauce over top. Cover and bake about 45 minutes or until chicken is tender.

CHICKEN CACCIATORE

Micro/Convection Style

1 medium onion, chopped
1 medium green pepper, thinly sliced
1 tablespoon butter or margarine
1 can (28 ounces) whole tomatoes
¼ cup all-purpose flour
1 bay leaf
1 clove garlic, minced
1 tablespoon parsley flakes
1 teaspoon paprika
½ teaspoon salt
½ teaspoon oregano
¼ teaspoon basil
½ cup dry red wine
1 frying chicken (about 3 pounds), cut up

Combine onion, green pepper, and butter in 3-quart microproof and heatproof casserole. Cover with casserole lid and cook (micro) on HI, 4 to 5 minutes or until onion is transparent.

Add tomatoes and flour. Stir until smooth. Blend in all remaining ingredients except chicken. Cover and cook (micro) on HI, 5 minutes.

Add chicken, covering pieces completely with sauce. Cover and cook (micro/convec) at 350°F, 25 to 30 minutes or until chicken is tender.

4 to 6 servings

REDUCING CALORIES

Scattered throughout the book are reduced-calorie suggestions and naturally low-calorie recipes. In general, you can reduce calories in many recipes by making the following substitutions.

Bouillon or water can be substituted for butter when sautéing onions or cooking vegetables and other foods.

Many vegetables can be substituted for rice, potatoes, or pasta. Try spaghetti squash or mashed cauliflower for an interesting change.

Well-trimmed meat offers far fewer calories and less cholesterol than fatty cuts.

A wide variety of skim milk-based cheeses is available today, and you'll never know the difference when substituting for whole milk cheeses.

If you take advantage of the natural juices produced when cooking rather than using flour, cream, or butter-based gravies and sauces, you can significantly reduce your calorie intake.

Fruits cooked in their natural juices are the "natural choice" for the calorie-counters among us. In fact, some people think sugar masks the taste of good fruit.

Removing the skins and fat from poultry is also a good way to cut calories. Skinned and boned turkey and chicken are readily available in a wide variety of packages at the market.

COOKING CASSEROLES

Microwaves are exceptionally good for cooking casseroles. Vegetables keep their bright fresh color and crisp texture. Meat is tender and flavorful. If you follow the information here and the specific instructions given with the many casserole recipes in this book, you will find yourself looking to the microwave method for your casserole cookery.

Casseroles are usually covered with glass lids or plastic wrap during microwave cooking. When using the micro/convection or convection methods, only glass lids should be used. These coverings trap moisture in the form of steam, keeping the casserole from drying out. But be sure to leave the dish uncovered if you add a cheese topping, crushed potato chips, or similar casserole toppings. Always follow recipe instructions concerning use of covers.

Allow casseroles to stand 5 to 10 minutes before serving, according to size. Standing time allows the center of the casserole to complete cooking.

You will obtain best results if you make ingredients uniform in size, stirring occasionally to distribute heat. If the ingredients are of different sizes, stir more often.

Casseroles containing less tender meats should be cooked on a low power setting, such as 50 or 30, for longer than usual microwave times. This provides an effect much like simmering on a stove top, providing tenderizing and flavor development.

REHEATING

Reheating is one of the major assets of this oven. Not only does most food reheat quickly, but it also retains moisture and its just-cooked flavor. Throughout the book, you will find charts that provide reheating information for many of the popular convenience foods. There are so many variances, however, that the best general guide will be the package itself. Always reheat for the minimum recommended time, then check.

Use 80 except when otherwise specified. You can use the temperature probe for reheating casseroles, beverages, and other appropriate food. Insert temperature probe into the largest or most dense piece of food and cook with the temperature probe set at 150°F to 160°F.

Dense food, such as mashed potatoes and casseroles, cooks more quickly and evenly if a depression is made in the center, or if the food is shaped in a ring.

To retain moisture during reheating, cover food with plastic wrap or a microproof lid.

Spread food out in a shallow container, rather than piling it high, for quicker and more even heating.

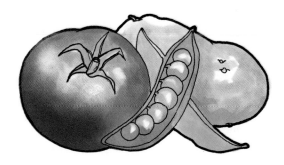

The familiar circular arrangement of food for microwave-method cooking is illustrated with Stuffed Mushrooms (page 42).

Until now, hot appetizers were a troublesome and time-consuming part of entertaining. With your new micro/convection oven, that's no longer true. Due to the speed of microwave reheating, you can assemble most appetizers in advance, and at the right moment simply "heat 'n serve." This chapter presents many recipes for entertaining your guests, but you'll also be tempted to prepare delicious snacks for yourself and your family.

ADAPTING RECIPES

Most of your favorite hot appetizers will adapt well to microwave cooking, except for those wrapped in pastry. For recipes that need a hot, dry environment for browning and crisping, micro/convection or convection are the methods of choice. You can reheat all appetizers using the microwave method.

The recipe for Rumaki (page 42) is an ideal guide for countless skewered appetizers containing seafood, chicken, vegetable, and fruit combinations. Miniature Hot Dog Treats (page 42) is another guide you can use for similar finger foods. There are probably more than 25 different popular approaches to stuffed mushrooms. We invite you to let the Stuffed Mushrooms (page 42) be your guide to cooking them with the microwave method. Also review the following suggestions for achieving greater success when adapting or cooking appetizers in your micro/convection oven.

- For many appetizers, the speed and convenience of the microwave method makes it the method of choice. However, when items need browning or crisping on the top or outside, the micro/convection method produces better results. The convection method is best for pastry-based appetizers that need a flaky crust. Appetizers generally don't need any ingredient changes to fit any of this oven's

cooking methods. Be sure, however, to match the cooking dish to the method you plan to use. Find a similar recipe in this chapter or refer to pages 9-11 for a review of recommended cookware.

- For a crisper bottom crust on items cooked on the wire rack by the micro/convection method, line the bottom of a glass baking dish with aluminum foil.

- Because of its very delicate nature, a sour cream dip should be covered and heated with the temperature probe to 115°F on 50.

- Toppings for canapés can be made ahead, but to assure a crisp base, do not place on bread or crackers until just before heating.

- Cover appetizers or dips only when the recipe specifies doing so. Use fitted glass lids, waxed paper, plastic wrap, or paper toweling.

- You can reheat two batches of the same or similar appetizers at one time with the microwave method by using both oven levels, the wire rack in the upper position and the bottom ceramic tray. Watch closely; those on top may cook more quickly than those on the bottom.

- The temperature probe set at 130°F on 70 provides an excellent alternative for heating hot dips containing seafood, cheese, or food to be served in a chafing dish or fondue pot.

To freshen corn chips and other snacks, just pop the serving bowl or basket in the oven and cook (micro) on HI, 15 seconds; let stand 3 minutes.

REHEATING GUIDE — APPETIZERS*

Food	Programming Method	Setting	First Cook Time	Second Cook Time	Probe Method	Special Notes
Dips, cheese, ½ cup	micro	10	1½ - 2½ min.		130°	Cover with plastic wrap.
Eggrolls, 6 oz. (12)	convec		follow package directions			Remove ceramic tray. Place rack in upper position. Preheat.
Meat spread, 4 oz. can	micro	80	30 - 60 sec.			Use microproof bowl.
Sausages, 5 oz. can	micro	80	1½ - 2½ min.			Use microproof casserole. Cover.
Tacos, mini, 5½ oz.	convec	400°	follow package directions			Remove ceramic tray. Place rack in upper position. Preheat. Use cookie sheet or foil tray.
Swiss fondue, 10 oz.	micro	80	5 - 7 min.		150°	Slit pouch. Set on microproof plate.

*Due to the tremendous variety in convenience food products available, times given here should be used only as guidelines. We suggest you cook food for the shortest recommended time and then check for doneness. Be sure to check the package for microwave and oven (convec) instructions.

NACHOS

Cooking Time: 4 to 6 minutes

> 1 bag (7 ounces) tortilla chips
> 1 can (16 ounces) refried beans
> ½ cup (2 ounces) shredded
>   Monterey jack cheese
> ½ cup (2 ounces) shredded sharp
>   Cheddar cheese
> Chopped green chilies (optional)

Arrange half of the tortilla chips in single layer on round microproof dish. Top each with scant teaspoon of beans. Sprinkle with cheeses and chilies.
   Cook (micro) on HI, 2 to 3 minutes or until cheese melts.
   Repeat with remaining chips.

10 to 15 servings

FRESH VEGETABLE DIP

Cooking Time: 5 minutes

> 1 package (10 ounces) frozen
>   chopped spinach
> 1 cup dairy sour cream
> ½ cup chopped fresh parsley
> ½ cup chopped green onions
> ½ cup mayonnaise
> 1 teaspoon fines herbes seasoning
> ½ teaspoon dill

Set spinach on microproof plate. (If spinach is in foil-lined package, remove foil.)
   Cook (micro) on HI, 5 minutes.
   Drain well; squeeze dry. Transfer to bowl. Add all remaining ingredients and blend thoroughly.
   Cover and refrigerate overnight.
   Serve with fresh vegetables, crackers, or chips.

about 3½ cups

SAUSAGE ROLLS

Cooking Time: 15 to 17½ minutes

> 1 medium onion, chopped
> 1 tablespoon vegetable oil
> ½ pound lean bulk sausage, crumbled
> 1 tablespoon tomato sauce or ketchup
> 1 teaspoon fresh lemon juice
> 1 container (8 ounces) refrigerated
>   crescent roll dough
> 1 egg, lightly beaten

Combine onion and oil in 1-quart glass measure or microproof bowl.

Cook (micro) on HI, 3 to 4 minutes. Stir through several times. Add sausage.

Cook (micro) on HI, 3 to 3½ minutes. Drain off fat. Stir in tomato sauce and lemon juice. Set aside; allow to cool.

Place wire rack in lower position of oven and preheat to 400°F.

Line bottom of 13x9-inch microproof and heatproof baking dish with aluminum foil. Cut pastry into 4 rectangles. Divide sausage mixture into fourths. Spread sausage mixture down center of dough. Brush edge of pastry with beaten egg and fold pastry over, enclosing sausage completely. Brush with egg yolk. Cut each length into 1-inch pieces. Arrange in prepared dish.

Cook (micro/convec) at 400°F, 9 to 10 minutes.

16 appetizers

MINIATURE HOT DOG TREATS

Cooking Time: 10 to 12 minutes

> 2 jumbo frankfurters
> 1 container (10 ounces) refrigerated
>   butterflake biscuit dough
> 1 egg, lightly beaten

Remove ceramic tray. Place wire rack in upper position of oven and preheat to 350°F.

Cut each frankfurter into 10 equal pieces. Separate and roll dough into 20 equal balls. Arrange 10 balls on aluminum tray or baking sheet. Push frankfurter slice firmly into each. Brush dough with beaten egg.

Cook (convec) at 350°F, 10 to 12 minutes or until golden brown.

Repeat with remaining dough and frankfurters.

20 appetizers

STUFFED MUSHROOMS

Cooking Time: 4 to 5 minutes

> 24 medium mushrooms (about
>   1 pound)
> 2 green onions, finely chopped
> ½ cup (2 ounces) finely shredded
>   Cheddar cheese
> ⅓ cup fine bread crumbs
> ¼ cup melted butter or
>   margarine
> ½ teaspoon salt
> ½ teaspoon Italian seasoning
> ½ teaspoon Worcestershire sauce
> ¼ teaspoon garlic powder
> ⅛ teaspoon freshly ground pepper

Snap out stems from mushrooms and finely chop; set caps aside. Transfer chopped stems to mixing bowl. Add onions and cheese; mix well. Blend in all remaining ingredients.

Spoon mixture into caps, mounding slightly in center. Arrange on 10-inch round microproof plate.

Cook (micro) on HI, 4 to 5 minutes or until heated through. (Mushrooms should still be firm.)

24 appetizers

RUMAKI

Cooking Time: 14 to 16 minutes

> ½ pound chicken livers,
>   rinsed and drained
> ¼ cup soy sauce
> ¼ teaspoon garlic powder
> 18 thin slices bacon, cut in half
> 1 can (8 ounces) sliced water
>   chestnuts, drained

Cut chicken livers into 36 one-inch pieces. Discard membranes; set livers aside. Combine soy sauce and garlic powder; set aside.

Place 1 piece liver on 1 piece bacon. Top with water chestnut. Roll up and fasten with wooden toothpick. Repeat with remaining liver pieces. Dip each piece into soy sauce mixture. Place 18 rumaki on microproof baking sheet and cover with paper towel. Place baking sheet on ceramic tray.

Cook (micro) on HI, 7 to 8 minutes. Turn over once. Repeat for remaining rumaki.

36 appetizers

SHRIMP KABOBS

Cooking Time: 6 to 8 minutes

- ½ **cup soy sauce**
- I **tablespoon rice vinegar or lemon juice**
- I **teaspoon sugar**
- ¼ **teaspoon ground ginger**
- I **can (8 ounces) whole water chestnuts, drained**
- 18 **large shrimp, peeled and deveined, tails intact**
- I **can (8 ounces) pineapple chunks, drained**
- I **tablespoon sesame seeds**
- 2 **fresh limes to serve**

Combine soy sauce, vinegar, sugar, and ginger in medium bowl and mix well. Cut 9 water chestnuts in half. Add shrimp and water chestnuts to marinade. Refrigerate I hour.

Push wooden skewer through I shrimp, I pineapple chunk, and I water chestnut half. Arrange half of the skewers on round microproof plate in circle with shrimp tail toward outer edge of plate. Sprinkle with sesame seeds.

Cook (micro) on HI, 3 to 4 minutes. Repeat with remaining skewers. Serve with lime wedges.

18 appetizers

SEAFOOD PUFFS

Cooking Time: 8 to 10 minutes

- 2 **egg whites**
- ½ **cup mayonnaise**
- I **can (6½ ounces) crabmeat, shrimp, or tuna, rinsed, drained, and flaked**
- ½ **teaspoon salt**
- ¼ **teaspoon paprika**
- ¼ **teaspoon dried tarragon**
- 50 **cheese or rye crackers**

Remove ceramic tray. Place wire rack in upper position of oven and preheat to 380°F.

Beat egg whites until stiff. Fold in remaining ingredients, except crackers. Spread crab mixture over crackers. Arrange half of the crackers on aluminum tray or baking sheet.

Cook (convec) at 380°F, 4 to 5 minutes or until puffy and brown. Repeat with remaining crackers. Serve immediately.

50 appetizers

**Hot Dog Wrap-Ups (below),
Shrimp Kabobs (left),
Seafarer Hors D'oeuvre (page 44)**

HOT DOG WRAP-UPS

Cooking Time: 13 to 15 minutes

- I **container (8 ounces) refrigerated crescent roll dough**
- 16 **cocktail-size frankfurters**
- I **egg, lightly beaten**
  Prepared mustard to serve

Remove ceramic tray. Place wire rack in upper position of oven and preheat to 360°F.

Divide dough into 8 wedges. Cut each wedge lengthwise through tip, making 16 equal triangles. Wrap each frankfurter in dough, rolling from wide end of wedge toward tip. Repeat with remaining dough and frankfurters. Brush with beaten egg. Transfer to aluminum tray or baking sheet.

Cook (convec) at 360°F, 13 to 15 minutes or until dough is golden brown and frankfurters are heated through. Serve hot with mustard.

16 appetizers

AMSTERDAM MEATBALLS

Cooking Time: 12 minutes

Meatballs:
- 1 pound lean ground beef
- ½ cup dry bread crumbs
- ⅓ cup chopped onion
- ¼ cup ketchup
- 1 egg, lightly beaten
- 1 teaspoon Worcestershire sauce
- ½ teaspoon garlic powder
- ¼ teaspoon salt
- ⅛ teaspoon freshly ground pepper

Sauce:
- ½ cup beef stock or broth
- 1 can (8 ounces) tomato sauce
- 2 tablespoons ketchup
- ½ cup dairy sour cream
- Paprika for garnish

Combine all ingredients for meatballs in large bowl and mix well. Shape into 1-inch balls. Arrange on microproof 10-inch pie plate. Cover with two lengths of paper towel and tuck each end under plate.

Cook (micro) on HI, 7 minutes. Drain on paper towel. Combine beef stock, tomato sauce, and ketchup in 10-inch microproof pie plate. Add meatballs.

Cook (micro) on 70, 5 minutes. Remove meatballs and set aside. Add sour cream to sauce and blend well. Return meatballs to dish. Cover with sauce. Sprinkle lightly with paprika and serve immediately.

4 to 6 servings

SEAFARER HORS D'OEUVRE

Cooking Time: 2½ to 4½ minutes

- 1 package (3 ounces) cream cheese
- 1 package (6½ ounces) frozen crabmeat or shrimp, thawed and drained
- 2 tablespoons fresh lemon juice
- 1 tablespoon ranch-style salad dressing mix
- 1 tablespoon mayonnaise
- 3 medium (about ¾ pound) zucchini, cut into ¼-inch rounds
- Paprika
- Chopped fresh parsley for garnish

To soften cheese, place in 1-quart glass measure and cook (micro) on HI, 30 seconds. Stir in crab, lemon juice, dressing mix, and mayonnaise. Blend well. Arrange half of the zucchini rounds in single layer on microproof serving dish. Top each with 1 teaspoonful crab mixture. Sprinkle with paprika.

Cook (micro) on HI, 1 to 2 minutes or until heated through. Repeat with remaining zucchini. Sprinkle with parsley before serving.

about 40 appetizers

If you are a fan of French Onion Soup with a baked cheese topping (page 47), the convection method provides excellent results.

The unique features of each cooking method — microwave, micro/convection, and convection — contribute to making lunch preparation easier than ever before. Convection is responsible for crisp crusts and grilled effects for sandwiches, pizzas, and other lunchtime favorites. The microwave method performs at its very best with sandwiches, hot drinks, soups, and chowders. For a quick pick-me-up all you need is a minute or two and a mug full of water for a cup of instant soup or coffee.

Begin your morning with breakfast cocoa and relax in the evening with after-dinner coffee made easily and quickly thanks to microwave reheating. What a convenience for fresh-brewed coffee lovers. No longer do you have to drink coffee that has bittered from being kept warm the conventional way. Brew your coffee as you normally would, pour what you want to drink now, and refrigerate the rest. Refrigerating will keep the coffee as fresh as when it was brewed. Then, throughout the day, pour single cups as you wish. Place in the oven and reheat (micro) on HI, 2 minutes. In a moment, you have truly fresh coffee.

ADAPTING RECIPES

To convert your soup or hot drink recipes to the microwave method, find a similar recipe in this chapter and follow the time and power level settings used here. Most soup is cooked on HI for an initial cooking sequence to heat the liquids rapidly. It is then usually reduced to 50, providing slower cooking for flavor development and tenderization. For best results, review the following suggestions for adapting or cooking soups, sandwiches, and hot drinks in your micro/convection oven.

- Soup is usually cooked covered. Large casseroles with lids are best, as the lids can be removed easily to check on the food.

- It is always permissible to interrupt cooking by opening the oven door to stir or add ingredients. Simply touch START after closing the door.

- Instead of soaking dried beans overnight, rinse beans in water. Place in a microproof casserole. Add water. Cover with the casserole lid and place in the oven. Cook (micro) on HI, 20 minutes, or until water comes to a full boil. Set aside, covered, for 1 hour. Proceed to cook soup according to your recipe.

- Remember, since there is no heat with the microwave method, there is less evaporation of liquid than with stove top simmering.

- Be careful with milk-based liquids and 2- or 3-quart quantities. They can boil over quickly. Always choose a large microproof container. Fill individual cups of milk-based liquids no more than two-thirds full.

Reheating Soup

To reheat canned soup, use a 1½- or 2-quart microproof casserole. Add milk or water as directed on the can. Cover with casserole lid and cook (micro) on HI, according to the guide. Stir cream-style soup halfway through the cooking time. Let stand, covered, 3 minutes.

Hamburgers are browned by the convection method. For varying doneness, simply make thick patties for rare, and thin for medium.

SOUPS, SANDWICHES, AND HOT DRINKS

- Instant soups and soup mixes are also easily prepared. Use a microproof soup mug or casserole. Add water, according to the guide. Cover with waxed paper or casserole lid and cook (micro) on HI, according to the guide. Let stand, covered, 5 minutes. (If noodles or rice are not tender, return to oven and cook another 1 to 1½ minutes.)

Sandwiches

- With the renewed interest in bread baking, as well as the whole grain and wonderful French and Italian breads available commercially, the enormous variety of sandwich combinations you can create will tickle your imagination. They are easy to heat in your oven. The best breads to use for sandwiches warmed by the microwave method are day-old, full-bodied breads such as rye and whole wheat, and breads rich in eggs and shortening.
- It is best to heat sandwiches on paper towels to absorb the steam and prevent sogginess. You will also discover that several thin slices of deli-style meat heat more quickly and evenly than one thick slice. The thick slice may also cause the bread to overcook before the meat is hot. Heat thick slices separately, then add the bread for a quick warming. The same is true for moist fillings, such as barbecued beef. The bread will overcook or become soggy if the filling and bread are heated together.
- A general guide to reheating sandwiches is to reheat (micro) on HI, 45 to 50 seconds for 1 sandwich. For 2 sandwiches, increase the time to 1 to 1½ minutes, and for 4 sandwiches, to 2 to 2½ minutes.
- For frozen pizza, remove ceramic tray, place wire rack in lower position, and preheat to 350°F. Cook (convec) at 350°F, 15 to 17 minutes or until brown and crisp.

REHEATING GUIDE — CANNED SOUP

Soup	Amount	Micro Power	Time (in minutes)	or	Probe Method	Special Notes
Broth	10¾ oz.	80	3 - 4	or	150°F	Use 1½-quart microproof casserole.
Cream Style: Tomato	10¾ oz.	80	5 - 6	or	140°F	Use 1½-quart microproof casserole.
	26 oz.	80	8 - 10	or	140°F	Use 2-quart microproof casserole.
Bean, Pea, or Mushroom	10¾ oz.	70	7 - 8	or	150°F	Use 1½-quart microproof casserole.
Undiluted chunk-style vegetable	10¾ oz.	80	2½ - 4	or	150°F	Use 1-quart microproof casserole.
	19 oz.	80	5 - 7	or	150°F	Use 1½-quart microproof casserole.

REHEATING GUIDE — QUICK SOUP

Soup	Number of Envelopes	Micro Power	Time (in minutes)	or	Probe Method	Special Notes
Instant soup, 1¼-ounce env.	1	HI	2 - 2½	or	150°F	Use ⅔ cup water in 8-ounce mug.
	2	HI	3 - 3½	or	150°F	Use ⅔ cup water per 8-ounce mug.
Soup mix, 2¾-ounce env.	1	HI	8 - 10	or	160°F	Use 4 cups water in 2-quart microproof casserole.

FRENCH ONION SOUP

Cooking Time: 59 minutes to 1 hour 3 minutes

>   2 **pounds onions, thinly sliced**
>   2 **tablespoons butter or margarine**
>   1½ **teaspoons vegetable oil**
>   ¼ **teaspoon sugar**
>   1½ **tablespoons all-purpose flour**
>   4 **cups beef broth**
>   ¼ **cup dry white wine**
>   1 **cup grated Parmesan cheese**
>   ½ **cup (2 ounces) shredded Swiss or Monterey jack cheese**
>   **Salt and pepper to taste**
>   **Croutons**

Combine onions, butter, and oil in 3-quart microproof and heatproof casserole or bowl. Cover with casserole lid and cook (micro) on HI, 8 minutes.

Stir in sugar. Cook (micro) on HI, 25 minutes or until onions begin to brown slightly.

Sprinkle with flour and mix well. Cook (micro) on HI, 1 minute. Remove onions and set aside.

Add stock to casserole and cook (micro) on HI, 6 to 7 minutes. Add onions and wine; stir well.

Cover and cook (micro/convec) at 400°F, 15 minutes or until soup is thickened.

Divide soup among individual heatproof serving bowls and sprinkle with half of the cheeses. Season with salt and pepper. Add croutons and sprinkle with remaining cheeses.

Remove ceramic tray carefully with hot pads. Place wire rack in upper position of oven. Set bowls on wire rack. Cook (convec) at 400°F, 5 to 8 minutes or until cheese is melted and brown.

4 servings

To make your own croutons, cut 6 to 8 ½-inch thick slices of French bread into cubes and arrange on microproof plate. Sprinkle with garlic powder. Cook (micro) on HI, 2 to 2½ minutes until bread is dry and crisp.

CREAM OF MUSHROOM SOUP

Cooking Time: 7 minutes

>   3 **cups chopped mushrooms**
>   2½ **cups chicken broth**
>   ½ **teaspoon onion powder**
>   ¼ **teaspoon salt**
>   ⅛ **teaspoon garlic powder**
>   ⅛ **teaspoon white pepper**
>   1 **cup heavy cream**

Combine mushrooms, broth, and seasonings in 2-quart microproof casserole or soup tureen. Place in oven.

Cook (micro) on HI, 5 minutes. Blend in cream. Cook (micro) on 60, 2 minutes.

6 servings

You can make a lower-calorie soup by substituting whole milk or undiluted evaporated skim milk for the heavy cream.

OLD WORLD LENTIL SOUP

Cooking Time: 1 hour

>   ¾ **cup dried lentils, rinsed and drained**
>   6 **cups water**
>   ½ **pound Polish sausage, cut into ½-inch slices**
>   1 **cup chopped onions**
>   ½ **cup chopped celery**
>   1 **medium tomato, peeled, seeded, and chopped**
>   1 **clove garlic, minced**
>   ¼ **teaspoon freshly ground pepper**
>   ¼ **teaspoon salt**
>   1 **bay leaf**

Combine lentils and water in 3-quart microproof and heatproof casserole and let soak 45 minutes. Add remaining ingredients and mix well.

Cover with casserole lid. Cook (micro/convec) at 320°F, 60 minutes. Discard bay leaf before serving.

4 to 6 servings

Celery leaves are useful. Include some, if you like, whenever chopped celery is used.

COUNTRY VEGETABLE SOUP

Cooking Time: 40 to 45 minutes

- 2 **medium potatoes, peeled and cut into ½-inch cubes**
- 2 **carrots, sliced**
- 2 **small onions, chopped**
- 1 **can (12 ounces) whole kernel corn, drained**
- 1 **can (16 ounces) stewed tomatoes, undrained**
- 4 **cups beef broth**
- 1 **bay leaf**
- 1 **teaspoon salt**
- ½ **teaspoon thyme**
- ⅛ **teaspoon freshly ground pepper**

Combine all ingredients except parsley in 4-quart microproof casserole. Cover with casserole lid and cook (micro) on HI, 20 minutes.

Stir through several times. Cover and cook (micro) on 50, 20 to 25 minutes.

Let stand 5 minutes. Discard bay leaf before serving.

6 *servings*

JAPANESE CAULIFLOWER SOUP

Cooking Time: 24 to 29 minutes

- 3 **tablespoons butter or margarine**
- ¼ **cup all-purpose flour**
- ⅛ **teaspoon ground nutmeg**
- 4 **cups chicken stock**
- 1 **large head cauliflower, broken into florets**
- ¼ **cup whipping cream or evaporated milk**
- 1 **egg yolk**
   Chopped fresh parsley for garnish

Place butter in 3-quart microproof casserole or soup tureen and cook (micro) on HI, 2 minutes. Stir in flour and nutmeg and mix until smooth. Blend in stock.

Cover with casserole lid and cook (micro) on HI, 7 minutes. Set aside a few cauliflower florets for garnish. Add remaining cauliflower to casserole.

Cover and cook (micro) on HI, 12 to 15 minutes or until cauliflower is tender. Transfer soup to blender in batches and purée.

Return to casserole and cook (micro) on HI, 3 to 5 minutes. Combine cream and egg yolk in small bowl, beating thoroughly. Add a little warm soup and blend well. Stir mixture into remaining soup a little at a time. Sprinkle with parsley, add reserved florets, and serve immediately.

4 *servings*

CHILI CON QUESO SOUP

Cooking Time: 18 to 20 minutes

- 3 **tablespoons butter or margarine**
- 1 **large onion, minced**
- 1 **can (28 ounces) peeled tomatoes, drained and cut into pieces, liquid reserved**
- 1 **can (4 ounces) diced green chilies**
- 1 **jar (2 ounces) pimientos, diced**
   Salt and freshly ground pepper to taste
- ½ **pound Cheddar cheese, shredded**
- ¼ **pound Monterey jack cheese, shredded**

Combine butter and onion in 2-quart microproof bowl or soup tureen. Cook (micro) on HI, 7 minutes, stirring once halfway through cooking time.

Add tomatoes and liquid, chilies, pimientos, salt and pepper, and blend well.

Cover and cook (micro) on HI, 9 to 10 minutes or until mixture comes to full boil. Stir in cheeses.

Cook (micro) on HI, 2 to 3 minutes or until cheeses are melted. Serve hot.

4 to 6 *servings*

Fish and Vegetable Bisque (right)

MICRO TIME

FISH AND VEGETABLE BISQUE

Cooking Time: 27 to 32 minutes

  ¾ **pound fish fillets,**
      cut into 1-inch chunks
  ¼ **pound ham, cut into ½-inch cubes**
  1 **can (8 ounces) whole kernel corn,**
      drained
  2 **stalks celery, cut into**
      thin strips
  2 **carrots, cut into thin**
      strips
  1 **small red pepper, cut into**
      thin strips
  1 **small green pepper, cut into**
      thin strips
  2 **small red potatoes, cubed**
  ⅓ **cup all-purpose flour**
  6 **cups hot milk, divided**
  2 **tablespoons chopped fresh parsley**
  1 **teaspoon tarragon**
    Salt and pepper to taste

Place fish and ham in 5-quart microproof casserole. Cover with casserole lid and cook (micro) on 50, 5 minutes.

Add corn, celery, carrots, peppers, and potatoes; stir. Combine flour and 2 cups of the milk in small bowl, blending well. Add to vegetable mixture. Cover and cook (micro) on HI, 10 to 12 minutes.

Gradually stir in remaining milk. Add parsley, tarragon, salt, and pepper. Cover and cook (micro) on 80, 12 to 15 minutes or until vegetables are crisp-tender.

6 to 8 servings

CHICKEN IN THE POT

Cooking Time: 1 hour

  Boiling water
1 4-pound chicken, cut up, giblets
   reserved (liver and kidney
   discarded)
5 to 6 cups hot water
4 large carrots, halved and cut
   into chunks
3 celery stalks, halved and cut
   into chunks
1 onion, quartered
1 small parsnip, halved and cut
   into chunks
1 tablespoon chicken bouillon
   granules
1/8 teaspoon freshly ground pepper
  Chopped fresh parsley for garnish

Pour boiling water over chicken to rinse well. Drain. Arrange chicken and giblets in 4-quart microproof casserole. Add all remaining ingredients except parsley, making sure water completely covers chicken.

Cover and cook (micro) on HI, 60 minutes. Let stand, covered, 15 minutes.

Divide parsley among bowls, fill with soup, and serve.

4 to 6 servings

The boiling water rinse reduces fat and helps eliminate foam. If desired, soup may be strained and broth served separately. Place chicken and vegetables on platter and sprinkle with parsley.

SPINACH SALAD

Cooking Time: 3 to 5 minutes

6 slices bacon, diced
1/4 cup vinegar
2 tablespoons water
1/2 teaspoon salt
1/4 teaspoon freshly ground pepper
1/4 teaspoon dry mustard
12 ounces fresh spinach, washed,
   stems removed
4 green onions, thinly sliced
1 cup sliced mushrooms
1 hard-cooked egg, chopped

Place bacon in 1-quart glass measure. Cover with double length of paper towel, ends tucked under glass

measure, and cook (micro) on HI, 2 to 3 minutes or until crisp. Remove with slotted spoon and let drain on paper towel. Add vinegar, water, salt, pepper, and mustard to drippings; blend well.

Cook (micro) on HI, 1 to 2 minutes or until mixture boils.

Combine spinach, onions, and mushrooms in large salad bowl. Pour hot dressing over top and toss lightly. Sprinkle with chopped egg and reserved bacon. Serve immediately.

6 to 8 servings

POTATO SALAD

Cooking Time: 10 to 12 minutes

2 pounds potatoes, peeled
   and cubed
1/2 cup water
1/4 teaspoon salt
1/4 cup Italian salad dressing
6 hard-cooked eggs,
   divided
1 cup mayonnaise
1 cup chopped celery
1/2 cup chopped onion
1/2 cup (8 tablespoons) chopped
   pimiento, divided
  Salt and freshly ground pepper
   to taste
  Chopped fresh parsley for garnish

Combine potatoes, water, and salt in 4-quart microproof casserole.

Cover and cook (micro) on HI, 10 to 12 minutes or until potatoes are fork tender.

Drain off water. Pour dressing over warm potatoes and toss lightly. Cover and set aside. Finely chop 5 eggs. Add to potatoes and toss again. Blend in mayonnaise, celery, onion, and all but 1 tablespoon pimiento. Season with salt and pepper.

Turn into serving bowl. Thinly slice remaining egg and arrange over potatoes. Sprinkle with parsley and remaining pimiento.

6 servings

BEEF TACOS

Cooking Time: 7 minutes

> 1 pound lean ground beef
> 1 small onion, chopped
> 1 envelope (1¼ ounces) taco
>   seasoning mix
> 10 taco shells
> 1½ cups (6 ounces) shredded Cheddar
>   cheese, divided
> 2 cups shredded lettuce
> 2 medium tomatoes, chopped
> 1 avocado, peeled and diced
>   Dairy sour cream (optional)
>   Hot pepper sauce (optional)

Crumble beef into 2-quart microproof casserole. Add onion. Cook (micro) on HI, 2 minutes. Stir to break up beef.

Cook (micro) on HI, 3 minutes. Remove from oven. Stir beef; drain. Stir in seasoning mix. Stand taco shells in large, shallow, microproof baking dish. Divide beef mixture among shells. Top each with about 1 tablespoon cheese.

Cook (micro) on HI, 2 minutes. Remove tacos from oven. Top each with lettuce, tomatoes, remaining cheese, and avocado. Pass sour cream and hot pepper sauce separately.

10 tacos

HAMBURGERS

Cooking Time: 11 to 15 minutes

> 1 pound lean ground beef
> ¼ cup ketchup
> 2 tablespoons minced onion
>   (optional)
> 1 large clove garlic, minced
>   (optional)
>   Salt and freshly ground pepper
>   to taste

Remove ceramic tray. Place wire rack in upper position of oven and preheat to 450°F.

Combine all ingredients in medium bowl and mix lightly. Shape into 4 patties. Place in aluminum broiling pan.

Cook (convec) at 450°F, 8 to 10 minutes. Turn hamburgers over and continue to cook (convec) at 450°F, 3 minutes for rare, 4 minutes for medium, or 5 minutes for well done.

4 servings

BACON-TOMATO-CHEESE GRILL

Cooking Time: 7 to 8 minutes

> 1 tablespoon butter or margarine
> 2 slices bread
> 2 slices Cheddar cheese
> 2 slices bacon, cooked
> 1 slice tomato, ½-inch thick

Remove ceramic tray. Place wire rack in upper position of oven and preheat to 450°F.

Butter both slices of bread on one side only. Place 1 slice of bread, buttered side down, on baking sheet or aluminum foil tray. Top with 1 slice cheese, then bacon, tomato, and remaining cheese. Top with remaining bread, buttered side up.

Cook (convec) at 450°F, 4 minutes. Turn sandwich over and continue to cook (convec) at 450°F, 3 to 4 minutes. Serve immediately.

1 serving

Up to 4 sandwiches can be grilled at the same time. Timing is not affected.

CONEY ISLAND HOT DOG

Cooking Time: 1¼ minutes

> 1 jumbo (3-ounce) hot dog
> 1 hot dog bun, split
>   Prepared mustard
> 2 tablespoons drained sauerkraut
>   Pickle relish, chili, grated
>   cheese, chopped onion
>   (optional)

Score opposite sides of hot dog in several places. Place on microproof plate.

Cook (micro) on HI, 1 minute. Place hot dog in bun.

Cook (micro) on HI, 15 seconds. Top with mustard, sauerkraut, and selected garnish.

1 serving

Because the hot dog is large, it takes longer to cook than it takes for the bun to become hot. The hot dog is cooked first, then added to the bun.

MEAL-IN-ONE SANDWICH

Cooking Time: 2 to 4 minutes

        1 loaf (1 pound) French bread
        1 to 2 tablespoons prepared mustard
        2 to 4 tablespoons mayonnaise
        2 jars (6 ounces each) marinated
             artichoke hearts, drained,
             liquid reserved
        1 small onion, thinly sliced
             into rings
        1 large tomato, thinly sliced
        1 pound sliced meat
     ½ pound sliced Monterey jack
             or mozzarella cheese

Place wire rack in lower position of oven and preheat to 450°F.

Slice loaf in half lengthwise. Spread one half with mustard and the other half with mayonnaise. Break up artichoke hearts and arrange over both halves. Overlap onion rings on bottom half; top with tomato slices. Arrange half of the meat on each bread half. Spoon some of the artichoke liquid over meat. Top with half of the cheese. Add another layer of meat and cheese to both halves.

Set halves directly on wire rack and cook (micro/convec) at 450°F, 2 to 4 minutes or until cheese begins to melt. Close sandwich, slice, and serve.

6 to 8 servings

Salami, corned beef, ham, turkey, roast beef, or bologna — choose your favorite, or combine them all for this king-size sandwich.

DEEP-DISH PIZZA

Cooking Time: 29 to 39 minutes

        1 loaf (1 pound) frozen white
             bread dough, thawed
        1 can (8 ounces) tomato sauce
        1 large clove garlic, minced
     ½ teaspoon sugar
     ½ teaspoon oregano
     ¼ teaspoon salt
     ⅛ teaspoon freshly ground pepper
     ¾ cup (3 ounces) shredded
             Monterey jack cheese
     ¾ cup (3 ounces) shredded
             mozzarella cheese
     ¼ cup grated Parmesan cheese

Roll out dough into 12-inch circle. Transfer to deep dish pizza pan. Cover with towel and let stand in warm draft-free area.

Combine tomato sauce, garlic, sugar, oregano, salt, and pepper in 1-quart glass measure. Cover with plastic wrap and cook (micro) on 70, 4 minutes. Stir through several times.

Remove ceramic tray. Place wire rack in lower position of oven and preheat to 350°F. Place crust on wire rack and cook (convec) at 350°F, 15 to 20 minutes. Cover with sauce, spreading evenly and leaving a 2-inch border. Top with cheeses and your choice of other toppings.

Cook (convec) at 350°F, 10 to 15 minutes or until brown and crisp. Cut pizza into wedges and serve hot.

6 to 8 servings

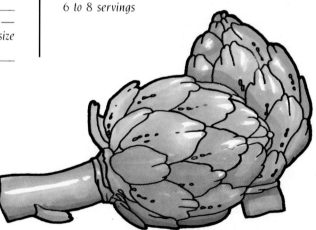

REUBEN SANDWICH

Cooking Time: 6 minutes

> Butter or margarine
> 4 slices rye or pumpernickel bread
> 6 ounces corned beef, thinly
>   sliced
> ½ cup drained sauerkraut
> 2 tablespoons Thousand Island
>   dressing
> 2 slices Swiss cheese

Remove ceramic tray. Place wire rack in lower position of oven and preheat to 450°F.

Lightly butter one side of each slice of bread. Place 2 slices buttered side down on baking sheet or aluminum foil tray. Layer remaining ingredients evenly over tops. Cover with remaining slices of bread buttered side up.

Cook (convec) at 450°F, 3 minutes. Turn sandwiches over.

Continue to cook (convec) at 450°F, 3 minutes. Serve immediately.

2 servings

SPICY APPLE DRINK

Cooking Time: 10 minutes

> 1 quart apple cider
> ¼ cup firmly-packed brown sugar
> 2 cinnamon sticks
> 8 whole cloves
> ½ lemon, thinly sliced
> ⅛ teaspoon mace
> ⅛ teaspoon nutmeg
> 1 orange, thinly sliced for garnish

Combine cider, sugar, cinnamon, cloves, lemon, mace, and nutmeg in 2-quart glass measure or microproof bowl.

Cook (micro) on HI, 10 minutes. Strain into heated mugs. Garnish with orange slices.

4 cups

ITALIAN MEATBALL SANDWICH

Cooking Time: 9 to 11 minutes

> 1 pound lean ground beef
> 1 cup cooked long grain rice
> 1 small onion, finely chopped
> 2 eggs, beaten
> 1 tablespoon Italian seasoning
> 1 jar (15 ounces) spaghetti sauce
>   or 2 cups Homemade Spaghetti
>   Sauce (page 114)
> 1 loaf (1 pound) French or Italian
>   bread, halved lengthwise
> Grated Parmesan cheese

Combine beef, rice, onion, eggs, and seasoning in mixing bowl and blend well. Shape mixture into eight equal meatballs. Arrange on microproof plate.

Cook (micro) on HI, 3 minutes.

Turn meatballs over and continue to cook (micro) on HI, 2 to 3 minutes or until meat just loses its pink color. Transfer meatballs to microproof baking dish and top with sauce.

Cover with plastic wrap and cook (micro) on HI, 4 to 5 minutes or until heated through. Spoon meatballs and sauce onto half of bread loaf and sprinkle generously with Parmesan cheese. Close sandwich with top of loaf. Serve hot.

4 servings

CAPPUCCINO

Cooking Time: 3 to 3½ minutes

> 2 cups milk
> ¼ cup semi-sweet chocolate morsels
> 2 teaspoons sugar
> 2 teaspoons instant coffee
> 8 tablespoons brandy
> Whipped cream for topping

Combine milk and chocolate in 1-quart glass measure.

Cook (micro) on HI, 3 to 3½ minutes or until hot, but not boiling. Add sugar and coffee and stir until dissolved. Divide among 4 mugs. Stir 2 tablespoons brandy into each mug. Top with dollop of whipped cream and serve.

4 servings

Oriental Beef (page 65) uses a special microwave stir-fry technique. The meat is cooked first and moved to the center when vegetables are added.

The convection method will be your first choice for steaks and chops. For convection, remember to remove the ceramic tray. Also for steaks and chops, you'll probably want to use the wire rack in the upper position of the oven. The fan-assisted hot air movement promotes crispness of the fat without drying out the meat.

The perfect method for cooking roasts is micro/convection. While the outside of the roast is browned by the constantly moving hot air (convection), the inside is being cooked quickly by the microwaves.

If guests or some family members prefer their beef rare and others medium, the microwave method solves the problem..After the roast is carved, just seconds of microwave cooking brings slices of rare roast to medium or well done. In addition, meat for the barbecue grill is enhanced by precooking with the microwave method. You still get that wonderful charcoal flavor without the extended attention that grilling often requires.

Microwave roasting methods are similar to dry roasting in your conventional oven. This means that more tender cuts of meat are recommended for best results. Less tender cuts should be marinated or tenderized and cooked at low power settings, such as 30 or 50. Easiest of all, the temperature probe can provide virtually automatic cooking, eliminating the need to calculate the cooking time. The best technique is to set the temperature probe at two (or more) temperatures, providing for a pause after the first temperature is reached. At the pause you can turn the meat over, baste, add ingredients, or do whatever is called for.

ADAPTING RECIPES

Guides on the following pages outline thawing and cooking times and power settings for most standard meat products. The temperature probe offers many cooking options as familiar as the use of a conventional meat thermometer. The advantage of course, is that the temperature probe will automatically call you to the kitchen when the temperature you set has been reached. If you're not ready to serve at that moment, no bother. The temperature probe automatically enters a "Hold" phase to keep your meat hot for up to an hour. You select and set your own desired cooking methods, temperatures, and power levels prior to cooking.

For best results when cooking meat, follow the suggestions provided below and on page 55.

■ Less tender cuts, such as chuck, bottom round, rump, or brisket are usually cooked with the microwave method by using HI for the initial cooking sequence, then changing to 50. This provides the tenderization such cuts require by slower final cooking. The initial HI power sequence aids browning and seals in the juices.

■ Lean ground beef should be used in microwave cooking because the extra fat is not required. If you use regular ground beef, be sure to drain the beef before adding other ingredients.

■ The temperature probe method is best for all tender cuts of meat, as well as meat loaf and pork.

The temperature probe eliminates error when roasting meat, such as Pork Loin Roast (page 69).

■ Recipe times in this book presume meat is at refrigerator temperature. If your meat requires lengthy preparation, during which the meat may reach room temperature, reduce cooking times.

■ Baste, marinate, or season meat in the same way you would for conventional cooking.

■ You can use a roasting rack appropriate to the cooking method to elevate meat from its drippings as it cooks.

■ Check dishes that use relatively long cooking times to be sure liquid has not evaporated. Add liquid as necessary.

■ For steaks, chops, and patties, you will have more surface browning if you preheat the oven to 450°F and cook at that temperature whenever you choose to use micro/convection or convection.

DEFROSTING MEAT

The microwave method is the method of choice for defrosting meat as well as a host of other foods. To help you achieve the best results when defrosting meat, we have prepared the following guidelines.

Meat Loaf (page 65) is cooked by the micro/convection method with the rack in the lower position of the oven. The temperature probe produces the most accurate cooking results.

■ To prepare for defrosting, remove meat from its original paper or plastic wrappings. Place meat in a micro-proof dish.

■ Defrost with the microwave method only as long as necessary, since standing time will complete the thawing process. Items like chops, bacon, and hot dogs should be separated as soon as possible. If some of the pieces are not thawed, distribute evenly in the oven and continue defrosting.

■ We recommend that you only slightly increase the time for weights larger than on the chart. Do not double, however. This conservative approach will help prevent the outside of meat from beginning to cook while the inside is still frozen.

■ If you don't plan to cook immediately, follow the guide for only one-half to three-fourths of the recommended time. Place meat in refrigerator until needed.

REHEATING GUIDE — MEAT*

Food	Micro Power	Time	Probe Method	Special Notes
Barbecued beef, chili, stews, hash etc., 16 oz. can	80	4 to 7 min.	150°F	Place in microproof dish. Cover. Stir halfway through cooking time.
Entrées, frozen, 5½ - 8 oz.		follow package directions		
Stuffed peppers, cabbage rolls, chow mein, etc., 16 - 32 oz.	80	6 to 10 min.	150°F	or follow package directions
Frozen dinners, 11½ - 14 oz.		follow package directions		
Meat pie, double crust, 8 oz.		follow package directions		

*Due to the tremendous variety in convenience food products available, times given here should be used only as guidelines. We suggest you cook food for the shortest recommended time and then check for doneness. Be sure to check the package for microwave instructions.

DEFROSTING GUIDE — MEAT

Meat	Amount	Micro Power	Time (in minutes per pound)	Standing Time (minutes)	Special Notes
Beef Ground beef	1 lb.	30	5 - 6	5	Turn over halfway through defrosting. Remove thawed portions with fork (top and bottom). Return remainder to oven to finish defrosting. Freeze in doughnut shape or depress center when freezing. Defrost on microproof plate.
	¼-lb. patty	30	1 per patty	2	
Pot roast, chuck	under 4 lbs.	30	3 - 5	10	Turn over halfway through defrosting.
	over 4 lbs.	70	3 - 5	10	Turn over halfway through defrosting.
Rib roast, rolled	2 to 4 lbs.	30	6 - 8	30 - 45	Turn over halfway through defrosting.
	6 to 8 lbs.	70	6 - 8	90	Turn over twice during defrosting.
Rib roast, bone in	4 to 5 lbs.	70	5 - 6	45 - 90	Turn over twice during defrosting.
Rump roast	3 to 4 lbs.	30	3 - 5	30	Turn over halfway through defrosting.
	6 to 7 lbs.	70	3 - 5	45	Turn over twice during defrosting.
Round steak	1 to 2 lbs.	30	4 - 5	5 - 10	Turn over halfway through defrosting.
Flank steak	1 lb.	30	4 - 5	5 - 10	Turn over halfway through defrosting.
Sirloin steak	½" thick	30	4 - 5	5 - 10	Turn over halfway through defrosting.
Tenderloin steak	2 to 3 lbs.	30	4 - 5	8 - 10	Turn over halfway through defrosting.
Stew beef	2 lbs.	30	3 - 5	8 - 10	Turn over halfway through defrosting. Separate.
Lamb Cubed for stew		30	7 - 8	5	Turn over halfway through defrosting. Separate.
Ground lamb	1 lb.	30	3 - 5	5	Turn over halfway through defrosting. Remove thawed portions with fork (top and bottom). Return remainder to oven to finish defrosting.
Chops	1" thick	30	5 - 8	15	Turn over twice during defrosting.
Leg	5 - 8 lbs.	30	4 - 5	15 - 20	Turn over twice during defrosting.
Pork Chops	½" thick	30	4 - 6	5 - 10	Separate chops halfway through defrosting.
	1" thick	30	5 - 7	10	
Spareribs, country-style ribs		30	5 - 7	10	Turn over halfway through defrosting.
Roast	under 4 lbs.	30	4 - 5	30 - 45	Turn over halfway through defrosting.
	over 4 lbs.	70	4 - 5	30 - 45	Turn over twice during defrosting.
Bacon	1 lb.	30	2 - 3	3 - 5	Defrost until strips separate.
Sausage, bulk	1 lb.	30	2 - 3	3 - 5	Turn over halfway through defrosting. Remove thawed portions with fork (top and bottom). Return remainder to oven to finish defrosting.
Sausage links	1 lb.	30	3 - 5	4 - 6	Turn over halfway through defrosting. Defrost until links can be separated.
Veal Roast	3 to 4 lbs.	30	5 - 7	30	Turn over halfway through defrosting.
	6 to 7 lbs.	70	5 - 7	90	Turn over twice during defrosting.
Chops	½" thick	30	4 - 6	20	Separate chops halfway through defrosting. Turn thawed side down and continue defrosting.
Variety Meat Hot dogs		30	5 - 6	5	Turn over halfway through defrosting.
Liver		30	5 - 6	10	Turn over halfway through defrosting.
Tongue		30	7 - 8	10	Turn over halfway through defrosting.

NOTE: Your oven is equipped with a Special Defrost feature. Please consult your Use & Care Manual for assistance in defrosting with this method. The timings in the chart here are for manual, or attended, defrosting techniques.

COOKING MEAT

For best results when cooking meat, follow the suggestions and guidelines below.

- Meat should be completely thawed before cooking, all fat should be trimmed, and most meat should be placed fat side down on a roasting rack in a baking dish safe for the cooking method planned. Rack and dish must be microproof for the microwave method, microproof and heatproof for the micro/convection method, and heatproof for convection.

- If you wish, for microwave-method cooking, meat may be covered lightly with waxed paper to stop splatters.

- We suggest that you use the temperature probe for the most accurate cooking of larger cuts. Insert temperature probe as horizontally as possible in the densest area, avoiding fat pockets or bone.

- Times given for steaks and patties will give medium doneness. Form thin patties for well done, and thick patties for rare. By doing this the cooking time for all three levels of doneness can remain the same.

- Ground meat to be used for casseroles should first be cooked briefly. Crumble it into a microproof dish and cook, covered with a paper towel. Then drain off any fat and add meat to the casserole.

- During standing time, the internal temperature of roasts will rise between 5°F and 15°F. Hence, standing time is considered an essential part of the time required to complete cooking.

- Cutlets and chops that are breaded are cooked with the same timing and at the same power control setting as shown in the guide for unbreaded.

TIPS FOR COOKING BACON

- Cook bacon by the microwave method on a paper towel-lined plate, and cover with additional paper towels to prevent splatters and absorb drippings.

- To reserve drippings, cook bacon on a microwave roasting rack in a microproof baking dish or on a microwave bacon rack. Bacon can also be cooked, in slices or cut up, in a casserole dish.

- For bacon that is soft rather than crisp, cook at the minimum timing.

- Bacon varies in quality. The thickness and amount of sugar and salt used in curing will affect browning and timing. Thicker slices take a bit longer to cook.

- High amounts of sugar in bacon may cause it to stick to paper towels. Use only white paper towels, because others may contain harmful dyes.

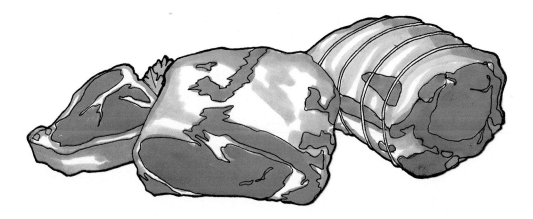

COOKING GUIDE — MEAT

Food	Programming Method	Setting	First Cook Time	Second Cook Time	Probe Method	Special Notes
Beef Ground beef bulk	micro	HI	2 min. per lb.	3 min. per lb.		Crumble in microproof dish.
Ground beef patties, 1 - 4 4 oz. each	convec	450°	Rare: 6 min.	2 - 3 min.		Remove ceramic tray. Place rack in upper position. Preheat. Use broiling pan or aluminum tray.
			Med: 7 min.	3 - 4 min.		
			Well: 8 min.	4 - 5 min.		
Meatloaf, 1½ - 1¾ lbs.	micro/convec	400°	25 min.		160°	Preheat. Let stand 5 - 10 minutes.
Beef rib roast, boneless	micro/convec	330°	6 min. per lb. turn over	6 min. per lb.	Rare: 120° Med: 130°	Place rack in lower position. Use microproof and heatproof dish with trivet.
Beef rib roast, bone-in, 5 lbs.	micro/convec	350°	8 min. per lb. fat-side down turn over	8 min. per lb.	Rare: 120° Med:130° Well: 140°	Place rack in lower position. Use microproof and heatproof dish.
Beef pot roast boneless, 3 lbs.	micro/convec	330°	7 min. per lb. turn over	7 min. per lb.	Med: 130° Well: 140°	Place rack in lower position. Use covered microproof and heatproof casserole or cooking bag.
Beef brisket, corned beef, flat cut, 2 - 3 lbs.	micro/convec	320°	15 - 20 min. per lb. check liquid add if necessary turn over	15 - 20 min. per lb.		Place rack in lower position. Use 4-quart microproof casserole, covered. Cover meat with water. Let stand 15 - 20 minutes after cooking.
Top round steak, 2 - 3 lbs.	micro/convec	350°	8 - 10 min. per lb. turn over check liquid	8 - 10 min. per lb.		Use microproof and heatproof casserole with tight cover or use browning bag. Needs liquid.
Sirloin steak, ¾" thick	convec	450°	Rare: 5 min.	5 - 6 min.		Remove ceramic tray. Place rack in upper position. Preheat. Use metal pan or foil tray.
			Med: 6 min.	6 - 7 min.		
			Well: 7 min.	7 - 8 min.		
			turn over			
Minute steak, cube steak, 4 - 6 oz.	convec	450°	3 - 4 min. turn over	3 - 6 min.		Remove ceramic tray. Place rack in upper position. Preheat. Use metal pan or foil tray.
Tenderloin steak, 4 - 8 oz. 1 inch thick	convec	450°	Rare: 5 min.	3 - 6 min.		Remove ceramic tray. Place rack in upper position. Preheat. Use metal pan or foil tray.
			Med: 5 min.	4 - 7 min.		
			Well: 6 min.	5 - 8 min.		
			turn over			
Rib eye or strip steak, 1 inch thick	convec	450°	Rare: 4 min.	3 - 6 min.		Remove ceramic tray. Place rack in upper position. Preheat. Use metal pan or foil tray.
			Med: 5 min.	4 - 7 min.		
			Well: 6 min.	5 - 8 min.		
			turn over			
Lamb Ground lamb patties, 4 4 oz. each	convec	450°	Rare: 8 min.	3 min.		Remove ceramic tray. Place rack in upper position. Preheat. Use metal pan or foil tray.
			Med: 9 min.	4 min.		
			Well: 10 min.	6 min.		
			turn over			
Lamb chops ¾" thick	convec	450°	Rare: 4 min.	3 - 5 min.		Remove ceramic tray. Place rack in upper position. Preheat. Use metal pan or foil tray.
			Med: 5 min.	4 - 6 min.		
			Well: 7 min.	4 - 6 min.		
Lamb leg or shoulder roast, bone in, 6½ lbs.	micro/convec	330°	3 min. per lb. fat side down turn over	5 - 6 min. per lb.	Rare: 145° Med: 155° Well: 165°	Place rack in lower position. Use microproof and heatproof dish with trivet.
Lamb roast, boneless 3 - 4 lbs.	micro/convec	330°	4 min. per lb. fat side down turn over	4 - 5 min. per lb.	150°	Place rack in lower position. Use microproof and heatproof dish with trivet.
Veal Shoulder or rump roast, boneless, 3 - 3½ lbs.	micro/convec	330°	3 - 5 min. per lb. turn over	4 - 5 min. per lb.	155°	Place rack in lower position. Use microproof and heatproof dish with trivet.
Veal chops ½" thick	convec	450°	4 min. turn over	3 - 4 min.		Remove ceramic tray. Place rack in upper position. Preheat. Use metal pan or foil tray.

COOKING GUIDE — MEAT (Cont'd)

Food	Programming Method	Setting	First Cook Time	Second Cook Time	Probe Method	Special Notes
Pork Pork chops, ½ - ¾" thick	convec	450°	Med: 7 min.	4 - 6 min.		Remove ceramic tray. Place rack in upper position. Preheat. Use metal pan or foil tray.
			Well: 9 min.	5 - 7 min.		
			turn over			
Spareribs, 3 - 4 lbs.	micro/convec	350°	15 - 20 min. per lb. turn over	2 - 3 min. per lb.		Place rack in lower position. Begin cooking in liquid in 3 - 4 quart casserole. Transfer to microproof and heatproof baking dish to finish.
Pork loin roast, boneless, 4 - 5 lbs.	micro/convec	320°	5 - 7 min. per lb. turn over	5 - 7 min. per lb.	165°	Place rack in lower position. Use microproof and heatproof baking dish.
Pork loin, center cut. 4 - 5 lbs.	micro/convec	320°	5 - 7 min. per lb. turn over	5 - 7 min. per lb.	165°	Place rack in lower position. Use microproof and heatproof baking dish.
Ham, boneless precooked	micro	70	5 - 6 min. per lb. turn over	5 - 6 min. per lb.	130°	Place rack in lower position. Use microproof baking dish.
Ham slice, center cut, precooked	convec	450°	4 - 5 min. turn over	5 - 6 min.		Remove ceramic tray. Place rack in upper position. Preheat. Use metal pan or foil tray.
Ham, canned 3 lbs. 5 lbs.	micro	70	5 - 6 min. per lb. turn over 4 - 5 min. per lb.	5 - 6 min. per lb.	130° 130°	Place rack in lower position. Use microproof baking dish.
Sausage patties, ½ - ¾" thick	convec	450°	5 - 7 min. turn over	7 - 9 min.		Remove ceramic tray. Place rack in upper position. Preheat. Use metal pan or foil tray.
Sausage, bulk 1 lb.	micro	HI	3 min. per. lb. stir	1 - 2 min. per lb.		Crumble in 1½-quart microproof dish. Cover with paper towel.
Pork sausage links, ½ - 1 lb.	convec	450°	5 min. rearrange	7 - 9 min.		Remove ceramic tray. Place rack in upper position. Preheat. Use metal pan or foil tray.
Precooked Polish sausage, Knockwurst, Ring bologna	micro	80	2 - 2½ min. per lb. rearrange	2 - 2½ min. per lb.		Pierce casing. Cover with paper towel.
Hot dogs - 1 2 4	micro	80	45 - 60 sec. 50 - 70 sec. 1½ - 2 min.			Use shallow microproof dish or wrap in paper towel.
Bacon: 1 slice 2 slices 4 slices 8 slices	micro	HI	45 sec. - 1 min. 2 - 2½ min. 4 - 4½ min. 5 - 6 min.			Use microproof dish or microwave bacon rack. Cover with paper towel with edges tucked under dish or rack.

ENCHILADA CASSEROLE

Cooking Time: 15 to 16 minutes

- 1¾ **pounds lean ground beef**
- 1 **large onion, chopped**
- 2 **cloves garlic, minced**
- 1 **can (16 ounces) tomato purée**
- 1 **package (1⅝ ounces) taco seasoning mix**
- 6 **corn tortillas**
- 3 **cups (12 ounces) shredded Cheddar cheese, divided**

Crumble beef into 1½-quart microproof casserole. Sprinkle with onion and garlic. Cook (micro) on HI, 3 minutes. Stir through several times.

Cook (micro) on HI, 2 to 3 minutes or until meat loses pink color. Pour off fat. Combine tomato purée and seasoning mix; pour over meat.

Cook (micro) on HI, 3 minutes, stirring several times. Alternate layers of tortillas, meat sauce, and 2½ cups of the cheese in 2-quart round microproof casserole or soufflé dish.

Cover and cook (micro) on HI, 7 minutes. Sprinkle with remaining cheese. To serve, cut into wedges and remove with pie server.

4 to 6 servings

CHUCK ROAST IN A BAG

Cooking Time: 1 hour 15 minutes

> 3 tablespoons all-purpose
>   flour
> 1 tablespoon brown sugar
> ½ teaspoon salt
> ½ teaspoon dry mustard
> ¼ teaspoon freshly ground pepper
> ¾ cup ketchup
> ½ cup water
> 2 tablespoons Worcestershire
>   sauce
> 1 tablespoon vinegar
> 1 lean beef chuck roast,
>   (about 4 pounds)
> 4 medium potatoes, peeled and
>   halved
> 2 large carrots, cut into
>   2-inch chunks
> 1 green pepper, sliced into
>   thin strips
> 1 large onion, sliced

Combine flour, brown sugar, salt, mustard, and pepper in small bowl. Stir in ketchup, water, Worcestershire, and vinegar. Place roast in large cooking bag.

Set bag in 2½-quart shallow microproof and heatproof baking dish. Spoon ketchup mixture over meat. Add remaining ingredients. Close bag with strip cut from open end of the bag.

Set baking dish on ceramic tray. Cook (micro/convec) at 350°F, 45 minutes. Turn bag over.

Continue to cook (micro/convec) at 350°F, 30 minutes.

Let stand 15 minutes before serving.

4 to 6 servings

PORTERHOUSE GRENADIER

Cooking Time: 22½ to 28½ minutes

> 3 tablespoons butter or margarine
> 2 tablespoons chopped green onion
> 1 cup sliced mushrooms
> 1 can (10¾ ounces) golden
>   mushroom soup
> ½ cup (2 ounces) shredded
>   Cheddar cheese
> ⅓ cup Madeira wine
> 1 teaspoon Worcestershire sauce
> ½ teaspoon bottled browning
>   sauce
> 1 beef loin Porterhouse steak
>   (about 1 pound), ¾ inch thick

Place butter in 1-quart glass measure and cook (micro) on HI, 1½ minutes or until melted.

Add onion. Cook (micro) on HI, 2 minutes or until onion is transparent.

Add mushrooms and stir. Cook (micro) on HI, 2 to 3 minutes or until mushrooms begin to soften.

Add soup, cheese, wine, Worcestershire, and browning sauce. Stir through several times. Cover with plastic wrap and cook (micro) on 70, 4 minutes.

Stir thoroughly. Cover and cook (micro) on 70, 4 to 5 minutes or until hot. (Sauce can be made ahead and refrigerated. Reheat (micro) on 70, 6 to 7 minutes, stirring twice during cooking time.)

Remove ceramic tray. Place wire rack in upper position of oven and preheat to 450°F.

Place steak on foil tray. Cook (convec) at 450°F, 5 to 6 minutes.

Turn steak over and continue to cook (convec) at 450°F, 4 minutes for rare, 5 to 6 minutes for medium, or 6 to 7 minutes for well done.

Serve immediately with sauce.

2 to 4 servings

PRIME RIB

Approximate Cooking Time: 45 minutes (rare)

- 1 **beef rib roast small end (5 pounds)**
- 3 **cloves garlic, minced**
- 1 **pound mushrooms, sliced (about 4 cups)**

Set roast fat side down in shallow microproof and heatproof dish. Rub entire surface with garlic. Cook (micro/convec) at 330°F, 20 minutes.

Turn roast on its side and continue to cook (micro/convec) at 330°F, 10 minutes.

Stand roast on bone, insert probe, and arrange mushrooms in dish around roast. Plug in probe. Continue to cook (micro/convec) at 330°F with probe set at 120°F for rare, 130°F for medium, or 140°F for well done.

Let stand 10 minutes before carving.

4 to 6 servings

SPICY BEEF SHORT RIBS

Cooking Time: 1 hour 35 minutes

- 3 **pounds beef short ribs, trimmed**
- 8 **to 10 cups hot water**
- 1 **large onion, thickly sliced into rings**
- 1 **teaspoon salt**
- 6 **celery tops with leaves Barbecue Sauce (page 114)**

Rinse ribs with hot water and drain well. Arrange in 4-quart microproof and heatproof casserole. Top with onion and sprinkle with salt. Arrange celery over onions. Add enough hot water to completely cover mixture.

Cover with casserole lid. Cook (micro/convec) at 350°F, 55 minutes.

Drain ribs, discarding onion and celery. Pour sauce over ribs, turning to coat evenly. Cover and cook (micro/convec) at 350°F, 15 minutes. Turn ribs over.

Cover and cook (micro/convec) at 350°F, 25 minutes.

4 servings

VEGETABLE-STUFFED FLANK STEAK

Cooking Time: 21½ minutes

- 1 **1½-pound flank steak**
- ¼ **cup chopped celery**
- ¼ **cup chopped green onion**
- 2 **cloves garlic, minced**
- 2 **teaspoons chopped fresh parsley**
- 1 **tablespoon butter or margarine**
- 1 **cup seasoned croutons, crushed**
- 2 **tablespoons dry white wine**
- 1 **tablespoon soy sauce**
- ⅛ **teaspoon freshly ground pepper**

Score both sides of steak using tip of sharp knife and set aside. Combine celery, onion, garlic, and parsley in small microproof bowl. Add butter and cook (micro) on HI, 1½ minutes.

Place wire rack in lower position of oven and preheat to 350°F.

Add crushed croutons to vegetable mixture and blend well. Spread stuffing over meat, leaving 1-inch border on all sides. Carefully roll up meat lengthwise; tie in 3 places. Arrange seam side down in microproof and heatproof dish.

Combine wine, soy sauce, and pepper; brush over meat.

Cook (mico/convec) at 350°F, 10 minutes. Brush meat with wine mixture, turn meat over, and brush again.

Continue to cook (micro/convec) at 350°F, 10 minutes. Brush with remaining wine mixture. Let stand, covered, 10 minutes before serving.

4 to 6 servings

For tasty stuffing, place ½ pound bulk pork sausage in microproof bowl and cook (micro) on HI, 3 minutes. Add ½ cup saltine cracker crumbs, ½ cup chopped tart apple, ¼ cup chopped celery, 1 tablespoon minced onion, ⅛ teaspoon salt, and ¼ teaspoon paprika. Stuff steak and cook as above.

Tenderloin of Beef Supreme (right)

TENDERLOIN OF BEEF SUPREME

Approximate Cooking Time: 35 minutes

> 1 **beef tenderloin roast
>   (2 to 2½ pounds)**
> 3 **tablespoons onion soup mix**
> ½ **pound mushrooms, finely chopped
>   (about 2 cups)**

Remove ceramic tray. Place wire rack in lower position of oven and preheat to 450°F.

Set meat in shallow heatproof baking dish and sprinkle with soup mix. Arrange mushrooms over and around roast. Cook (convec) at 450°F, 18 minutes.

Turn meat over and baste with mushrooms and drippings. Insert temperature probe horizontally into thickest part of roast. Plug in probe. Cook (convec) at 450°F with probe set at 120°F.

Let stand 5 minutes before serving.

4 to 6 servings

NEW ENGLAND BOILED DINNER

Cooking Time: 1 hour 33 minutes to
            1 hour 35 minutes

> 1 **3- to 3¼-pound flat cut corned
>   beef brisket, rinsed**
> 5 **to 6 whole new potatoes, rinsed**
> 4 **medium carrots, quartered**
> 1 **medium head cabbage, cut
>   into wedges**
>   **Water**

Preheat oven to 350°F.

Place meat in 5-quart microproof and heatproof casserole. Add potatoes and carrots. Pour in enough water to cover completely.

Cover with casserole lid and cook (micro/convec) at 350°F, 40 minutes. Turn meat over and add water as necessary to keep ingredients covered.

Cover and continue to cook (micro/convec) at 350°F, 50 minutes or until meat is tender. Let stand, covered, 20 to 30 minutes. Arrange cabbage over top.

Cover and cook (micro) on HI, 3 to 5 minutes or until cabbage is crisp-tender. Transfer meat to platter and slice thinly. Surround with vegetables. Serve hot.

4 to 6 servings

BRISKET OF BEEF

Cooking Time: 2 hours

- 3 large onions, sliced into rings
- 1 2- to 3-pound flat cut brisket of beef
- 1 envelope (1½ ounces) onion soup mix
- 1 cup water or dry white wine
- 12 large mushrooms, finely chopped
- 4 medium potatoes, peeled

Arrange half of the onions in 4-quart microproof and heatproof casserole. Set brisket on top, cutting in half if necessary. Sprinkle with onion soup mix. Arrange remaining onions on top. Pour in water or wine.

Cover with casserole lid and cook (micro/convec) at 320°F, 40 minutes. Turn meat over. Add mushrooms and potatoes. Spoon onions and accumulated liquid over top, adding more water if necessary.

Cover and continue to cook (micro/convec) at 320°F, 20 minutes. Turn meat and potatoes over. Cover and cook (micro/convec) at 320°F, 40 minutes.

Transfer meat to cutting board. Keep potatoes and sauce covered. Slice meat thinly across the grain and return to dish.

Cook (micro/convec) at 320°F, about 20 minutes or until heated through.

4 to 6 servings

JUMBO MEATBALLS

Cooking Time: 15 to 16 minutes

- 1 pound lean ground beef
- 1 medium potato, peeled and coarsely grated
- 2 tablespoons onion soup mix
- 3 tablespoons chopped fresh parsley
- 1 egg, beaten
- 2 cups beef broth
- 1 tablespoon Worcestershire sauce
- 2 tablespoons cornstarch
- 2 tablespoons water

Combine beef, potato, soup mix, parsley, and egg in large bowl and blend well. Shape into 12 1½-inch meatballs. Combine broth and Worcestershire in 2-quart microproof casserole. Add meatballs and stir.

Cover and cook (micro) on 70, 10 minutes. Combine cornstarch and water in small bowl and mix until smooth. Stir into broth.

Cover and cook (micro) on 70, 5 to 6 minutes or until sauce is thickened. Stir through several times.

4 servings

STUFFED ONIONS

Cooking Time: 28 minutes

- 4 large onions
- ¼ cup water
- ½ pound lean ground beef
- 1 can (8 ounces) tomato sauce, divided
- ½ teaspoon chili powder
- ¼ teaspoon freshly ground pepper
- ¼ cup Italian bread crumbs
- ½ cup (2 ounces) shredded Cheddar cheese
- Chopped fresh parsley for garnish

Peel onions and cut thin section off bottoms so they stand upright, keeping layers intact so they will not separate. Cut tops from onions; set aside 3 slices.

Arrange onions stem side down in 1½-quart microproof casserole. Pour in water.

Cover and cook (micro) on HI, 10 minutes. Turn onion stem side up. Cover with casserole lid and cook (micro) on HI, 3 minutes. Set aside to cool.

Scoop out centers of onions, leaving 3 layers (about ⅓-inch shell). Chop pulp and reserved slices and measure ¾ cup. Transfer to 1½-quart microproof casserole. Crumble in beef.

Cook (micro) on HI, 3 minutes or just until meat loses pink color. Drain off liquid. Blend in half of tomato sauce, chili powder, pepper, and bread crumbs. Cover and cook (micro) on HI, 4 minutes.

Place wire rack in lower position of oven and preheat to 350°F.

Mound stuffing in shells; do not pack tightly. Arrange in microproof and heatproof baking dish just large enough to accommodate onions. Spoon remaining tomato sauce evenly over tops.

Cook (micro/convec) at 350°F, 5 minutes. Sprinkle with cheese. Continue to cook (micro/convec) at 350°F, 3 minutes or until cheese is melted.

Sprinkle with parsley and serve.

4 servings

SPECIAL SWISS STEAK

Cooking Time: 1 hour 4 minutes

        2   **pounds beef top round steak,**
              ½ inch thick
        2   **tablespoons butter or margarine**
        1   **medium onion, minced**
        1   **tablespoon cornstarch**
        1   **can (8 ounces) tomato sauce**
        ½   **cup beef broth**
        1   **tablespoon Worcestershire sauce**
        ½   **teaspoon Italian herb seasoning**
        2   **cups (1 pint) whole cherry tomatoes**
        1   **package (10 ounces) frozen**
              whole green beans
        1   **package (10 ounces) frozen**
              pearl onions

Pound steak on both sides with meat mallet or flat side of cleaver. Cut into 4 pieces and set aside.

Place butter and chopped onion in 5-quart shallow microproof and heatproof casserole. Cook on HI, 4 minutes or until onions are transparent.

Add cornstarch and stir until well blended. Stir in tomato sauce, broth, Worcestershire, and Italian seasoning. Add steak. Spoon sauce over steak. Cover with casserole lid. Cook (micro) on 50, 35 minutes.

Rearrange steak. Arrange beans and pearl onions on top. Cover and cook (micro) on 50, 20 minutes.

Add cherry tomatoes. Cover and cook (micro) on 80, 5 minutes or until heated through.

4 servings

BAKED BEEFY MACARONI

Cooking Time: 21 minutes

        1   **pound lean ground beef**
        1   **jar (15 ounces) spaghetti**
              sauce or 2 cups Homemade
              Spaghetti Sauce (page 114)
      10   **ounces elbow macaroni, cooked**
        1½ **cups (6 ounces) shredded**
              Cheddar cheese

Crumble beef into 8-inch round microproof and heatproof baking dish. Cook (micro) on HI, 6 minutes. Remove from oven. Stir through meat once. Drain well.

Place wire rack in lower position of oven and preheat to 350°F.

Add spaghetti sauce and macaroni to meat and mix well. Cook (micro/convec) at 350°F, 10 minutes. Sprinkle cheese over top.

Cook (micro/convec) at 350°F, 5 minutes. Serve immediately.

4 to 6 servings

Special Swiss Steak (left)

ORIENTAL BEEF

Cooking Time: 15 minutes

- ½ **cup soy sauce**
- ½ **cup dry sherry**
- ½ **cup water**
- 1 **tablespoon sugar**
- 1 **clove garlic, minced**
- 2 **thin slices fresh ginger, minced**
- 1 **beef loin sirloin steak boneless (1½ to 2 pounds), cut into thin strips**
- ½ **medium bunch broccoli**
- 1 **package (6 ounces) frozen snow peas**
- 1 **red pepper, cut into thin strips**
- 1 **small zucchini (about 4 ounces) sliced**
  Cooked rice to serve

Combine soy sauce, sherry, water, sugar, garlic, and ginger in 3-quart microproof casserole. Add steak and stir to coat. Cover with casserole lid and let stand at room temperature 2 hours, stirring occasionally.

Cut broccoli stems diagonally into thin slices and break florets into individual pieces. Combine broccoli, snow peas, red pepper, and zucchini. Arrange marinated steak in center of casserole. Arrange vegetables around steak. Cover and cook (micro) on HI, 5 minutes.

Stir. Cook (micro) on 50, 10 minutes.
Serve with rice.

4 to 6 servings

MEAT LOAF

Approximate Cooking Time: 30 minutes

- 1½ **pounds lean ground beef**
- 2 **eggs, lightly beaten**
- 1 **medium onion, finely chopped**
- 1 **can (8 ounces) tomato sauce, divided**
- 2 **slices bread, rinsed with warm water, squeezed dry and torn into pieces**
- 1 **teaspoon Worcestershire sauce**
- ½ **teaspoon salt**
- ¼ **teaspoon freshly ground pepper**
- 1 **clove garlic, crushed**
- 3 **hard-cooked eggs**

Place wire rack in lower position of oven and preheat to 400°F.

Combine beef, beaten eggs, onion, ⅓ cup of the tomato sauce, bread, Worcestershire, salt, pepper, and garlic in large bowl. Mix to blend well.

Turn half of the beef mixture into 9x5-inch microproof and heatproof loaf dish, spreading evenly. Arrange hard-cooked eggs in center. Cover with remaining meat mixture, smoothing top. Brush remaining tomato sauce over meat.

Insert temperature probe in center of meat loaf.

Plug in probe. Cook (micro/convec) at 400°F with probe set at 160°F. Pour off juices before serving.

6 to 8 servings

A unique surprise! Each slice of this special loaf contains a cross section of egg.

ROLLED VEGETABLE MEAT LOAF

Cooking Time: 25 to 32 minutes

- 1¾ **pounds lean ground beef**
- 2 **eggs, lightly beaten**
- 2 **tablespoons ketchup**
- ¼ **cup dry bread crumbs**
- 1 **teaspoon salt**
- ¼ **teaspoon freshly ground pepper**

Filling:
- ¾ **cup chopped onions**
- ½ **cup chopped green pepper**
- ½ **cup chopped celery**
- 1 **jar (2 ounces) pimiento, drained**
- ½ **teaspoon garlic powder**

Place wire rack in lower position of oven and preheat to 380°F.

Combine beef, eggs, ketchup, bread crumbs, salt, and pepper; mix lightly. Turn mixture out onto waxed paper and shape into 8x10-inch rectangle. Combine remaining ingredients in medium bowl. Spread evenly over meat, leaving 1-inch border on all sides. Carefully roll up meat from short end, pressing edges together to seal.

Arrange roll seam side down in 9x5-inch microproof and heatproof loaf dish.

Cook (micro/convec) at 380°F, 12½ to 16 minutes.

Rotate dish and continue to cook (micro/convec) at 380°F, 12½ to 16 minutes. Let stand 3 minutes before serving.

4 to 6 servings

VEAL CORDON BLEU

Cooking Time: 12 to 14 minutes

> 6 slices prosciutto ham
> 6 slices mozzarella cheese
> 6 slices veal (about 1 to 1¼
>   pounds), pounded thin
> 1 cup seasoned bread crumbs
> ¼ teaspoon salt
> ⅛ teaspoon freshly ground pepper
> 1 egg, lightly beaten
> 3 tablespoons vegetable oil
> 2 tablespoons chopped fresh parsley

Place wire rack in lower position of oven and preheat to 350°F.

Place slice of ham and cheese on each veal slice. Roll up and secure with toothpick. Combine bread crumbs, salt, and pepper in shallow dish. Coat each veal roll with bread crumbs, dip in beaten egg, and coat again with bread crumbs, covering completely. Pour half of the oil into bottom of microproof and heatproof baking dish. Arrange veal rolls in dish and drizzle with remaining oil.

Cook (micro/convec) at 350°F, 12 to 14 minutes. Spoon any cheese from bottom of dish over veal. Sprinkle with parsley and serve immediately.

4 servings

MEDALLIONS OF VEAL

Cooking Time: 10 minutes

> ¼ cup all-purpose flour
>   Salt and freshly ground pepper
>   to taste
> 8 slices veal (about ¾ pound),
>   pounded thin
> 3 tablespoons vegetable oil
> 2 tablespoons finely minced shallots
> ½ pound fresh mushrooms,
>   thinly sliced
> ¼ cup dry white wine

Remove ceramic tray. Place wire rack in upper position of oven and preheat to 450°F.

Combine flour, salt, and pepper in shallow dish. Coat veal on both sides with flour mixture, covering completely. Combine oil and shallots in shallow heatproof baking dish.

Place shallot mixture in oven. Cook (convec) at 450°F, 2 minutes. Add veal to dish.

Cook (convec) at 450°F, 4 minutes. Turn veal over. Add mushrooms and wine.

Continue to cook (convec) at 450°F, 4 minutes. Let stand, covered, 5 minutes before serving.

2 to 3 servings

VEAL PARMIGIANA

Cooking Time: 17 minutes

> 4 veal cutlets (1 pound)
> ½ cup cracker meal or dry
>   bread crumbs
> ½ cup grated Parmesan cheese
> 1 egg, beaten with ¼ teaspoon
>   salt
> ½ cup chopped onions
> 1 can (8 ounces) tomato sauce
> 3 tablespoons tomato paste
> ½ teaspoon sugar
> ⅛ teaspoon oregano
> ⅛ teaspoon freshly ground pepper
> 4 slices mozzarella cheese
> 2 tablespoons grated Parmesan
>   cheese
> 2 tablespoons chopped fresh
>   parsley

Place wire rack in lower position of oven and preheat to 300°F.

Pound veal lightly to even thickness. Mix cracker meal and ½ cup Parmesan cheese in shallow dish. Dip veal in egg, then roll in crumb mixture, coating completely. Sprinkle onions in bottom of microproof and heatproof baking dish. Arrange veal in single layer over onions.

Cook (micro/convec) at 300°F, 12 minutes. Combine tomato sauce, tomato paste, sugar, oregano, and pepper. Spoon tomato mixture over veal. Top with mozzarella cheese.

Cook (micro/convec) at 300°F, 5 minutes. Sprinkle veal with remaining Parmesan cheese and parsley. Serve immediately.

4 servings

California Lamb Chops (right)

CALIFORNIA LAMB CHOPS

Cooking Time: 17½ to 23½ minutes

  4 **lamb shoulder arm chops
       (4 ounces each)**
  ½ **cup butter or margarine**
  1 **cup white wine or chicken broth**
  2 **teaspoons chopped chives**
  ½ **teaspoon Dijon-style mustard**
  ½ **teaspoon tarragon**
  ½ **teaspoon rosemary**
  ⅛ **teaspoon freshly ground pepper**
  2 **eggs, lightly beaten**

Trim all fat from lamb chops. Set aside.

Combine remaining ingredients, except eggs, in 2-cup glass measure. Cook (micro) on HI, 2½ minutes. Slowly beat hot liquid into eggs.

Remove ceramic tray. Place wire rack in lower position of oven and preheat to 450°F.

Arrange chops on broiler pan. Cook (convec) at 450°F, 8 minutes.

Turn chops over and continue to cook (convec) at 450°F, 6 minutes for rare, 8 minutes for medium, and 12 minutes for well done.

Remove rack carefully with hot pads. Place ceramic tray in oven. To reheat sauce, cook (micro) on 50, 1 minute. Pour sauce evenly onto 4 serving plates. Place meat on sauce.

2 servings

LAMB SHANKS FOR TWO

Cooking Time: 20 to 22 minutes

  2 **lamb shanks (about 1½ pounds)**
  1 **teaspoon lemon juice**
  1 **clove garlic, finely minced
       Freshly ground pepper to taste**

Place wire rack in upper position of oven and preheat to 450°F.

Sprinkle lamb with lemon juice, garlic, and pepper. Arrange in microproof and heatproof baking dish. Cook (micro/convec) at 450°F, 15 minutes. Turn shanks over and continue to cook (micro/convec) at 450°F, 5 to 7 minutes.

2 servings

SHISH KABOBS

Cooking Time: 17 to 18 minutes

　　1　cup prepared chili sauce
　½　cup ketchup
　　1　tablespoon honey
　　1　tablespoon prepared red
　　　　horseradish
　　1　tablespoon chopped chutney
　　　　(optional)
　　1　pound lamb, cut into 12 cubes
　　1　green pepper, cut into 12
　　　　pieces
　　1　large onion, cut into 12
　　　　chunks
　12　small mushrooms
　　4　12-inch bamboo skewers

Combine chili sauce, ketchup, honey, horseradish, and chutney in 1-quart microproof bowl. Cover and cook (micro) on HI, 3 to 4 minutes or until sauce just begins to boil.

Place wire rack in lower position of oven and pre-heat to 350°F.

Alternate lamb, green pepper, onion, and mushrooms on each skewer. Set skewers in 13x9-inch microproof and heatproof baking dish. Brush generously with sauce. Cook (micro/convec) at 350°F, 7 minutes.

Turn kabobs over and baste with sauce. Cook (micro/convec) at 350°F, 7 minutes or until meat is tender.

4 servings

PORK RIBS

Cooking Time: 50 minutes

　　4　pounds country-style pork ribs
　　7　cups water
　　1　jar (24 ounces) sauerkraut,
　　　　drained and rinsed
　　1　jar (16 ounces) sweet-sour red
　　　　cabbage
　　1　medium onion, chopped
　　　　Salt and freshly ground pepper
　　　　to taste

Arrange ribs in 4-quart microproof casserole. Add water.

Cover with casserole lid and cook (micro) on HI, 20 minutes. Stir once during cooking. Drain well and set aside.

Place wire rack in lower position of oven and pre-heat to 300°F.

Combine sauerkraut and red cabbage in 13x9-inch microproof and heatproof baking dish. Arrange ribs over top. Sprinkle with onion and season with salt and pepper.

Cook (micro/convec) at 300°F, 30 minutes.

6 servings

SWEET AND SOUR PORK

Cooking Time: 41 to 46 minutes

　　4　medium carrots, thinly sliced
　¼　cup vegetable oil
　　2　pounds lean pork, cut into
　　　　½-inch cubes
　　1　medium onion, sliced
　　2　green peppers, seeded and sliced
　　1　can (16 ounces) pineapple chunks
　¼　cup cornstarch
　½　cup soy sauce
　½　cup firmly packed light
　　　　brown sugar
　¼　cup vinegar
　　1　tablespoon Worcestershire sauce
　¼　teaspoon hot pepper sauce
　½　teaspoon freshly ground pepper
　　　　Chow mein noodles or
　　　　　hot cooked rice to serve

Combine carrots and oil in 3-quart microproof and heatproof casserole.

Cover with casserole lid and cook (micro) on HI, 6 minutes. Add pork, onion, and green peppers.

Cover and cook (micro) on HI, 5 minutes. Drain pineapple chunks, reserving ½ cup syrup. Transfer syrup to bowl. Stir in cornstarch. Blend in remaining ingredients. Add to pork with pineapple chunks, mixing thoroughly.

Cover and cook (micro/convec) at 350°F, 15 minutes.

Stir through several times and continue to cook (micro/convec) at 350°F, 15 to 20 minutes or until sauce has thickened and pork is done.

Serve over chow mein noodles or cooked rice.

4 to 6 servings

PORK LOIN ROAST

Approximate Cooking Time: 1 hour 45 minutes

  1 **4- to 5-pound pork loin roast**
  2 **tablespoons honey**
  1 **tablespoon Worcestershire sauce**
  6 **unpeeled, medium potatoes,**
      halved lengthwise
  2 **medium onions, quartered**
  ½ **cup water**

Place pork fat side up in 13x9-inch microproof and heatproof baking dish. Combine honey and Worcestershire in small bowl. Brush on roast.

Cook (micro/convec) at 320°F, 25 minutes. Remove pork from dish and set aside.

Arrange potatoes cut side down in dish. Add water. Set roast over potatoes and surround with onions.

Insert temperature probe horizontally into thickest part of roast. Plug in probe. Cook (micro/convec) at 320°F, with probe set at 130°F.

Turn roast over, being careful not to dislodge probe. Continue to cook (micro/convec) at 320°F, with probe set at 165°F.

Let stand in oven 10 minutes before serving.

6 to 8 servings

BAKED HAM WITH PINEAPPLE

Approximate Cooking Time: 28 minutes

  1 **5-pound canned ham**
     Whole cloves
  1 **can (8 ounces) crushed**
      pineapple, undrained
  ½ **cup firmly-packed brown sugar**
  1 **tablespoon fresh lemon juice**
  1 **tablespoon cornstarch**
  2 **teaspoons dry mustard**

Set ham fat side up in microproof and heatproof baking dish. Score top in checkerboard pattern and stud with cloves where lines intersect.

Cook (micro/convec) at 320°F, 18 minutes. Remove ham from oven and drain off excess liquid.

Mix all remaining ingredients in small microproof bowl. Cook (micro) on HI, 2 minutes, stirring halfway through cooking time. Continue to cook (micro) on HI, 1 minute or until mixture thickens and begins to clear. Remove bowl from oven and spoon mixture over ham, keeping pineapple on top.

Insert temperature probe horizontally into center of ham. Return ham to oven. Plug in probe. Cook (micro/convec) at 320°F, with probe set at 130°F, basting twice during cooking.

Let stand 10 minutes before serving.

8 to 10 servings

When preparing the glaze, the oven will be hot. Be sure to use hot pads even though only microwave energy is being used for this step.

STUFFED PORK CHOPS

Cooking Time: 21 to 23 minutes

  ¼ **cup butter or margarine,**
      divided
  ¼ **cup minced onion**
  ¾ **cup chopped peeled apples**
  3 **tablespoons chopped raisins**
  1 **cup coarse dry bread crumbs**
  ¼ **cup hot water**
  2 **tablespoons sugar**
  ⅛ **teaspoon sage, rosemary, and thyme**
  ½ **teaspoon salt**
  ¼ **teaspoon freshly ground pepper**
  4 **rib or loin pork chops, 1½-inch**
      thick, with pockets

Combine 2 tablespoons of the butter and minced onion in 1-quart microproof bowl. Cook (micro) on HI, 2 minutes.

Stir in apples and raisins. Cook (micro) on HI, 1 minute.

Stir in remaining ingredients except chops. Fill pockets with equal amounts of stuffing. Arrange in 8-inch round microproof and heatproof baking dish.

Cook (micro/convec) at 320°F, 18 to 20 minutes.

4 servings

SCALLOPED HAM AND POTATOES

Cooking Time: 26½ to 31½ minutes

>   2 large onions, thinly sliced
>   2 tablespoons butter or margarine
>   4 medium red potatoes (about
>   2 pounds), peeled and thinly
>   sliced, divided
> 1½ to 2 cups cubed cooked ham,
>   divided
>   3 tablespoons all-purpose flour
>   ⅛ teaspoon salt
>   ⅛ teaspoon freshly ground pepper
> 1½ cups (6 ounces) shredded sharp
>   Cheddar cheese, divided
>   Paprika
>   1 cup milk

Combine onions and 2 tablespoons butter in 2-quart microproof casserole. Cover with casserole lid and cook (micro) on HI, 10 minutes, stirring once during cooking.

Remove onions from dish and set aside. Layer half of the potatoes and half of the ham in bottom of same dish.

Combine flour, salt, and pepper in small bowl. Sprinkle half of the flour mixture over ham. Top with half of the onion and half of the cheese. Sprinkle with paprika. Repeat layering.

Pour milk into 2-cup glass measure and cook (micro) on HI, 1½ minutes or until scalded. Pour over top.

Cover and cook (micro) on HI, 15 to 20 minutes or until potatoes in center of dish are fork tender. Serve hot.

4 to 6 servings

Potatoes vary greatly in moisture content and density. You may need to adjust timing.

LIVER, BACON, AND ONIONS

Cooking Time: 18 to 19 minutes

>   4 slices bacon
>   1 large onion, sliced into rings
>   1 pound liver, about ½ to
>   ¾ inch thick

Arrange bacon in shallow microproof and heatproof dish and cover with paper towel.

Cook (micro) on HI, 4 to 5 minutes or until bacon is crisp. Remove bacon and set aside.

Add onion slices to bacon drippings, stirring to coat. Cook (micro) on HI, 4 minutes. Set aside.

Place wire rack in upper position of oven and preheat to 320°F.

Push onions to outer edge of dish and place liver in center.

Cook (micro/convec) at 320°F, 5 minutes. Turn liver over and continue to cook (micro/convec) at 320°F, 5 minutes or until liver is medium rare. Sprinkle with crumbled bacon.

2 to 3 servings

FRANKS AND BEANS

Cooking Time: 23 minutes

>   ½ pound bacon, chopped
>   ½ cup chopped onion
>   1 can (28 ounces) baked beans
>   ¼ cup firmly-packed brown sugar
>   1 teaspoon Worcestershire sauce
>   1 pound frankfurters

Place bacon in 2-quart microproof casserole and cover with paper towel. Cook (micro) on HI, 5 minutes.

Add onion. Cover and cook (micro) on HI, 3 minutes. Stir in beans, sugar, and Worcestershire. Cut franks in half lengthwise and score to prevent curling.

Arrange half of the cut franks in single layer in 8-inch square microproof and heatproof baking dish. Spread half of the bean mixture over top. Repeat layering.

Place wire rack in lower position of oven. Cook (micro/convec) at 350°F, 15 minutes or until heated through. Serve hot.

4 servings

An uncoated chicken breast (left center) and a few of the possible coatings: seasoned bread crumbs, barbecue sauce, cornflake crumbs, and honey-soy glaze.

Chicken Breasts Miyako (page 76) are rolled and placed along outer edge of a microproof baking dish for even cooking.

Poultry turns out crisper, browner, and juicier than ever, thanks to the micro/convection cooking method. If you've never tried your hand at a duck or goose, now's the time.

You can also avoid the frustrations of long barbecue cooking by partially cooking poultry with the microwave method, then finishing it off on the charcoal grill. Try the tasty recipes suggested here and then adapt your own. You'll even want to experiment with new recipes when you discover how much easier it is to cook poultry in your micro/convection oven. The nicest thing of all is that most poultry recipes cook with little or no attention from the cook. What's more, many of them can be cooked using the temperature probe, eliminating the need for you to calculate the cooking time.

ADAPTING RECIPES

Poultry recipes for which you select the micro/convection method will not need ingredient changes in preparing them for this oven. Compare using a similar recipe in this chapter and review the conversion explanation on page 38. If you want an extra-crisp, well-browned skin (on your duckling or turkey, for example), cook for additional time using the convection method.

For best results when cooking poultry, follow these easy guidelines.

- To obtain uniform doneness and flavor, cook poultry weighing no more than 10 pounds in the micro/convection oven. Poultry over 10 pounds should be cooked conventionally.

- The temperature probe may be used in cooking whole poultry. Insert the probe in the fleshy part of the inside thigh muscle without touching the bone.

- Poultry pieces prepared in a cream sauce should be cooked (micro) on 70 to prevent the cream from separating or curdling.

- Chicken coated with a crumb mixture cooks to crispness more easily if left uncovered.

- Less tender game birds should be cooked on a microwave roasting rack, placed in a microproof baking dish. Cook (micro) on 70 to provide tenderizing. Pour off fat as necessary. For best results, marinate game birds before cooking.

- Conventional pop-up indicators for doneness do not work correctly with the microwave or micro/convection methods.

- Standing time is essential to complete cooking. Allow up to 15 minutes standing time for whole poultry, depending upon size. The internal temperature will rise approximately 15°F during 15 minutes standing time. Chicken pieces and casseroles need only 5 minutes standing time.

DEFROSTING POULTRY

To prepare for defrosting, remove poultry from original paper or plastic wrappings. Metal leg clamps of frozen turkey need not be removed until after thawing. Keep metal at least 1 inch from oven walls.

Defrost only as long as necessary. Poultry should be cool in the center, in fact still a bit icy. Standing time completes the thawing process.

Wing and leg tips and area near breastbone may need to be shielded to prevent cooking. As soon as they appear thawed, cover with small strips of foil, keeping foil at least 1 inch from oven walls.

Turn all poultry over between the first and second stages of defrosting (at the pause signal, if you use the PAUSE touch pad and set both defrosting sequences before touching START).

COOKING POULTRY

There are just a few basic recommendations in cooking poultry, many of which apply as well to conventional cooking.

When cooking whole birds, place on a roasting rack set in a baking dish that is safe for the cooking method planned. Rack and dish must be microproof for the microwave method; microproof and heatproof for the micro/convection method; heatproof for convection.

We recommend that during microwave cooking you cook whole poultry covered loosely with a waxed paper tent to prevent splattering. Toward the end of the cooking time, small pieces of aluminum foil may be used for shielding to cover legs, wing tips, or breastbone area to prevent overcooking. Foil should be at least 1 inch from oven walls.

Use the temperature probe inserted in thickest part of thigh, set at 180°F for whole poultry, and at 170°F for parts, including turkey breasts. Standing time completes the cooking of poultry.

DEFROSTING GUIDE — POULTRY

Food	Amount	Minutes (per pound)	Micro Power	Standing Time (in minutes)	Special Notes
Capon	6 - 8 lbs.	2	70	60	Turn over halfway through defrosting. Immerse in cold water for standing time.
Chicken, cut up	2 - 3 lbs.	5 - 6	30	10 - 15	Rearrange every 5 minutes. Separate pieces when partially thawed.
Chicken, whole	2 - 3 lbs.	6 - 8	30	25 - 30	Turn over halfway through defrosting. Immerse in cold water for standing time.
Cornish hen	1 - 1½ lbs.	6 - 8	30	20	Turn over halfway through defrosting.
Duckling	4 - 5 lbs.	4	70	30 - 40	Turn over halfway through defrosting. Immerse in cold water for standing time.
Turkey	Under 8 lbs.	3 - 5	30	60	Turn over halfway through defrosting. Shield warm areas. Immerse in cold water for standing time.
	Over 8 lbs.	3 - 5	70	60	
Ground turkey, bulk	1 lb.	4 - 5	30	5	Turn over halfway through defrosting.
Turkey fillets	1 - 2 lbs.	3 - 4	30	5	Turn over halfway through defrosting. Separate fillets when partially thawed.
Turkey breast	Under 4 lbs.	3 - 5	30	20	Turn over halfway through defrosting.
	Over 4 lbs.	1 / 2	70 / 30	20	Start at 70, turn over, continue on 30.
Turkey parts	1 - 2 lbs.	5 - 6	30	15 - 20	Rearrange every 5 minutes. Separate pieces when partially thawed.
Turkey roast, boneless	2 - 4	3 - 4	30	10	Remove from foil pan. Cover with waxed paper.

NOTE: Your oven is equipped with a Special Defrost feature. Please consult your Use & Care Manual for assistance in defrosting with this method. The timing in this chart is for manual, or attended, defrosting.

COOKING GUIDE — POULTRY

Food	Programming Method	Setting	First Cook Time	Second Cook Time	Probe Method	Special Notes
Chicken, whole, 3 - 4 lbs.	micro/convec	400°	5 - 6 min. per lb. breast down, turn over	6 min. per lb.	180°F	Place rack in lower position. Use microproof and heatproof dish with trivet.
Chicken, pieces, 3 - 4 lbs.	micro/convec	350°	6 min. skin down turn over	4 - 5 min. per lb.	170°F	Place rack in lower position. Preheat. Use microproof and heatproof baking dish.
Cornish hens, 1 - 1½ lbs.	micro/convec	350°	10 min. breast up turn over	8 - 9 min.	180°F	Place rack in lower position. Preheat. Use microproof and heatproof baking dish.
Duckling, 4 - 5 lbs.	micro/convec	400°	5 - 6 min. breast down turn over	6 min. per lb.	170°F	Place rack in lower position. For additional browning, cook (convec) at 400°.
Turkey, whole 10 lbs.	micro/convec	330°	5 - 6 min. per lb. breast up turn over	6 min. per lb.	170°F	Place rack in lower position. Use microproof or heatproof dish with trivet.
Turkey breast, 3 - 4 lbs.	micro/convec	350°	4 min. per lb. skin down turn over	3½ - 4½ min. per lb.	170°F	Place rack in lower position. Preheat. Use microproof and heatproof baking dish.
Turkey roast, boneles, 2 - 4 lbs.	micro/convec	400°	4 min. per lb. turn over	4 - 5 min. per lb.	170°F	Place rack in lower position. Use microproof and heatproof baking dish with trivet.
Turkey parts, 3 lbs.	micro/convec	350°	3 - 4 min. per lb.	4 - 5 min. per lb.		Place rack in lower position. Preheat. Use microproof and heatproof baking dish. Start skin side down.

REHEATING GUIDE — POULTRY*

Food	Programming Method	Setting	First Cook Time	Second Cook Time	Probe Method	Special Notes
Chicken, frozen fried, 1½-2 lbs.	micro/convec	350°	7 min.	7 - 8 min.		Place rack in lower position. Preheat. Use 12x7-inch microproof and heatproof baking dish.
Chicken Kiev, 1 - 2 pieces	micro/convec	350°	10 min.	6 - 8 min.		Place rack in lower position. Preheat. Use microproof and heatproof baking dish.
Chicken à la King, frozen, 5 oz.	micro	HI	3 - 4 min.			Place on microproof plate.
Creamed chicken, 10½ oz. can	micro	80	2 - 4 min.		150°F	Stir halfway through cooking time.
Chicken chow mein, 14 - 24 oz. can	micro	80	4 - 6 min.			Stir halfway through cooking time.
Turkey tetrazzini, frozen, 12 oz.	micro	HI	3 - 4 min.			Place on microproof plate.
Turkey, sliced in gravy, frozen, 5 oz.	micro	HI	3 - 5 min.			Slit pouch. Place in microproof dish.

*Due to the tremendous variety in convenience food products available, times given here should be used only as guidelines. We suggest you cook food for the shortest recommended time and then check for doneness. Be sure to check the package for microwave and oven (convec) instructions.

HOT CHICKEN SALAD FOR ONE

Cooking Time: 10 minutes

- 1 **cup cubed cooked chicken**
- 1 **stalk celery, chopped**
- ¼ **cup toasted slivered almonds**
- 1 **green onion, chopped**
- 2 **tablespoons grated Parmesan cheese**
- 2 **tablespoons grated Monterey Jack cheese**
- ½ **teaspoon dill**
- ¼ **teaspoon Italian herb seasoning**
  Salt and freshly ground pepper to taste
- 1 **teaspoon lemon juice**
- ½ **cup mayonnaise**
- 1 **tablespoon dry bread crumbs**

Place wire rack in lower position of oven. Lightly grease shallow 1-quart microproof and heatproof casserole.

Combine all ingredients except bread crumbs in 2-quart mixing bowl; mix thoroughly. Spoon salad into prepared casserole and sprinkle with bread crumbs. Cook (micro/convec) at 350°F, 10 minutes.

1 serving

CHICKEN PAUPIETTES

Cooking Time: 25 minutes

- ¼ **cup butter or margarine**
- 2 **tablespoons chopped green pepper**
- 2 **tablespoons chopped celery**
- 1 **clove garlic, minced**
- 1 **tablespoon chopped green onion**
- ½ **teaspoon salt**
- ¼ **teaspoon freshly ground pepper**
- 2 **cups fresh bread crumbs**
- 4 **whole boneless chicken breasts, pounded thin**
  Paprika
  Basic White Sauce (page 113)
- 1 **tablespoon chopped fresh parsley for garnish**

Combine butter, green pepper, celery, garlic, onion, salt, and pepper in 2-quart glass measure or microproof bowl.

Cook (micro) on HI, 2 minutes. Stir through several times.

Place wire rack in lower position of oven and preheat to 350°F.

Add bread crumbs to vegetable mixture and fold in lightly. Divide into 4 equal portions. Place 1 portion in center of each chicken breast and roll up.

Arrange in 8-inch microproof and heatproof baking dish, seam side down. Sprinkle lightly with paprika. Cook (micro/convec) at 350°F, 13 minutes.

Remove ceramic tray carefully with hot pads. Cook (convec) at 350°F, 10 minutes.

Top with Basic White Sauce, sprinkle with parsley, and serve.

4 servings

CHICKEN CAFE

Cooking Time: 42 minutes

- 4 **pounds chicken parts**
- 1 **teaspoon garlic salt**
- ½ **teaspoon ground ginger**
- 1 **can (8 ounces) pineapple chunks, drained, syrup reserved**
- ½ **cup coffee-flavored liqueur**
- 1 **tablespoon fresh lemon juice**
- 2 **tablespoons cornstarch**
- 2 **tablespoons coffee-flavored liqueur**
- 1 **can (11 ounces) mandarin orange segments, drained**
- ¼ **cup thinly sliced green onions**

Place wire rack in lower position of oven and preheat to 400°F.

Rinse chicken and pat dry with paper towel. Arrange skin side down in 13x9-inch microproof and heatproof baking dish. Sprinkle with garlic salt and ginger.

Cook (micro/convec) at 400°F, 20 minutes. Drain off liquid. Turn chicken skin side up. Combine pineapple syrup, ½ cup liqueur, and lemon juice and pour over chicken.

Cook (micro/convec) at 400°F, 20 minutes or until chicken is tender. Transfer chicken to platter. Skim off fat from drippings in dish. Combine cornstarch with 2 tablespoons liqueur and stir until cornstarch is completely dissolved. Blend into drippings.

Cook (micro) on HI, 2 minutes, stirring once. Add oranges and pineapple.

Return chicken to dish, spooning sauce and fruit over top. Sprinkle with green onions and serve. (If chicken has cooled, cook (micro) on HI, 2 to 3 minutes.)

4 servings

OVEN-FRIED CHICKEN

Cooking Time: 30 minutes

>   2 cups cornflake crumbs
>   1 tablespoon cornstarch
>   2 teaspoons onion powder
>   ¼ teaspoon salt
>   ⅛ teaspoon freshly ground pepper
>   1 broiler-fryer chicken (3 pounds),
>   cut up, rinsed, and patted dry
>   1 egg, lightly beaten

Place wire rack in lower position of oven and preheat to 350°F.

Combine cornflake crumbs, cornstarch, onion powder, salt, and pepper in large bowl. Dip each chicken piece in egg, then roll in crumb mixture, covering completely. Arrange chicken skin side down in 12x7-inch shallow microproof and heatproof baking dish.

Cook (micro/convec) at 350°F, 15 minutes. Turn chicken pieces over and continue to cook (micro/convec) at 350°F, 15 minutes or until chicken tests done.

4 servings

CHICKEN PAPRIKASH

Cooking Time: 30 minutes

>   1 broiler-fryer chicken (2½ to
>   3 pounds), cut up
>   1 tablespoon paprika
>   1 cup milk
>   1 tablespoon all-purpose flour
>   ¼ cup dairy sour cream

Place wire rack in lower position of oven and preheat to 350°F.

Rinse chicken and pat dry with paper towel. Arrange chicken skin side down in 2½-quart microproof and heatproof casserole, placing thicker portions toward outer edge of casserole and chicken wings at center. Sprinkle with paprika. Cook (micro/convec) at 350°F, 15 minutes.

Turn chicken skin side up. Pour milk around chicken. Cook (micro/convec) at 350°F, 15 minutes. Transfer chicken to serving platter.

Stir flour into sour cream. Stir sour cream mixture into milk in casserole. Pour around chicken before serving.

4 servings

CHICKEN WITH OLD FASHIONED DRESSING

Cooking Time: 42 minutes

>   ¼ cup diced onion
>   ¼ cup diced celery
>   1 tablespoon butter or margarine
>   1 cup diced fresh mushrooms
>   ⅔ cup hot chicken stock
>   1½ cups cornbread stuffing mix
>   2 tablespoons minced fresh parsley
>   1 3- to 4-pound chicken
>   1 slice white bread
>   Vegetable oil
>   Garlic powder
>   Paprika

Combine onion, celery, and butter in 1-quart microproof bowl. Cook (micro) on 90, 2 minutes. Stir in mushrooms and stock.

Combine stuffing mix and parsley; mix lightly. Spoon into cavity and neck. Tuck bread inside cavity to seal opening. Brush chicken with oil. Sprinkle with garlic powder and paprika.

Place wire rack in lower position and preheat to 400°F.

Set chicken breast side down on roasting rack and place in shallow microproof and heatproof baking dish.

Cook (micro/convec) at 400°F, 20 minutes. Turn chicken over; baste with drippings and sprinkle with additional paprika.

Cook (micro/convec) at 400°F, 20 minutes.

If additional crispness is desired, remove ceramic tray with hot pads and cook (convec) at 450°F until done.

4 to 6 servings

You can make your own chicken stock for this recipe by combining 1 teaspoon instant chicken bouillon and ⅔ cup hot water.

CHICKEN BREASTS MIYAKO

Cooking Time: 7 to 9 minutes

> 2 whole chicken breasts (1 pound
>   each), skinned, boned, and split
> 2 teaspoons Dijon-style mustard
> 8 fresh snow peas
> 1 small sweet red pepper, cut into
>   thin strips
> 4 ounces Brie cheese
> 1 teaspoon cornstarch
> ¼ cup chicken broth
> 1 green onion, chopped
> 1 tablespoon lemon juice

Lightly pound each chicken breast with meat mallet. Spread one side with mustard, and top with two snow peas and one-fourth the pepper strips. Cut Brie into 4 pieces. Place over red pepper strips. Roll up each chicken breast and place in 1-quart microproof casserole. Set aside.

Combine cornstarch, broth, and lemon juice in 1-cup glass measure. Stir until cornstarch dissolves. Cook (micro) on HI, 1 minute.

Stir. Pour hot broth mixture over chicken. Sprinkle onion over chicken. Cover with casserole lid and cook (micro) on 70, 6 to 8 minutes or until chicken is tender.

4 servings

BARBECUED CHICKEN

Cooking Time: 30 minutes

> 3 to 4 pounds chicken parts
> ½ cup Barbecue Sauce (page 114)

Place wire rack in lower position of oven and preheat to 350°F.

Arrange chicken skin side down in 12x7-inch microproof and heatproof baking dish. Brush generously with sauce. Cook (micro/convec) at 350°F, 15 minutes.

Turn chicken over and brush with sauce. Cook (micro/convec) at 350°F, 15 minutes or until chicken is tender.

4 servings

This recipe works equally well with two chicken halves. Timing will vary with size of the chicken. Substitute bottled barbecue sauce for homemade if you're in a hurry.

Chicken Breasts Miyako (left)

CHICKEN MARENGO

Cooking Time: 50 minutes

    1 broiler-fryer chicken (3½ pounds),
         cut up, rinsed, and patted dry
  ¼ cup vegetable oil
    2 cups soft bread crumbs
    1 package (3 ounces) spaghetti
         sauce mix
  ½ pound mushrooms, sliced
         (about 2 cups)
    1 can (16 ounces) tomatoes,
         cut up
    1 cup dry white wine

Brush chicken parts with oil. Mix bread crumbs and sauce mix in plastic bag. Add chicken, 1 piece at a time, and shake to coat well. Arrange chicken in 3-quart round or oval microproof and heatproof casserole with thickest portions toward outer edge of casserole.

Cook (micro/convec) at 350°F, 20 minutes.

Add remaining ingredients. Cover and continue to cook (micro/convec) at 350°F, 30 minutes.

4 to 6 servings

CHICKEN WINGS PARMESAN

Cooking Time: 14 to 15 minutes

    6 chicken wings
  10 buttery crackers
  ¼ cup grated Parmesan cheese
    3 tablespoons minced fresh parsley
    1 teaspoon garlic powder
  ½ teaspoon salt
  ⅛ teaspoon freshly ground pepper
  ½ teaspoon paprika
  ¼ cup butter or margarine, melted

Cut wings in half, discarding tips. Rinse; pat dry with paper towel and set aside.

Place wire rack in lower position and preheat to 350°F.

Mix crackers in blender or food processor to make fine crumbs; pour into bowl. Add all remaining ingredients except butter and blend well. Dip chicken into melted butter; then roll in crumbs, coating evenly. Arrange chicken pieces skin side up in spoke pattern on 9-inch round microproof and heatproof pie plate with thickest parts toward outer edge of plate.

Cook (micro/convec) at 350°F, 14 to 15 minutes or until chicken is tender and crisp. Serve hot.

2 to 4 servings

HAWAIIAN CHICKEN FOR TWO

Cooking Time: 15½ to 17½ minutes

    1 whole chicken breast (1 pound), split
    1 can (11 ounces) chunk pineapple,
         drained, juice reserved
    1 can (6½ ounces) mandarin oranges,
         drained, juice reserved
    2 tablespoons brown sugar
    1 tablespoon vinegar
    1 teaspoon soy sauce
  ½ teaspoon grated orange peel
    1 teaspoon cornstarch

Place chicken in 9-inch round microproof and heatproof baking dish. In 2-cup glass measure, combine equal amounts of reserved juices to total ¼ cup. Add brown sugar, vinegar, soy sauce, and orange peel; stir. Add cornstarch and stir until mixture is well blended.

Cook (micro) on HI, 1½ minutes, stirring once.

Place wire rack in lower position of oven and preheat to 370°F.

Pour sauce mixture over chicken. Cook (micro/convec) at 370°F, 12 to 14 minutes.

Spoon pineapple chunks and orange sections over chicken. Baste with sauce. Cook (micro/convec) at 370°F, 2 minutes. Let stand, covered, 5 minutes before serving.

2 servings

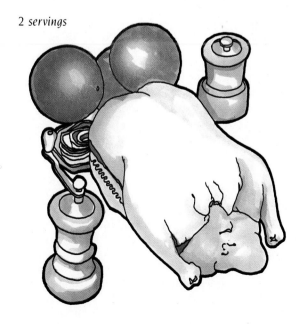

ROAST CHICKEN WITH WILD RICE

Cooking Time: 51 to 56 minutes

> 1 medium onion, chopped
> ¼ cup butter or margarine
> 1 package (10 ounces) frozen white
> and wild rice, thawed
> ½ cup coarsely chopped mushrooms
> 1 broiler/fryer chicken (3 to 4 pounds)
> Vegetable oil
> Paprika

Combine onion and butter in 1-quart microproof bowl. Cook (micro) on HI, 3 minutes.

Stir in rice and mushrooms. Cover with plastic wrap. Cook (micro) on HI, 3 minutes.

Spoon rice mixture into cavity and neck. Tuck bread inside cavity to seal opening. Brush chicken with oil. Sprinkle with paprika.

Place wire rack in lower position of oven and preheat to 400°F. Set chicken breast side down on microproof and heatproof roasting rack; place rack in shallow microproof and heatproof baking dish. Cook (micro/convec) at 400°F, 20 minutes.

Turn chicken over; baste with drippings and sprinkle with additional paprika. Cook (micro/convec) at 400°F, 25 to 30 minutes.

If additional crispness is desired, remove ceramic tray carefully with hot pads and cook (convec) at 450°F.

4 to 6 servings

CORNISH HENS WITH CITRUS GLAZE

Cooking Time: 35 minutes

> 2 Cornish hens (1½ pounds each)
> 1 onion, quartered
> 1 stalk celery, cut into pieces
> 2 slices lemon
> 2 tablespoons butter or margarine,
> melted
> Citrus Glaze (page 115)

Place wire rack in lower position of oven and preheat to 450°F.

Rinse Cornish hens in cool water and pat dry with paper towel. Place onion, celery, and lemon in hen cavities.

Place hens breast side up in oval microproof and heatproof baking dish with thickest parts toward outer edge of dish. Brush each hen with 1 tablespoon butter. Cook (micro/convec) at 350°F, 15 minutes.

Turn hens over and continue to cook (micro/convec) at 350°F, 15 minutes.

Turn hens breast side up and brush with Citrus Glaze. Cook (micro/convec) at 350°F, 5 minutes or until glaze is set.

2 servings

CORNISH HENS WITH WILD RICE DRESSING

Approximate Cooking Time: 25 minutes

> ¾ cup chopped onion
> ¼ cup butter or margarine
> 1 package (10 ounces) frozen white
> and wild rice, thawed
> ½ cup coarsely chopped mushrooms
> 2 Cornish hens (1½ pounds each)
> Salt
> Paprika

Combine onion and butter in 1-quart microproof bowl. Cook (micro) on HI, 3 minutes. Stir in rice and mushrooms. Cover with plastic wrap. Cook (micro) on HI, 3 minutes. Stir and set aside.

Place wire rack in lower position of oven and preheat to 350°F.

Rinse hens and pat dry with paper towel. Sprinkle cavities with salt and stuff with dressing. Tie legs together with string. Place hens breast side up in microproof and heatproof baking dish. Sprinkle with paprika.

Cook (micro/convec) at 350°F, 15 minutes.

Turn hens over and sprinkle with paprika. Insert temperature probe into fleshy part of thigh or breast. Plug in probe. Cook (micro/convec) at 350°F, with probe set at 170°F.

Remove from oven. Cover with aluminum foil and let stand 5 minutes. Remove foil and string. Serve breast side up.

2 servings

TURKEY FLORENTINE

Cooking Time: 9 to 10 minutes

> 1 package (10 ounces) frozen
>   chopped spinach or 8 ounces
>   fresh spinach, cooked and chopped
> ¼ cup chopped water chestnuts
> 1 green onion, chopped
> 2 tablespoons chopped pimiento
> ¼ teaspoon nutmeg
>   Basic White Sauce (page 113)
> 4 slices turkey breast (2 ounces each)
> ¼ cup grated Parmesan cheese

Place package of spinach on microproof plate. (If spinach is in foil-lined package, remove foil.) Cook on HI, 5 minutes. Let stand 5 minutes. Squeeze dry.

Combine spinach, water chestnuts, onion, pimiento, nutmeg, and Basic White Sauce; mix well.

Place turkey slices in 8-inch round microproof baking dish with thickest portions toward outer edge of dish. Pour sauce evenly over turkey. Sprinkle with Parmesan cheese.

Cover with waxed paper and cook (micro) on HI, 4 to 5 minutes or until meat is done and sauce is hot.

2 *to 4 servings*

TURKEY WITH CORNBREAD STUFFING

Approximate Cooking Time: 2 hours 10 minutes

> ½ cup diced onion
> ½ cup diced celery
> 2 tablespoons butter or margarine
> 2 cups diced mushrooms
> 1 cup hot chicken stock
> 2 cups cornbread stuffing mix
> 1 10- to 12-pound turkey, cleaned,
>   rinsed, and patted dry
>   Vegetable oil
>   Paprika

Combine onion, celery, and butter in 3-quart microproof bowl. Cook (micro) on HI, 4 minutes.

Stir in mushrooms. Continue to cook (micro) on HI, 2 minutes.

Turkey Florentine (left)

Add stock and blend well. Add stuffing mix and blend lightly, adding more liquid if mixture seems too dry. Spoon stuffing into turkey cavities. Tuck in wings. Rub outside with oil and sprinkle with paprika. Place turkey breast side up in shallow microproof and heatproof baking dish.

Cook (micro/convec) at 350°F, 15 minutes. Rotate one-half turn and continue to cook (micro/convec) at 350°F, 15 minutes. Baste turkey with drippings.

Turn turkey breast side down. Cook (micro/convec) at 350°F, 15 minutes.

Insert probe into fleshy part of thigh. Plug in probe. Cook (micro/convec) at 350°F with probe set at 170°F. Tent turkey with aluminum foil and let stand 15 minutes before carving.

8 *to 10 servings*

BREAST OF TURKEY JARDINIERE

Cooking Time: 24 to 30 minutes

- 1 medium carrot, cut into thin
  2-inch strips
- 1 celery stalk, cut into thin
  2-inch strips
- 1 small onion, cut into thin
  2-inch strips
- 1 small potato, cut into thin
  2-inch strips
- 1 tablespoon minced fresh parsley
- 2 tablespoons butter or margarine
  Salt and freshly ground pepper
  to taste
- ½ turkey breast (3½ to 4 pounds),
  boned and skinned (if desired)
  Paprika

Combine carrot, celery, onion, potato, and parsley in small microproof and heatproof casserole, just large enough to accommodate all ingredients. Dot with butter. Season lightly with salt and pepper.

Preheat oven to 350°F. Set turkey breast on vegetables and sprinkle with paprika.

Cover and cook (micro/convec) at 350°F, 12 to 15 minutes.

Rotate dish one-half turn and continue to cook (micro/convec) at 350°F, 12 to 15 minutes. Serve immediately.

3 to 4 servings

Boned chicken breasts also work well for this recipe.

ROAST RASPBERRY DUCKLING

Approximate Cooking Time: 55 minutes

- 1 duckling (4 pounds), giblets removed
- 1 carrot, peeled and cut into chunks
- 1 medium onion, cut into quarters
- 1 jar (10 ounces) raspberry jelly
- ¼ cup raspberry liqueur
- 2 tablespoons fresh lemon juice

Rinse duckling and pat dry with paper towel. Place carrot and onion pieces in body cavity. Secure neck skin with wooden toothpicks or skewers. Tie legs together with string; tie wings to body. Pierce skin in several places with fork to allow fat to drain.

Remove ceramic tray. Place wire rack in lower position of oven and preheat to 400°F.

Place duckling breast side up on microproof and heatproof roasting rack in 12x7-inch microproof and heatproof baking dish.

Cook (micro/convec) at 400°F, 15 minutes.

Combine remaining ingredients in small bowl and stir until smooth. Turn duckling over and brush with glaze.

Insert temperature probe into fleshiest part of thigh. Plug in probe. Cook (micro/convec) at 400°F, to 170°F.

Remove probe. Turn duckling breast side up. Baste with glaze and drippings.

Cook (convec) at 400°F, 10 minutes.

2 servings

Your new micro/convection oven gives you a variety of options for cooking fish, each of which has its own strengths and advantages. For poaching and steaming, where moisture retention is needed, the microwave method clearly is the method of choice. As you will recall, little or no evaporation occurs with microwave cooking because no hot air is present to dry the surface of food. For baking fish, the micro/convection method is superior. And for preparing breaded fish, where browning and crisping are desirable, the convection method delivers the best results.

All aspects of cooking fish and seafood in your micro/convection oven are fast and easy. Cooking times are short. Standing time required to complete the cooking process is short. Even clean up is quick, as fish does not stick or burn, particularly when the microwave and micro/convection methods are used. In general, fish should be prepared at the last minute, after all of the other elements of your meal are done or nearly done. Often standing time can complete the cooking process in the time it takes to remove fish from the oven and serve it at the table.

ADAPTING RECIPES

Use the cooking guides and the recipes as references for adapting your own dishes. If you don't find a recipe that matches or comes close to the conventional recipe you want to adapt, follow this general rule of thumb: Begin cooking (micro) at 70 or at HI for one-fifth of the time that the conventional recipe recommends. Check frequently. If the dish is not done, continue cooking 30 seconds at a time. As in conventional cooking, the secret to cooking seafood is to watch it carefully, since fish can overcook in seconds.

For best results when cooking fish and seafood, observe these useful guidelines.

■ For fish steaks with a browned appearance or fish that is coated with your favorite mix of crumbs or crackers and seasoning, use a preheated oven (400°F is best) and the convection method. Remove the ceramic tray and place the wire rack in the lower position. Do not cover. No alterations are necessary to suit a conventional seafood recipe to this oven. Simply consult the Guides or find a similar recipe in this chapter to help you determine the cooking time. As a general reminder, be conservative. Seafood cooks very quickly, and there's no way to rescue overcooked food.

■ Most recipes that specify a particular variety of fish will work when any white fish is substituted. When a recipe calls for fresh or thawed frozen fish fillets, use sole, flounder, bluefish, cod, scrod, or any similar fish.

■ When cooking whole fish, the dish should be rotated one-quarter turn twice during the cooking process to help provide even cooking. The uneven shape of the fish makes this procedure necessary.

■ Cook fish covered unless it is coated with crumbs, which seal in the juices.

■ Fish is done when the flesh becomes opaque and barely flakes with a fork. Shellfish is done when flesh is opaque and just firm.

■ To remove seafood odors from the oven, combine I cup water with lemon juice and a few cloves in a small bowl. Cook (micro) on HI, 3 to 5 minutes.

Lake Country Trout (page 87) cooks best in a microproof au gratin dish. Notice the foil covering to prevent overcooking.

For microwave cooking, shrimp are arranged with the tails toward the center of a microproof baking dish. They cook more evenly this way.

DEFROSTING FISH AND SHELLFISH

To prepare for defrosting, remove seafood from its original wrapper and place in a microproof dish.

To prevent the outer edges from drying out or beginning to cook, remove seafood from the oven before it has completely thawed. Even if it is a bit icy, that's fine. Standing time will complete the thawing process. Seafood is so delicate that you must be the final judge.

Finish defrosting under cold running water, separating fillets.

All seafood profits from approximately 5 minutes standing time. However, if you are adding it to a chowder or seafood casserole, standing time can be eliminated.

Cover the head of whole fish with aluminum foil during thawing. There is so little flesh in that area that it will begin to cook unless shielded.

We recommend turning seafood over or rearranging during defrosting. Remove any pieces that are nearly thawed.

COOKING FISH AND SHELLFISH

For microwave-method cooking, place seafood in a microproof baking dish with thick edges of fillets and steaks and thick ends of shellfish toward the outer edge of the dish. Cover the dish with plastic wrap or waxed paper. Test often during the cooking period to avoid overcooking. The timing is the same for seafood in the shell or without the shell.

DEFROSTING GUIDE — FISH AND SHELLFISH

Food	Amount	Micro Power	Time (in minutes)	Standing Time (in minutes)	Special Notes
Fish fillets	1 lb.	30	4 - 6	4 - 6	Defrost on microproof dish. Turn over halfway through defrosting. Carefully separate under cold water.
	2 lbs.	30	5 - 7	5	
Fish steaks	1 lb.	30	4 - 6	5	Defrost on microproof dish. Turn over halfway through defrosting. Carefully separate under cold running water.
Whole fish	8 - 10 oz.	30	4 - 6	5	Defrost on shallow microproof dish. Cover head with aluminum foil. Turn over halfway through defrosting. Should be icy when removed. Finish at room temperature.
	1½ - 2 lbs.	30	5 - 7	5	
Lobster tails	8 oz.	30	5 - 7	5	Remove wrapping. Place in microproof baking dish. Separate and rearrange during thawing as necessary.
Crab legs	8 - 10 oz.	30	3 - 4	5	Remove wrapping. Place in microproof baking dish. Separate and rearrange during thawing as necessary.
Crab meat	6 oz.	30	4 - 5	5	Defrost on microproof dish. Break apart and rearrange during thawing as necessary.
Shrimp	1 lb.	30	3 - 4	5	Remove from package to microproof dish. Spread out loosely. Rearrange during thawing as necessary.
Scallops	1 lb.	30	3 - 4	5	Defrost on microproof dish. Spread out loosely if in pieces. Turn over and rearrange during thawing as necessary.
Oysters, shucked	12 oz.	30	3 - 4	5	Remove from package to microproof dish. Turn over and rearrange during thawing as necessary.

NOTE: Your oven is equipped with a Special Defrost feature. Please consult your Use & Care Manual for assistance in defrosting with this method. The timing in this chart is for manual, or attended, defrosting.

COOKING GUIDE — FISH AND SHELLFISH

Food	Micro Power	Time (in minutes)	Probe Method	Special Notes
Fish fillets, 1 lb. ½ inch thick, 2 lbs.	HI HI	4 - 5 7 - 8	140°F 140°F	Use 6x9-inch microproof dish, covered with waxed paper.
Fish steaks, 1 inch thick, 1 lb.	HI	5 - 6	140°F	Use 6x9-inch microproof dish, covered with waxed paper.
Whole fish 8 - 10 oz. 1½ - 2 lbs.	HI HI	3½ - 4 5 - 7	170°F 170°F	Use shallow microproof dish shaped to accommodate whole fish. Rotate dish twice during cooking time.
Crab legs 8 - 10 oz. 16 - 20 oz.	HI HI	3 - 4 5 - 6		Use shallow microproof dish, covered with waxed paper. Rotate dish halfway through cooking time.
Shrimp, scallops 8 oz. 1 lb.	70 70	3 - 4 5 - 7		Use shallow microproof dish, covered with waxed paper. Rearrange halfway through cooking time.
Snails, clams, oysters, 12 oz.	70	3 - 4		Use shallow microproof dish, covered with waxed paper. Rearrange halfway through cooking time.
Lobster tails 1: 8 oz. 2: 8 oz. each 3: 8 oz. each	HI HI HI	3 - 4 5 - 6 9 - 11		Use shallow microproof dish. Split shell to reduce curling.

REHEATING GUIDE — FISH AND SHELLFISH*

Food	Programming Method	Setting	First Cook Time	Second Cook Time	Special Notes
Fish sticks frozen, (12)	micro/convec	400°	5 min. turn over	change to convec 400° 4 - 5 min.	Place wire rack in lower position. Preheat. Use foil-lined microproof and heatproof baking dish.
Shrimp or crab newburg, frozen, 6½ oz.	micro	HI	4 - 6		Slit pouch. Place on microproof plate. Flex pouch to mix halfway through cooking time.
Scallops or fish kabobs, 7 oz.	micro/convec	400°	5 min. turn over	change to convec 400° 4 - 5 min.	Place wire rack in lower position. Preheat. Use foil-lined microproof and heatproof baking dish.
Tuna casserole, frozen, 16 oz.	micro	HI	4 - 6		Remove from package to 1-quart microproof casserole. Stir once during cooking.

*Due to the tremendous variety in convenience food products available, times given here should be used only as guidelines. We suggest you cook food for the shortest recommended time and then check for doneness. Be sure to check the package for microwave and oven (convec) instructions.

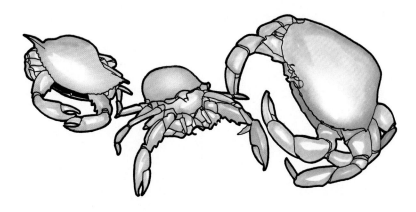

Salmon in Parchment (right)

MICRO TIME

SALMON IN PARCHMENT

Cooking Time: 4 to 5 minutes

>   1 **piece parchment, 12 inches square**
>   1 **salmon fillet (5 to 6 ounces)**
>   1 **carrot, cut into thin strips**
>   ½ **stalk celery, cut into thin strips**
>   2 **tablespoons butter or margarine,**
>   **melted**
>   1 **tablespoon lemon juice**
>   1 **sprig fresh dill or ¼ teaspoon**
>   **dill weed**

Place salmon in center of parchment. Arrange carrots and celery around salmon. Drizzle butter over fish and vegetables. Sprinkle with lemon juice and top with dill. Seal parchment, butcher-wrap style. Place on microproof plate.

Cook (micro) on HI, 4 to 5 minutes or until parchment is steaming, but not dry.

1 serving

This is a wonderful way to serve any fish. Vary the vegetable combination and herbs to suit your moods. The parchment remains sealed until you tear it open at the table.

MICRO/CONVEC TIME

LOBSTER TAILS SUPREME

Cooking Time: 7½ minutes

>   2 **8-ounce lobster tails**
>   2 **tablespoons butter or margarine,**
>   **melted**
>   **Clarified Butter (page 116)**
>   **Lemon wedges**

Place wire rack in lower position of oven and preheat to 450°F.

Split each lobster tail through top shell and carefully remove meat, leaving small end attached to shell.

Arrange lobster in microproof and heatproof dish. Brush meat with melted butter.

Cook (micro/convec) at 450°F, 7½ minutes. Serve immediately with Clarified Butter and lemon wedges.

2 servings

To prepare 1 lobster tail, cook (micro/convec) at 450°F, 3 minutes 15 seconds to 4 minutes. To prepare 4 lobster tails, cook (micro/convec) at 450°F, 10 to 11 minutes.

SCALLOPS AU VIN

Cooking Time: 7½ to 8½ minutes

> 2 **tablespoons butter or margarine**
> 2 **large cloves garlic, minced**
> 2 **green onions, chopped**
> ⅛ **teaspoon paprika**
> 2 **tablespoons dry white wine**
> ¾ **pound large sea scallops**
> I **tablespoon lemon juice**

Combine butter, garlic, onions, paprika, and wine in I-cup glass measure. Cook (micro) on HI, 2½ minutes. Cover with plastic wrap and set aside.

Preheat browning dish according to manufacturer's instructions. Place scallops in dish and cook (micro) on HI, 5 to 6 minutes. Transfer to serving dish. Drizzle hot butter sauce over scallops, and sprinkle with lemon juice.

2 servings

STEAMED CLAMS WITH GARLIC BUTTER

Cooking Time: 10½ to 11 minutes

> 2 **dozen clams in the shell,**
> **well scrubbed**
> ½ **cup butter or margarine**
> 2 **cloves garlic, minced**
> 2 **tablespoons chopped fresh parsley**
> I **teaspoon lemon juice**

Arrange half of the clams in circle on microproof pie plate or serving dish, placing hinges toward outer edge of plate. Cook (micro) on HI, 4½ minutes or until shells open, removing clams as soon as they open; discard any that do not open.

Repeat with remaining clams.

Combine butter, garlic, parsley, and lemon juice in small microproof serving bowl. Cook (micro) on HI, 1½ to 2 minutes or until butter bubbles.

Arrange clams on individual serving plates and pass garlic butter separately.

4 servings

Scallops Au Vin (left)

SHRIMP VERACRUZ

Cooking Time: 12 to 13 minutes

> 1 large onion, cut into chunks
> 1 large green pepper, seeded
>   and cut into chunks
> 2 cloves garlic, crushed
> 2 tablespoons vegetable oil
> 1 can (8 ounces) tomato sauce
> ¼ cup dry white wine
> ½ teaspoon oregano
> ½ teaspoon salt
> ¼ teaspoon cumin
> ⅛ teaspoon hot pepper sauce
> 1 pound jumbo shrimp, shelled
>   and deveined
>   Chopped fresh parsley for garnish

Combine onion, green pepper, garlic, and oil in oval microproof baking dish.

Cook (micro) on HI, 3 minutes. Stir through several times. Add tomato sauce, wine, oregano, salt, cumin, and hot pepper sauce.

Cover with plastic wrap and cook (micro) on HI, 5 minutes. Add shrimp, spooning sauce to cover.

Cook (micro) on HI, 4 to 5 minutes or until shrimp are pink. (If several shrimp are done before remainder, move to center of dish.) Garnish with parsley.

4 servings

Use a shallow au gratin or other microproof baking dish just large enough to accommodate shrimp and sauce. Too large a dish may cause uneven cooking patterns.

SCAMPI

Cooking Time: 4 to 5 minutes

> 3 tablespoons vegetable oil
> 2 large cloves garlic, minced
> 3 tablespoons minced fresh parsley
> 2 tablespoons dry white wine
> ⅛ teaspoon paprika
> 12 ounces large shrimp (¾ pound),
>   shelled, deveined, butterflied,
>   tails intact
>   Juice of ½ lemon
>   Salt and freshly ground pepper
>   to taste
>   Chopped fresh parsley for garnish

Combine oil and garlic in oval microproof baking dish just large enough to accommodate all ingredients.

Cook (micro) on HI, 1 minute. Add parsley, wine, and paprika. Continue to cook (micro) on HI, 1 minute. Add shrimp, lemon juice, salt, and pepper. Stir to coat shrimp well.

Arrange shrimp in dish with tails toward center. Cover with plastic wrap and cook (micro) on HI, 3 to 4 minutes or until shrimp turn pink, stirring once or twice during cooking time.

Garnish with additional parsley and serve immediately.

2 servings

It is important not to overcook shrimp or use too large a dish.

CRAB FLORENTINE

Cooking Time: 23½ to 28½ minutes

> 1 package (10 ounces) frozen
>   chopped spinach
> 1 medium onion, chopped
> 3 tablespoons butter or margarine
> 6 eggs, lightly beaten
> 1 cup cream or half and half
> 3 tablespoons dry white wine
> ¼ teaspoon salt
> ⅛ teaspoon freshly ground pepper
> ⅛ teaspoon cayenne
> 6 ounces chopped crabmeat, rinsed
>   and drained
> ¼ cup grated Parmesan cheese

Set package of spinach on microproof plate. (If spinach is in foil-lined package, remove foil.) Cook (micro) on HI, 2½ minutes. Turn package on side and continue to cook (micro) on HI, 2 minutes. Set aside.

Combine onion and butter in 2-quart microproof bowl. Cook (micro) on HI, 4 minutes. Let cool slightly. Add eggs, cream, wine, salt, pepper, and cayenne. Mix well.

Place wire rack in lower position of oven and preheat to 330°F.

Drain spinach well and squeeze dry. Stir into onion mixture. Stir in crabmeat. Turn into 8-inch round microproof and heatproof baking dish and sprinkle with cheese.

Cook (micro/convec) at 330°F, 15 to 20 minutes or until almost set.

Let stand 5 minutes before serving.

6 to 8 servings

ORANGE ROUGHY FOR TWO

Cooking Time: 5 to 7 minutes

> 2 orange roughy or haddock fillets
>   (4 ounces each)
> 1 small tomato, diced
> 1 green onion, sliced
> 2 tablespoons chopped green pepper
> 2 tablespoons chopped celery
> 2 tablespoons chopped fresh parsley
> 2 tablespoons dry white wine
>   Juice of 1 lime
> 2 tablespoons butter or margarine,
>   melted

Place wire rack in upper position of oven and preheat to 450°F.

Place fish fillets in 7x11-inch microproof and heatproof baking dish. Combine tomato, green onion, green pepper, celery, and parsley in small bowl. Spoon vegetables over fillets. Combine wine, lime juice, and melted butter in 1-cup glass measure. Pour over vegetables and fish.

Cook (micro/convec) at 450°F, 5 to 7 minutes or until fish flakes easily with a fork.

2 servings

LAKE COUNTRY TROUT

Cooking Time: 13 minutes

> 2 8-ounce trout
> 1 small onion, chopped
> 3 tablespoons butter or margarine
> 6 mushrooms, sliced
> 2 tablespoons slivered almonds
> 2½ tablespoons chopped fresh parsley
>   Salt and freshly ground pepper
>   to taste

Rinse trout and pat dry with paper towel. Arrange in oval microproof and heatproof baking dish. Set aside.

Combine onion and butter in microproof dish. Cook (micro) on HI, 3 minutes.

Place wire rack in upper position of oven and preheat to 400°F.

Add mushrooms, almonds, and 2 tablespoons parsley to butter mixture. Mix well. Stuff trout cavities with half of the mixture, sprinkling remainder over tops of trout. Season with salt and pepper. Sprinkle trout with remaining parsley.

Cook (micro/convec) at 400°F, 10 minutes or until trout are done.

2 servings

HALIBUT STEAKS

Cooking Time: 16 minutes

> 2 tablespoons dry white wine
> 1 tablespoon lemon juice
> 1 tablespoon olive oil
> ⅛ teaspoon salt
> ⅛ teaspoon freshly ground pepper
> 2 halibut steaks (6 to 8 ounces each),
>   1 inch thick

Combine wine, lemon juice, olive oil, salt, and pepper in shallow dish. Add fish, turning several times to coat. Cover and marinate in refrigerator 3 hours, turning twice to recoat.

Remove ceramic tray. Place wire rack in upper position of oven and preheat to 450°F.

Set fish on aluminum foil or broiling pan, reserving marinade. Cook (convec) at 450°F, 8 minutes.

Turn fish over and brush with marinade. Cook (convec) at 450°F, 8 minutes or until fish flakes easily with a fork.

2 servings

Be careful not to overcook or fish will be tough. Shark or swordfish can be substituted for halibut.

FISH STEAK SURPRISE

Cooking Time: 10 minutes

> 2 8-ounce fish steaks
>   (swordfish, halibut, or salmon)
> 2 tablespoons onion soup mix
> ½ cup mayonnaise

Place wire rack in lower position of oven and preheat to 450°F.

Arrange steaks in 8-inch square microproof and heatproof baking dish. Sprinkle evenly with soup mix and cover completely with mayonnaise.

Cook (micro/convec) at 450°F, 10 minutes or until fish tests done.

2 servings

CIOPPINO

Cooking Time: 25 to 27 minutes

- ¼ cup olive oil
- 2 cloves garlic, minced
- 1 large onion, finely chopped
- 2 cups hot water
- 1 can (28 ounces) peeled pear-shaped tomatoes
- 2 cans (8 ounces each) tomato sauce
- 1 package (3 ounces) dry spaghetti sauce mix
- ¼ teaspoon freshly ground pepper
- 1 cup dry white wine
- 1½ pounds rockfish or other firm-fleshed white fish, cut into chunks
- 12 scallops
- 8 to 10 large shrimp, cleaned and deveined, tails intact
- 8 to 10 clams, washed and scrubbed

Combine oil, garlic, and onion in 4-quart microproof casserole.

Cook (micro) on HI, 4 minutes. Add water, tomatoes, tomato sauce, sauce mix, and pepper.

Cover and cook (micro) on HI, 10 minutes or until mixture comes to a full boil. Stir in wine. Add fish, scallops, and shrimp.

Cover and cook (micro) on HI, 10 minutes or until fish is just translucent. Remove from oven and let stand, covered, while preparing clams.

Arrange clams in circle on microproof plate. Cook (micro) on HI, 1 to 3 minutes or just until clams open, watching constantly and removing from oven immediately as they open; discard any that do not open. Stir soup and add clams. Serve hot.

8 to 10 servings

BREADED FISH FILLETS

Cooking Time: 10 to 12 minutes

- 1½ pounds fish fillets, about ½ inch thick
- ¾ cup crushed corn flakes
- 2 tablespoons minced fresh parsley
- ¼ teaspoon salt
- ⅛ teaspoon freshly ground pepper
- 1 egg, lightly beaten

Remove ceramic tray. Place wire rack in lower position of oven and preheat to 400°F.

Rinse fillets with cold water and pat dry with paper towel. Combine corn flakes, parsley, salt, and pepper in shallow oval dish. Dip each fillet in beaten egg, then roll in corn flake mixture, covering completely. Arrange in metal pan.

Cook (convec) at 400°F, 10 to 12 minutes or until fish flakes easily with a fork. Serve immediately.

4 servings

TUNA CASSEROLE

Cooking Time: 21 minutes

- 10 ounces elbow macaroni, cooked
- 3 cups Basic Cheese Sauce (page 113)
- 1 can (6½ ounces) tuna, drained
- ½ cup chopped onion
- ¼ cup chopped green pepper
- ¼ cup chopped celery
- 1 cup fresh bread crumbs
- 2 tablespoons butter or margarine

Combine macaroni, sauce, tuna, onion, green pepper, and celery in large bowl and blend well. Turn into 13x9-inch microproof and heatproof baking dish.

Place butter in small microproof bowl and cook (micro) on HI, 1 minute or until melted. Stir bread crumbs into butter and blend well. Sprinkle over macaroni mixture.

Place wire rack in lower position of oven and preheat to 350°F.

Cook (micro/convec) at 350°F, 20 minutes or until top is golden.

6 to 8 servings

Sunny-Side-Up Eggs (page 91) are a convection method treat. Also shown is a handy method for poaching a number of eggs at one time in a microproof muffin ring.

Whether you're preparing simple scrambled eggs or a fancy quiche, you'll find that the microwave, micro/convection, and convection methods of your oven offer you a wide variety of choices for cooking egg or cheese dishes. The micro/convection method is especially good for cooking quiches, such as Quiche Lorraine shown on this page. The microwave mode cooks the filling quickly, while the convection mode helps to brown the top and crispen the crust. When used all by itself, the microwave method is excellent for scrambling and poaching eggs. A word of caution, however: do not cook eggs in the shell in this oven. Pressure builds up inside the shell, which causes the egg to burst. Eggs must be removed from their shells and egg yolks should be carefully pierced before cooking in order to prevent them from popping. In general, keep in mind that eggs and cheese are delicate ingredients. Handle them with care and you will have delightful results.

ADAPTING RECIPES

The best advice for adapting recipes that use eggs and cheese as primary ingredients is to be conservative. It's better to undercook than overcook. Cheese and eggs cook so quickly that a few seconds can make the difference between airy excellence and a rubbery disaster. That's not to make you shy away from adapting your own recipes. You will be able to make countless variations on the recipes here, substituting vegetables and cooked meat, and adding your own spices and sauces. To help you along, we have prepared a list of guidelines for you to follow:

- We recommend that you undercook eggs slightly and allow standing time to complete cooking. Eggs become tough when overcooked. Always check doneness to avoid overcooking.

- Cover poaching or baking eggs to trap steam and ensure even cooking. Eggs are usually cooked (micro) at 60.

- If you want a soft yolk, remove egg from oven before whites are completely cooked. A brief standing time allows whites to set without overcooking yolks.

- Omelets and scrambled eggs should be stirred at least once during cooking. Fondues and sauces profit from occasional stirring during the cooking time.

- Cheese melts quickly and makes an attractive topping for casseroles and sandwiches. Cook cheese (micro) on 70 or a lower setting for short periods of time to avoid separation and toughening.

- Add ⅛ to ¼ teaspoon vinegar to the water when poaching eggs to help the white coagulate.

Quiches are placed on the wire rack, lower position, and cooked the micro/convection way. Quiche Lorraine (page 93) can be the basis for a great, out-of-the-ordinary brunch.

COOKING EGGS

Eggs should be at refrigerator temperature before cooking. If they are at room temperature, somewhat less cooking time will be required.

To scramble: Break eggs into a 4-cup glass measure. Add milk or cream and beat with a fork. Add butter, cover with waxed paper, and cook (micro) on 60, according to the guide. Stir once during cooking, and just before serving. Let stand 1 minute before serving.

To poach: Bring water and ¼ teaspoon vinegar to a boil in a 1-cup glass measure or appropriate microproof dish. Break egg carefully into hot water and pierce yolk lightly with a toothpick. Cover with waxed paper and cook (micro) on 50, according to the guide. Let stand 1 minute.

COOKING GUIDE — SCRAMBLED EGGS
Cook (MICRO) on 60

Number of Eggs	Liquid (Milk or Cream)	Butter	Minutes to Cook	Special Notes
1	1 tablespoon	1 teaspoon	1 to 1½	
2	2 tablespoons	2 teaspoons	2 to 2½	Lightly stir egg halfway through cooking time.
4	3 tablespoons	3 teaspoons	4½ to 5½	
6	4 tablespoons	4 teaspoons	7 to 8	

COOKING GUIDE — POACHED EGGS
Cook (MICRO) on HI to boil water, on 50 upon adding egg

Number of Eggs	Water	Container	Minutes to Boil Water on HI	Minutes to Cook on 50
1	¼ cup	6-ounce microproof custard cup	1½ to 2	1
2	¼ cup	6-ounce microproof custard cups	2	1½ to 2
3	¼ cup	6-ounce microproof custard cups	2 to 2½	2 to 2½
4	1 cup	1-quart microproof dish	2½ to 3	2½ to 3

SHIRRED EGGS

Cooking Time: 3½ minutes

> 1   **teaspoon butter or margarine**
> 2   **eggs**
> 1   **tablespoon cream or half and half**
>   **Salt and freshly ground pepper to taste**

Place butter in microproof ramekin or small cereal bowl. Cook (micro) on HI, 30 seconds. Break eggs into ramekin. Pierce yolks carefully with toothpick. Add cream.

Cover tightly with plastic wrap and cook (micro) on 30, 3 minutes or until set.

Let stand 1 minute before serving.

1 to 2 servings

POACHED EGG

Cooking Time: 2½ minutes

> ¼   **cup water**
> ¼   **teaspoon vinegar**
> ⅛   **teaspoon salt**
> 1   **large egg**

Combine water, vinegar, and salt in 6-ounce microproof custard cup. Cook (micro) on HI, 1½ minutes.

Carefully break egg into hot liquid. Pierce yolk carefully with toothpick.

Cover with waxed paper and cook (micro) on 50, 1 minute.

Let stand 1 minute before serving.

1 serving

SUNNY-SIDE-UP EGGS

Cooking Time: 7 minutes

> 1 tablespoon butter or margarine
> 2 large eggs
> Salt and freshly ground pepper
> to taste

Remove ceramic tray. Place wire rack in upper position of oven and preheat to 450°F.

Place butter in shallow aluminum foil baking pan. Cook (convec) 450°F, 1 minute.

Break eggs into pan. Season with salt and pepper. Cook (convec) at 450°F, 6 minutes.

1 to 2 servings

CHEESED HAM AND EGGS

Cooking Time: 12 minutes

> ¼ cup butter or margarine
> ¼ cup all-purpose flour
> 2 cups milk
> 1 cup (4 ounces) shredded Cheddar cheese
> 2 teaspoons Worcestershire sauce
> 1½ teaspoons prepared mustard
> 6 hard-cooked eggs, diced
> 1 cup diced cooked ham
> 4 to 6 slices toast to serve

Place butter in 1½-quart microproof casserole. Cook (micro) on HI, 1 minute. Blend in flour. Whisk milk into butter-flour mixture; blend until smooth. Cook (micro) on 80, 7 minutes, stirring frequently during cooking time.

Add cheese, Worcestershire sauce, and mustard; stir until smooth. Carefully stir in eggs and ham. Cook (micro) on 50, 4 minutes.

Serve on toast.

4 to 6 servings

SCRAMBLED EGG

Cooking Time: 2½ minutes

> 1 tablespoon butter or margarine
> 1 large egg
> 2 tablespoons low-fat milk
> 6 tablespoons (1½ ounces) shredded Monterey jack or Cheddar cheese
> Salt and freshly ground pepper
> to taste

Place butter in small microproof bowl. Cook (micro) on HI, 30 seconds. Swirl butter to coat sides of bowl.

Break egg into prepared bowl. Add milk; mix well with fork. Add cheese, salt, and pepper; blend well.

Cover with waxed paper and cook (micro) on 60, 1 minute. Stir.

Cover and continue to cook (micro) on 60, 1½ minutes. Stir before serving.

1 serving

OMELET FOR TWO

Cooking Time: 2½ minutes

> 1 **tablespoon butter or margarine**
> 4 **eggs**
> 4 **tablespoons water**
> ⅛ **teaspoon salt**
> ⅛ **teaspoon freshly ground pepper**

Place butter in 9-inch microproof pie plate. Cook (micro) on HI, 30 seconds or until melted.

Combine eggs, water, salt, and pepper. Beat lightly with a fork. Pour into pie plate.

Cover with waxed paper and cook (micro) on 60, 2 minutes or until center is nearly set.

Let stand, covered, 1 to 2 minutes. Fold in half and serve immediately.

2 servings

Before folding omelet, add crumbled cooked bacon, grated Cheddar cheese, chopped cooked ham, chopped tomato, or whatever filling you choose.

CHEESE FONDUE

Cooking Time: 7 to 8 minutes

> 4 **cups (16 ounces) shredded Swiss cheese**
> ¼ **cup all-purpose flour**
> ⅛ **teaspoon salt**
> ¼ **teaspoon nutmeg**
> ⅛ **teaspoon freshly ground pepper**
> 2 **cups dry white wine**
> 2 **tablespoons kirsch**
> 1 **loaf French bread, cut into cubes**

Combine cheese, flour, salt, nutmeg, and pepper in 1½-quart microproof casserole. Stir gently to coat cheese with flour. Blend in wine.

Cover and cook (micro) on 50, 6 minutes, stirring frequently during cooking time. Stir through several times to finish melting cheese. Blend in kirsch.

Serve immediately with cubes of French bread for dipping. If fondue cools, cook (micro) on 50, 1 to 2 minutes.

6 to 8 servings

Omelet for Two (left)

EGGS BENEDICT

Cooking Time: 2 minutes

> 2 **English muffins, split and toasted**
> 4 **slices ham, about ¼ inch thick**
> 4 **poached eggs (page 90)**
> 1 **cup Hollandaise Sauce (page 113)**

Set muffin halves split side up on microproof serving plate. Top each with ham slice.

Cook (micro) on HI, 2 minutes.

Top each with poached egg and hot Hollandaise Sauce. Serve immediately.

4 servings

SAUSAGE AND LEEK QUICHE

Cooking Time: 28 to 29 minutes

  1½ **pounds leeks, white and tender part of leaves, well rinsed, drained, and finely chopped**
  ⅓ **cup butter or margarine**
  ½ **pound bulk pork sausage**
  1 **cup half and half**
  3 **egg yolks**
  1 **egg**
  ⅛ **teaspoon salt**
  ⅛ **teaspoon freshly ground pepper**
  1 **prebaked Basic Pie Crust (page 128)**
    Paprika

Combine leeks and butter in 2-quart microproof bowl. Cover with plastic wrap and cook (micro) on HI, 10 minutes, stirring halfway through cooking time. Stir again, cover, and set aside.

Place sausage in separate 2-quart microproof bowl and cook (micro) on HI, 5 minutes, stirring halfway through cooking time. Remove sausage with slotted spoon and drain thoroughly on paper towel.

Place wire rack in lower position of oven and preheat to 350°F.

Combine half and half, egg yolks, egg, salt, and pepper in medium bowl. Beat well. Stir in leeks. Spoon mixture into pie crust, spreading evenly. Arrange sausage over top and sprinkle with paprika.

Cook (micro/convec) at 350°F, 13 to 14 minutes, rotating quiche halfway through cooking time.

Let stand in oven 5 to 10 minutes or until set. Cut into wedges and serve.

6 to 8 servings

QUICHE LORRAINE

Cooking Time: 22 to 24 minutes

 10 **slices bacon**
  1½ **cups (6 ounces) shredded Swiss cheese**
  ½ **cup thinly sliced green onions**
  1 **prebaked Basic Pie Crust (page 128)**
  1 **tall can evaporated milk or evaporated skim milk**
  4 **eggs**
  ⅛ **teaspoon salt**
  ¼ **teaspoon nutmeg**
  ⅛ **teaspoon ground red pepper**

Arrange 5 slices bacon on paper towel-lined microproof plate. Cover with 2 sheets paper towel and arrange second layer of bacon on top. Cover with paper towel.

Cook (micro) on HI, 7 to 9 minutes. Remove bacon from oven. Crumble and set aside.

Place wire rack in lower position of oven and preheat to 350°F.

Sprinkle bacon, cheese, and onion over crust, reserving 1 teaspoon of each. Beat milk, eggs, salt, nutmeg, and red pepper in 1-quart bowl. Carefully pour into pie crust. Sprinkle top with reserved bacon, cheese, and onion.

Cook (micro/convec) at 350°F, 7½ minutes. Rotate dish one-half turn and continue to cook (micro/convec) at 350°F, 7½ minutes.

Let stand in oven 10 minutes to set. Cut into wedges and serve.

6 to 8 servings

A quiche is especially pretty in a microproof and heatproof quiche dish, but you can also prepare the crust in any 9-inch microproof and heatproof pie plate.

CHEESE SOUFFLE

Cooking Time: 40 to 46 minutes

    1 teaspoon butter or margarine
    ¼ cup grated Parmesan cheese
    ¼ cup butter or margarine
    ¼ cup all-purpose flour
    ½ teaspoon dry mustard
    ¼ teaspoon salt
    ¼ teaspoon freshly ground pepper
    1 cup milk
    1½ cups (6 ounces) shredded
       Cheddar cheese
    6 eggs, separated
    ½ teaspoon cream of tartar

Coat bottom and sides of 2-quart soufflé dish with 1 teaspoon butter. Sprinkle with Parmesan, rotating dish to cover evenly and letting excess cheese remain in bottom. Refrigerate.

Place ¼ cup butter in 2-quart glass measure or microproof bowl and cook (micro) on HI, 3 minutes or until melted.

Stir in flour. Add mustard, salt, and pepper. Slowly blend in milk, mixing until smooth. Cook (micro) on HI, 2 to 3 minutes or until thickened, stirring every 30 seconds.

Add cheese and stir until melted. Beat egg yolks until smooth and lemon-colored. Add to cheese mixture and blend well.

Remove ceramic tray. Place wire rack in lower position of oven and preheat to 330°F.

Beat egg whites in large mixing bowl until foamy. Add cream of tartar and continue beating until stiff peaks form. Stir ⅓ of the whites into cheese mixture. Gently fold in remaining whites. Turn into prepared dish.

Cook (convec) at 330°F, 35 to 40 minutes or until knife inserted midway between center and edge of soufflé comes out clean. Serve immediately.

6 servings

Refrigerating prepared dish helps ensure an even-rising soufflé. The center will still be moist when soufflé is checked.

MACARONI AND CHEESE

Cooking Time: 27½ minutes

    ½ cup butter or margarine
    ½ cup all-purpose flour
    ½ teaspoon salt
    ¼ teaspoon freshly ground pepper
    2 cups milk
    2 cups (8 ounces) shredded sharp
       Cheddar cheese
    1 package (8 ounces) elbow
       macaroni, cooked
    2 tablespoons butter or margarine
    1 cup fresh bread crumbs

Place ½ cup butter in 2-quart microproof and heat-proof bowl and cook (micro) on HI, 1½ minutes. Stir in flour, salt, and pepper, and blend well. Whisk milk into butter-flour mixture, blending until smooth. Slowly stir in cheese.

Cover with plastic wrap and cook (micro) on HI, 5 minutes. Add macaroni and toss thoroughly with fork. Set aside.

Place 2 tablespoons butter in 2-cup glass measure. Cook (micro) on HI, 1 minute. Add bread crumbs and mix well. Sprinkle evenly over macaroni and cheese.

Preheat oven to 300°F. Cook (micro/convec) at 300°F, 20 minutes or until macaroni is heated through and top is golden.

6 to 8 servings

WELSH RABBIT ON TOAST

Cooking Time: 12 minutes

 4 **cups (16 ounces) shredded sharp
   Cheddar cheese**
 4 **teaspoons butter or margarine**
 ¾ **teaspoon Worcestershire sauce**
 ¼ **teaspoon salt**
 ½ **teaspoon paprika**
 ¼ **teaspoon dry mustard**
 ¼ **teaspoon cayenne**
 2 **eggs, lightly beaten**
 1 **cup flat beer or ale, room
   temperature
   Toasted French bread slices**

Combine cheese, butter, Worcestershire, salt, paprika, mustard, and cayenne in 2-quart microproof casserole; mix well.

Cover and cook (micro) on 50, 6 minutes, stirring halfway through cooking time.

Stir part of cheese mixture into beaten eggs. Slowly stir eggs back into remaining cheese, blending until smooth. Gradually blend in beer.

Cover and cook (micro) on 50, 6 minutes, stirring frequently during cooking time. Cheese mixture should be smooth. Stir thoroughly and briskly.

Arrange bread in individual shallow bowls. Ladle cheese mixture over top and serve.

4 to 6 servings

LOX AND EGGS

Cooking Time: 6¾ to 7¾ minutes

 2 **tablespoons butter or margarine**
 1 **small onion, finely diced**
 2 **ounces lox (smoked salmon), diced**
 6 **eggs**
 6 **tablespoons milk
   Chopped fresh parsley for garnish**

Place butter in 8-inch microproof pie plate. Cook (micro) on HI, 45 seconds. Swirl butter to coat bottom.

Sprinkle with onion. Cook (micro) on HI, 2 to 3 minutes or until onion is transparent and begins to brown slightly.

Add lox. Cook (micro) on HI, 1 minute.

Beat eggs with milk in medium bowl; pour into lox mixture. Cook (micro) on HI, 3 minutes or until set, stirring from outside to center to cook evenly. Sprinkle with parsley and serve.

4 servings

MEXICAN SCRAMBLED EGGS

Cooking Time: 9½ minutes

 2 **tablespoons butter or margarine**
 1 **can (4 ounces) diced green chilies**
 1 **large tomato, peeled, coarsely
   chopped, and drained**
 4 **tablespoons minced onion**
 6 **eggs**
 6 **tablespoons milk**
 ⅛ **teaspoon garlic powder
   Salt and freshly ground pepper
   to taste**
 1 **cup (4 ounces) shredded
   Cheddar cheese
   Chopped fresh parsley for garnish**

Place butter in microproof dish or pie plate. Cook (micro) on HI, 1 minute. Swirl butter to coat bottom.

Add chilies, tomato, and onion. Cover with plastic wrap and cook (micro) on HI, 2 minutes.

Beat eggs, milk, garlic powder, salt, and pepper in medium bowl until well blended. Pour over tomato mixture. Cook (micro) on 80, 5 minutes, stirring frequently from outer edge toward center of dish.

Sprinkle with cheese. Cook (micro) on 80, 1½ minutes.

Sprinkle with parsley for garnish.

3 to 4 servings

You can substitute ½ cup chopped green pepper for chilies. Cook on HI, 1 minute before adding to butter.

One-Step Lasagna (page 100) and Vegetarian Lasagna (page 99) cook in a microproof baking dish, covered tightly with plastic wrap.

The stove top method for cooking rice and pasta has never really been improved upon, as it takes just as long for these ingredients to rehydrate by the microwave method as it does by conventional means. Once rice and pasta are prepared and added to other ingredients, however, the microwave method can be a definite cooking time saver. Moreover, "one step" recipes, such as our own One-Step Lasagna on page 100, take advantage of the speed and ease of microwave cooking by integrating rehydration time into the total cooking time of the recipe. The noodles actually rehydrate as they would in boiling water, but they do so right in the casserole itself. In this chapter, you'll find several such convenient "one-step" recipes using pasta or rice. Moreover, there are many convenience rice and pasta products on the market today designed specifically for taking advantage of the speed of the microwave method. From those and the many fine recipes in this chapter, you will undoubtedly be pleased by the microwave mode of your micro/convection oven.

ADAPTING RECIPES

You will discover that your conventional rice or noodle-based casseroles can be easily adapted to microwave and micro/convection cooking. When you find a similar recipe here, adjust your ingredients, but follow only about three-quarters of the recommended microwave cooking times in the similar recipe. Then check, and extend the cooking time by 1-minute segments until done. Make a note of the final cooking time for future reference. Also observe the following guidelines.

- Cooked pasta or rice to be used in a casserole should be slightly firmer than if it is to be eaten at once. Simply cook a bit less.

- Quick-cooking rice may be substituted when converting from conventional recipes that call for uncooked rice. This will allow the rice to cook in the same short time as the rest of the ingredients. Otherwise, precook regular rice to a firm stage and add to the dish.

- To reheat pasta, rice, and cereals, use the microwave method with a power setting of 80.

- **To cook pasta:** Place spaghetti in 13x9-inch baking dish. Add 2½ cups hot water for 2 ounces of uncooked spaghetti; 4 cups for 4 ounces of spaghetti. Cook (micro) on HI, 6 to 9 minutes or until water comes to a boil. Then finish cooking on 50 (6 minutes for 2 ounces; 8 minutes for 4 ounces).
  To cook rice: Add 2 cups water to 1 cup of uncooked rice. Cook (micro) on HI, 4 to 5 minutes or until water comes to a boil. Finish cooking on 50, 13 to 15 minutes. Allow 5 minutes standing time.
  To cook grits or other hot cereals: Cook on HI, 6 to 7 minutes for ⅓ cup grits (uncooked). Follow package directions for liquid.

Leftover pasta dishes no longer mean difficult reheating or scorched casserole bottoms. Reheat right on a serving platter with no added moisture using your oven's microwave mode.

COOKING GUIDE — RICE

Food	Amount Uncooked	Water	Micro Power	Time (minutes)	Standing Time (minutes)	Special Notes
Short grain	1 cup	2 cups	HI	12	5	Use 3-quart microproof casserole.
Long grain	1 cup	2 cups	HI	14	5	Use 3-quart microproof casserole.
Wild rice	1 cup	3 cups	50	40 - 45	5	Use 3-quart microproof casserole.
Brown rice	1 cup	3 cups	50	45 - 50	5	Use 3-quart microproof casserole.
Quick-cooking	1 cup	1 cup	HI	3 - 4	5	Use 1-quart microproof casserole.

BARLEY-RICE CASSEROLE

Cooking Time: 45 to 50 minutes

- ½ **cup butter or margarine**
- ½ **pound mushrooms, sliced**
- 2 **stalks celery, chopped**
- 1 **medium onion, chopped**
- 1 **cup long grain rice**
- 1 **cup barley**
- 1 **envelope (1½ ounces) onion soup mix**
- 2 **cans (10¾ ounces each) beef broth**
- 1 **soup can (10¾ ounces) water**

Combine butter, mushrooms, celery, and onion in 3-quart microproof and heatproof casserole. Cover with casserole lid and cook (micro) on HI, 5 minutes, stirring halfway through cooking time.

Stir in rice and barley. Cover and cook (micro) on HI, 5 minutes.

Add soup mix, broth, and water. Cover and cook (micro) on HI, 20 minutes. Stir through several times.

Cook (micro/convec) at 300°F, 15 to 20 minutes or until most of the liquid is absorbed. Let stand 10 minutes or until remaining liquid is absorbed.

8 servings

SPANISH RICE

Cooking Time: 34 minutes

- ¼ **cup butter or margarine**
- 1 **medium onion, chopped**
- ¼ **cup chopped green pepper**
- 1 **stalk celery, chopped**
- 1 **cup long grain rice**
- 1 **cup water**
- 1 **cup tomato sauce**
- 1 **can (14½ ounces) tomatoes, drained and chopped**
- 1 **can (4 ounces) diced green chilies (optional)**

Place butter and onion in 3-quart microproof and heatproof casserole. Cook (micro) on HI, 2 minutes.

Add green pepper and celery. Cook (micro) on HI, 2 minutes.

Add in rice, water, tomato sauce, tomatoes, and chilies; stir. Cover with casserole lid and cook (micro/convec) at 350°F, 30 minutes.

Let stand, covered, 10 minutes before serving.

6 to 8 servings

Oriental Rice Medley (right)

SIMPLE HERBED RICE

Cooking Time: 12 to 14 minutes

> 2 cups chicken or beef broth
> 1 cup long grain rice
> ¼ cup minced onion
> 2 tablespoons chopped fresh parsley

Combine broth, rice, onion, and parsley in 2-quart microproof casserole. Cover and cook (micro) on HI, 12 to 14 minutes.

Remove from oven and let stand, covered, 10 minutes or until all broth is absorbed.

4 servings

Vary rice to suit your taste and complement the other dishes on the menu. Substitute vegetable or onion bouillon for the chicken broth, or substitute any fresh herbs you prefer.

ORIENTAL RICE MEDLEY

Cooking Time: 17 to 18 minutes

> 1 cup long grain white rice
> 2 cups chicken broth
> 1 package (10 ounces) oriental-style frozen vegetables, thawed
> 1 can (4 ounces) sliced mushrooms, drained
> 2 green onions, chopped
> ¼ cup butter or margarine
> 2 tablespoons soy sauce

Combine rice and broth in 3-quart microproof casserole. Cover with casserole lid and cook (micro) on HI, 12 minutes.

Stir in oriental vegetables, mushrooms, onions, butter, and soy sauce. Cover and cook (micro) on HI, 5 to 6 minutes or until hot.

4 servings

CHEESY VEGETABLES AND RICE

Cooking Time: 17 to 20 minutes

> 1 cup long grain rice
> 2 cups hot water
> 2 cups (8 ounces) shredded Monterey jack cheese, divided
> 1 large zucchini, sliced
> 1 medium tomato, chopped
> 1 green onion, chopped
> 1 teaspoon Italian herb seasoning
> 1 container (8 ounces) dairy sour cream

Place rice and water in 1½-quart microproof casserole. Cover with casserole lid and cook (micro) on HI, 8 to 10 minutes.

In layers over rice, place half of the cheese, zucchini, tomato, green onion, Italian seasoning, and remaining cheese. Cover and cook (micro) on 80, 8 to 9 minutes.

Spread sour cream evenly over top. Cover and continue to cook (micro) on 80, 1 minute.

Remove from oven and let stand, covered, 5 minutes.

4 servings

This protein-rich dish can be the focus of a meatless meal, or it can be a side dish. A green salad and crusty bread round out the meal.

VEGETARIAN LASAGNA

Cooking Time: 38½ to 43½ minutes

1	**large onion, chopped**
½	**pound carrots, shredded**
½	**pound mushrooms, coarsely chopped (about 2 cups)**
1	**container (15 ounces) ricotta cheese**
2	**eggs**
¼	**cup grated Parmesan cheese**
1	**cup spaghetti sauce**
6	**uncooked lasagna noodles**
1	**package (20 ounces) frozen chopped spinach, thawed and drained**
½	**pound tomatoes, peeled and coarsely chopped**
2	**cups (8 ounces) shredded mozzarella cheese**

Place onion in 1-quart microproof casserole. Cover with casserole lid and cook (micro) on HI, 2½ minutes. Spread onions on paper towel to absorb excess moisture. Place carrots in same casserole. Cover and cook (micro) on HI, 3 minutes. Spread out on paper towel. Repeat with mushrooms, cooking (micro) on HI, 3 minutes.

In the same casserole, stir together ricotta, eggs, and Parmesan cheese. Set aside.

Spoon spaghetti sauce into 12x7-inch microproof casserole. Add remaining ingredients in layers as follows.

Form first layer with 3 lasagna noodles, spinach, onions, and half of the ricotta mixture.

Form second layer with 3 lasagna noodles, carrots, mushrooms, and half of the ricotta mixture.

Top with tomatoes and mozzarella. Double-wrap casserole tightly with plastic wrap. Refrigerate 6 to 12 hours.

Remove casserole from refrigerator and let stand 1 hour. Cook (micro) on HI, 10 minutes.

Rotate dish one-half turn. Cook (micro) on 50, 20 to 25 minutes or until hot and bubbly.

Remove from oven and let stand 10 minutes before serving.

8 servings

This is a truly original dish — a delight to the eye as well as the palate. While it does require some effort on your part, we're sure you'll think the results are well worth it.

Vegetarian Lasagna (left)

ONE-STEP LASAGNA

Cooking Time: 37 minutes

> 1 pound lean ground beef
> 1 jar (15 ounces) spaghetti
> sauce or 2 cups Homemade
> Spaghetti Sauce (page 114)
> ½ cup hot water
> 1 package (7 ounces) uncooked
> lasagna noodles, trimmed to fit
> 12x7-inch baking dish
> 1 container (15 ounces) ricotta cheese,
> divided
> 3 cups (12 ounces) shredded
> mozzarella cheese, divided
> ½ cup grated Parmesan cheese
> Chopped fresh parsley for garnish

Crumble beef in 2-quart microproof casserole. Cover with casserole lid and cook (micro) on HI, 5 minutes, stirring once during cooking time.

Pour off fat. Add spaghetti sauce and water. Mix well.

Spread one-third of the meat sauce in 12x7-inch microproof baking dish. Arrange half of the uncooked noodles over sauce. Spread with half of the ricotta. Spread one-third of the meat sauce over ricotta. Sprinkle with 1 cup of the mozzarella.

Repeat with remaining noodles, ricotta, and meat sauce. Top with Parmesan cheese. Double wrap with plastic wrap.

Cook (micro) on HI, 15 minutes. Rotate casserole and cook (micro) on 50, 15 minutes.

Uncover and sprinkle with remaining mozzarella. Leave uncovered and cook (micro) on 50, 2 minutes or until cheese is melted. Sprinkle with parsley and serve with additional Parmesan if desired.

6 servings

STROGANOFF CASSEROLE

Cooking Time: 28 minutes

> 1 pound lean ground beef
> 1 small onion, chopped
> 2 cloves garlic, minced
> 3 cups (4 ounces) uncooked medium-
> width egg noodles
> 1 cup sliced mushrooms
> 1 can (13¾ ounces) beef broth
> ⅛ teaspoon freshly ground pepper
> 1 container (8 ounces) dairy
> sour cream
> 2 tablespoons chopped fresh parsley
> for garnish

Combine beef, onion, and garlic in 2-quart microproof casserole. Cook (micro) on HI, 6 minutes, stirring halfway through cooking time.

Add noodles, mushrooms, broth, and stir. Cover with casserole lid and cook (micro) on 50, 22 minutes, stirring halfway through cooking time.

Let stand 5 minutes. Blend in sour cream and sprinkle with parsley before serving.

6 servings

When preparing vegetables for cooking with the microwave method, cut pieces as uniform in size as possible for more even cooking results.

The microwave method of your micro/convection oven excels in the art of cooking vegetables. Because very little water is used, sometimes none at all, vegetables emerge from the oven freshly-colored, full of flavor, tender and nutritious. Even reheated, fresh vegetables retain their original flavor and color. Because the steam that heats them is primarily generated within the vegetables themselves, they don't dry out. Canned vegetables heat well, too, as they can be drained to retain their full fresh taste after cooking.

ADAPTING RECIPES

Cooked vegetables are best when still slightly crisp. If you prefer a softer texture, simply cook a bit longer.

To adapt a conventional recipe, find a similar recipe in this chapter and also check the cooking guides. The following tips offer additional thoughts for you as you go about creating your own recipes and adapting your new and old favorites.

- Celery, onions, green peppers, and carrots are usually precooked before being added to other vegetable casserole ingredients.

- The temperature probe can also be used for cooking vegetables. Insert temperature probe into center of dish and cook (micro) on HI with probe set at 150°F.

Broccoli cooks much more evenly when stalks are split and florets placed toward the center of the dish. Other vegetables that are not uniform in shape or density can profit from similar preparation and arrangement.

- Frozen vegetables in foil-wrapped or lined cartons must be removed from their original packaging. Cook others in their original packages.

- To reheat packaged frozen vegetables in pouches, make a small slit in center of pouch. Place pouch on microproof plate. Cook (micro) on HI, 4 to 5 minutes. Flex pouch to rearrange contents. Continue to cook (micro) on HI, 4 to 5 minutes.

- Freeze small portions of your favorite vegetable dishes in boilable plastic pouches. Tie with string or rubber bands, not wire twist ties, for defrosting/ reheating later with the microwave method.

COOKING VEGETABLES

It is not difficult to remember the microwave method cooking instructions for vegetables. **All vegetables are cooked (micro) on HI.** Choose a microproof casserole or baking dish or use a microwave roasting rack when appropriate. Cover all vegetables during cooking, with the exception of whole vegetables (potatoes, squash, etc.).

Most vegetables profit from 2 to 3 minutes of standing time before serving.

COOKING GUIDE — VEGETABLES
Cook (micro) on HI

Food	Amount	Fresh Vegetable Preparation	Time (in minutes)	Water	Standing Time (in minutes)	Special Notes
Artichokes 3½" in diameter	Fresh: 1 2	Wash thoroughly. Cut off very top part.	7 - 8 11 - 12	¼ cup ½ cup	2 - 3 2 - 3	When done, leaves will peel off easily.
	Frozen: 10 oz.	Slit pouch.	5 - 6			
Asparagus spears and cut pieces	Fresh: 1 lb.	Wash thoroughly. Snap off tough base and discard.	2 - 3	¼ cup	None	Stir or rearrange halfway through cooking time.
	Frozen: 10 oz.		7 - 8	None	2 - 3	
Beans: green, wax, French-cut	Fresh: 1 lb.	Remove ends. Wash well. Leave whole or break in pieces.	12 - 14	¼ cup	2 - 3	Stir or rearrange as necessary during cooking time.
	Frozen: 6 oz.		7 - 8	None	None	
Beets	4 medium	Scrub beets. Leave 1" of top on beet.	16 - 18	¼ cup	None	After cooking, peel. Cut or leave whole.
Broccoli	Fresh, whole 1 - 2½ lbs.	Remove outer leaves. Slit stalks.	9 - 10	¼ cup	3	Stir or rearrange as necessary during cooking time.
	Frozen, whole		8 - 10	¼ cup	3	
	Fresh, chopped 1 - 1½ lbs.		9 - 10	¼ cup	2	
	Frozen, chopped 10 oz.		8 - 9	None	2	
Brussels sprouts	Fresh: 1 lb.	Remove outside leaves if wilted. Cut off stems. Wash.	8 - 9	¼ cup	2 - 3	Stir or rearrange halfway through cooking time.
	Frozen: 10 oz.		6 - 7	None	None	
Cabbage	½ medium head, shredded	Remove outside wilted leaves.	5 - 6	¼ cup	2 - 3	Rearrange wedges after 7 minutes.
	1 medium head, wedges		13 - 15	¼ cup	2 - 3	
Carrots	4: sliced or diced	Peel and cut off tops.	7 - 9	1 Tb.	2 - 3	Stir halfway through cooking time.
	6: sliced or diced	Fresh young carrots cook best.	9 - 10	2 Tbs.	2 - 3	
	8: tiny, whole		8 - 10	2 Tbs.	2 - 3	
	Frozen: 10 oz.		8 - 9	None	None	
Cauliflower	1 medium, in florets	Cut tough stem. Wash. Remove outside leaves.	7 - 8	¼ cup	2 - 3	Stir after 5 minutes.
	1 medium, whole	Remove core.	8 - 9	½ cup	3	Turn over halfway through cooking time.
	Frozen: 10 oz.		8 - 9	½ cup	3	Stir after 5 minutes.
Celery	2½ cups, 1" slices	Clean stalks thoroughly.	8 - 9	¼ cup	2	
Corn: kernel	Frozen: 10 oz.		5 - 6	¼ cup	2	Stir halfway through cooking time.
On the cob	1 ear	Husk. Cook no more than 4 at a time.	3 - 4	None	2	Place in microproof dish. Add ¼ cup water. Cover with plastic wrap. After cooking, let stand, covered, 2 minutes.
	2 ears		6 - 7	None	2	
	3 ears		9 - 10	None	2	
	4 ears		11 - 12	None	2	
Eggplant	1 medium, sliced	Wash and peel. Cut into slices or cubes.	5 - 6	2 Tbs.	3	
	1 medium, whole	Wash and pierce skin.	6 - 7			Place on microwave roasting rack.
Greens: collard, kale, etc.	Fresh: 1 lb.	Wash. Remove wilted leaves or tough stems.	6 - 7	None	2	
	Frozen: 10 oz.		7 - 8	None	2	

COOKING GUIDE — VEGETABLES (cont'd)
Cook (micro) on HI

Food	Amount	Fresh Vegetable Preparation	Time (in minutes)	Water	Standing Time (in minutes)	Special Notes
Mushrooms	Fresh: ½ lb. sliced	Add butter.	2 - 4		2	Stir halfway through cooking time.
Okra	Fresh: ½ lb.	Wash thoroughly. Leave whole or cut in thick slices.	3 - 5	¼ cup	2	
	Frozen: 10 oz.		7 - 8	None	2	
Onions	1 lb., tiny whole	Peel. Add 1 Tb. butter.	6 - 7	None	3	Stir halfway through cooking time.
	1 lb., medium to large	Peel and quarter. Add 1 Tb. butter.	7 - 9	None	3	
Parsnips	4 medium, quartered	Peel and cut.	8 - 9	¼ cup	2	Stir halfway through cooking time.
Peas: green	Fresh: 1 lb.	Shell peas. Rinse well.	7 - 8	¼ cup	2	Stir halfway through cooking time.
	Fresh: 2 lbs.		8 - 9	½ cup	2 - 3	
	Frozen: 6 oz.		5 - 6	None	None	
Peas and onions	Frozen: 10 oz.		6 - 8	2 Tbs.	2	
Potatoes, sweet 5 - 6 oz. ea.	1	Wash and scrub well. Pierce with fork. Place on microwave roasting rack or paper towel in circle, 1" apart.	4 - 4½	None	3	
	2		6 - 7	None	3	
	4		8 - 10	None	3	
	6		10 - 11	None	3	
Potatoes, white baking 6 - 8 oz. ea.	1	Wash and scrub well. Pierce with fork. Place on microwave roasting rack or paper towel in circle, 1" apart.	4 - 6	None	3	
	2		6 - 8	None	3	
	3		8 - 12	None	3	
	4		12 - 16	None	3	
	5		16 - 20	None	3	
red, boiling	3	Peel potatoes, cut in quarters.	12 - 16	½ cup	None	Stir halfway through cooking time.
Rutabaga	Fresh: 1 lb.	Wash well. Remove tough stems or any wilted leaves.	6 - 7	None	2	Stir halfway through cooking time.
	Frozen: 10 oz.		7 - 8	None	2	
Snow peas	Frozen: 6 oz.		3 - 4	2 Tbs.	3	
Spinach	Fresh: 1 lb.	Wash well. Remove tough stems. Drain.	6 - 7	None	2	Stir halfway through cooking time.
	Frozen: 10 oz.		7 - 8	None	2	
Squash, acorn or butternut	1 - 1½ lbs. whole	Scrub. Pierce with fork.	10 - 12	None		Cut and remove seeds to serve.
Spaghetti squash	2 - 3 lbs.	Scrub, pierce with fork. Place on microwave roasting rack.	6 per lb.	None	5	Serve with butter, Parmesan cheese, or spaghetti sauce.
Turnips	4 cups cubed	Peel, wash.	9 - 11	¼ cup	3	Stir after 5 minutes.
Zucchini	3 cups sliced	Wash; do not peel. Add butter.	7 - 8		2	Stir after 4 minutes.

BLANCHING GUIDE — VEGETABLES
Cook (micro) on HI

Food	Amount	Water	Approximate Time (in minutes)	Microproof Casserole Size
Asparagus (cut in 1-inch pieces)	4 cups	¼ cup	4½	1½ quart
Beans, green or wax (cut in 1-inch pieces)	1 pound	½ cup	5	1½ quart
Broccoli (cut in 1-inch pieces)	1 pound	⅓ cup	6	1½ quart
Carrots (sliced)	1 pound	⅓ cup	6	1½ quart
Cauliflower (cut in florets)	1 head	⅓ cup	6	2 quart
Corn (cut from cob)	4 cups	none	4	1½ quart
Corn-on-the-cob (husked)	6 ears	none	5½	1½ quart
Onions (quartered)	4 medium	½ cup	3 - 4½	1 quart
Parsnips (cubed)	1 pound	¼ cup	2½ - 4	1½ quart
Peas (shelled)	4 cups	¼ cup	4½	1½ quart
Snow peas	4 cups	¼ cup	3½	1½ quart
Spinach (washed)	1 pound	none	4	2 quart
Turnips (cubed)	1 pound	¼ cup	3 - 4½	1½ quart
Zucchini (sliced or cubed)	1 pound	¼ cup	4	1½ quart

REHEATING GUIDE — VEGETABLES*

Food	Programming Method	Setting	Time (in minutes)	Special Notes
Au gratin vegetables, frozen, 11½ oz.	micro	70	10 - 12 min.	Use microproof loaf dish, covered.
Onion Rings, 9 oz.	convec	follow package directions		Remove ceramic tray. Place wire rack in upper position. Preheat. Use cookie sheet or foil tray.
Potatoes, Country-cut fries, 1 lb.	convec	follow package directions		Remove ceramic tray. Place wire rack in upper position. Preheat. Use cookie sheet or foil tray.
French fries, 1 lb.	convec	follow package directions		Remove ceramic tray. Place wire rack in upper position. Preheat. Use cookie sheet or foil tray.
Instant mashed, potatoes 4 servings	micro	HI	5 - 6 min.	Follow package directions. Reduce liquid by 1 tablespoon.
Stuffed potatoes, 12 oz. (2)	micro/convec	400°	10 - 12 min.	Place wire rack in lower position. Place potatoes in oven during preheat. Use microproof and heatproof container.
Tater tots, 1 lb.	convec	follow package directions		Remove ceramic tray. Place wire rack in upper position. Preheat. Use cookie sheet or foil tray.
Vegetable crêpes, 6½ oz.	micro/convec	300°	7 - 8 min.	Place wire rack in lower position. Use heatproof paper tray.
Vegetable soufflé, 12 oz.	micro	HI	12 - 15 min.	Transfer to microproof paper tray.
Vegetables, frozen in pouch, 10 - 12 oz.	micro	HI	8 - 10 min.	Slit pouch. Place on microproof plate. Flex halfway through cooking time to mix.

*Due to the tremendous variety in convenience food products available, times given here should be used only as guidelines. We suggest that you cook food for the shortest recommended time and then check for doneness. Be sure to check the package for microwave and oven (convec) instructions.

COOKING GUIDE — CANNED VEGETABLES Cook (micro) on 80	Size	Minutes Drained	Minutes Undrained	Special Notes
	8 ounces	1½ - 2	2 - 2½	Regardless of quantity, use a 4-cup microproof casserole, covered. Stir once. Let stand, covered, 2 - 3 minutes before serving.
	15 ounces	2½ - 3	3 - 4	
	17 ounces	3½ - 4	4 - 5	

Note: Temperature probe may be used. Cook (micro) on 80 with probe set at 150°F. Place probe in center of dish. Stir halfway through cooking time.

Microwave Vegetable Variety

MICRO TIME   CONVEC TIME

ZUCCHINI SOUFFLE

Cooking Time: 49 to 55 minutes

1 **teaspoon butter or margarine**
¼ **cup grated Parmesan cheese**
½ **cup butter or margarine**
1 **zucchini (about 1 pound),
   shredded**
3 **green onions or 1 medium onion,
   finely chopped**
2 **cloves garlic, minced**
¼ **cup dry white wine**
3 **tablespoons minced fresh parsley**
1 **tablespoon fresh lemon juice**
⅛ **teaspoon nutmeg
   Salt and freshly ground pepper
   to taste**
1 **jar (2 ounces) pimientos, drained,
   finely diced**
6 **eggs, separated**
2 **tablespoons grated Parmesan cheese**
½ **teaspoon cream of tartar**

Coat bottom and sides of 2-quart soufflé dish with 1 teaspoon butter. Sprinkle with ¼ cup Parmesan, rotating dish to cover evenly and letting excess cheese remain on bottom. Refrigerate dish.

Combine ½ cup butter, zucchini, green onions, and garlic in 2-quart microproof bowl. Cook (micro) on HI, 4 minutes or just until limp.

Add wine, parsley, lemon juice, nutmeg, salt, and pepper. Cook (micro) on HI, 5 to 6 minutes or until zucchini is tender. Drain. Add pimientos and mix well. Set aside to cool.

Remove ceramic tray. Place wire rack in lower position of oven and preheat to 330°F.

Beat egg yolks with 2 tablespoons grated Parmesan cheese until thick and lemon colored. Blend in zucchini mixture. Beat egg whites in large mixing bowl until foamy. Add cream of tartar and continue beating until stiff. Stir ⅓ of the egg whites into zucchini mixture. Gently fold in remaining whites. Turn into prepared dish.

Cook (convec) at 330°F, 40 to 45 minutes or until knife inserted midway between center of soufflé and edge of dish comes out clean. Serve immediately.

6 servings

EGGPLANT PIZZAS

Cooking Time: 30 to 32 minutes

- 1 **large eggplant (about 10 inches long)**
  Salt
- ¼ **cup chopped onion**
- 1 **large clove garlic, minced**
- 1 **tablespoon olive oil**
- 1 **can (8 ounces) tomato sauce**
- 1 **can (6 ounces) tomato paste**
- ½ **teaspoon sugar**
- ¼ **teaspoon grated lemon peel**
- ¼ **teaspoon oregano**
- ¼ **teaspoon salt**
- ⅛ **teaspoon freshly ground pepper**
- ¼ **cup olive oil**
- 1 **cup shredded mozzarella cheese**
- ⅓ **cup grated Parmesan cheese**

Cut eggplant into slices ⅜-inch thick (do not peel). Sprinkle both sides with salt. Arrange on double thickness of paper towels and let drain 30 to 45 minutes.

Combine onion, garlic, and 1 tablespoon olive oil in 1½-quart microproof bowl. Cover with plastic wrap and cook (micro) on HI, 3 minutes.

Add tomato sauce, paste, sugar, lemon peel, oregano, ¼ teaspoon salt, and pepper. Mix well. Cover with paper towel and cook (micro) on 50, 6 minutes, stirring halfway through cooking time. Set aside.

Rinse eggplant in cold water and pat dry with paper towel. Brush each side generously with remaining olive oil. Layer in 3-quart microproof and heatproof casserole.

Remove ceramic tray. Place wire rack in upper position of oven.

Cover and cook (micro/convec) at 350°F, 15 minutes. Drain off any excess oil.

Preheat oven to 380°F.

Arrange eggplant slices in single layer on baking sheet or aluminum tray. Spoon tomato sauce evenly over top. Sprinkle with cheeses. Cook (convec) at 380°F, 6 to 8 minutes or until cheese begins to brown. Serve hot.

8 to 10 servings

RATATOUILLE

Cooking Time: 39 to 41 minutes

- 1 **eggplant (about 1½ pounds), peeled or unpeeled**
  Salt
- ¼ **cup olive oil**
- 2 **medium onions, thinly sliced**
- 2 **cloves garlic, minced**
- 1 **green pepper, sliced into thin strips**
- 4 **zucchini (about 1 pound), cut into ¼-inch slices**
- ¼ **cup chopped fresh parsley**
- ½ **teaspoon freshly ground pepper**
- ½ **teaspoon basil leaves, crumbled**
- ½ **teaspoon oregano, crumbled**
- ½ **pound mushrooms, sliced**
- 3 **large tomatoes, peeled, seeded, and cut into wedges**
- ¼ **cup grated Parmesan cheese**

Cut eggplant into 1-inch cubes. Transfer to colander and sprinkle with salt. Let stand 20 minutes. Rinse with cold water. Drain and pat dry with paper towel.

Combine oil, onion, garlic, and green pepper in 4-quart microproof and heatproof casserole. Cover with casserole lid and cook (micro) on HI, 4 to 6 minutes. Stir through several times. Add eggplant, zucchini, parsley, pepper, basil, oregano and toss lightly.

Place wire rack in lower position of oven and preheat to 350°F.

Cover and cook (micro/convec) at 350°F, 20 minutes.

Stir in mushrooms and tomatoes. Cover and cook (micro/convec) at 350°F, 5 minutes. Sprinkle with cheese.

Remove ceramic tray carefully with hot pads. Cook (convec), uncovered, at 350°F, 10 minutes. Serve hot.

6 to 8 servings

ASPARAGUS CASSEROLE

Cooking Time: 10 minutes

- 20 saltine crackers, crushed
- 1 can (15 ounces) asparagus pieces
- 3 cups (12 ounces) shredded Cheddar cheese, divided
- 4 hard-cooked eggs, chopped, divided
- ½ cup milk
- 1 can (10¾ ounces) condensed cream of mushroom soup

Place wire rack in lower position of oven and preheat to 350°F.

Sprinkle half of the cracker crumbs into 2-quart microproof and heatproof casserole.

Drain asparagus, reserving 3 tablespoons liquid.

Arrange half of the cheese, asparagus, and eggs over crumbs. Repeat layering.

Combine milk, mushroom soup, and reserved liquid in small bowl and blend well. Pour over top.

Cook (micro/convec) at 350°F, 10 minutes. Serve immediately.

6 to 8 servings

GREEN BEANS AMANDINE

Cooking Time: 9 minutes

- 1 package (10 ounces) frozen French-cut green beans
- ½ cup sliced almonds
- 2 tablespoons butter or margarine
  Salt and freshly ground pepper to taste

Set package of beans on microproof plate and cook (micro) on HI, 6 minutes.

Transfer to microproof serving dish and set aside.

Combine almonds and butter in 1-cup glass measure. Cook (micro) on HI, 2 minutes or until nuts are lightly brown, stirring after 1 minute.

Add nut mixture to beans, season with salt and pepper, and toss lightly. Cook (micro) on HI, 1 minute. Serve hot.

3 to 4 servings

STUFFED TOMATOES

Cooking Time: 14 to 16 minutes

- 1 package (10 ounces) frozen chopped spinach
- 4 large firm tomatoes
- 1 cup (4 ounces) shredded mozzarella cheese, divided
- ¼ cup finely minced onions
- ¼ cup grated Parmesan cheese
- ½ teaspoon salt
- ⅛ teaspoon freshly ground pepper
- 2 tablespoons chopped fresh parsley

Set spinach on microproof plate. Cook (micro) on HI, 8 minutes. Let stand 5 minutes. Drain well; squeeze dry. Transfer to large bowl and set aside.

Slice ½-inch piece from top of each tomato. Carefully hollow out centers, discarding seeds and leaving ½-inch shell. Invert shells on paper towels to drain.

Chop pulp finely and add to spinach. Add ½ cup mozzarella, onion, Parmesan, salt, and pepper to spinach mixture; blend well. Spoon evenly into tomato shells. Sprinkle with remaining mozzarella and parsley. Arrange in 8-inch round microproof and heatproof baking dish.

Place wire rack in lower position of oven.

Cook (micro/convec) at 350°F, 6 to 8 minutes or until heated through. Serve immediately.

4 servings

STATE FAIR CORN

Cooking Time: 11 to 12 minutes

- 4 unhusked ears of corn
  Butter or margarine
  Salt to taste

Discard any soiled outer pieces of husk. Soak corn in cold water 5 to 10 minutes to clean and moisten. Drain. Set unhusked corn directly on microproof serving dish.

Cook (micro) on HI, 11 to 12 minutes. Let stand 3 minutes. Husk and serve hot with butter.

4 servings

CHEESE BROCCOLI

Cooking Time: 8½ minutes

> 1 **package (10 ounces) frozen broccoli spears**
> ¼ **cup (1 ounce) shredded Monterey jack cheese**

Unwrap broccoli; place in shallow 2-cup microproof dish. Cover with plastic wrap. Cook (micro) on HI, 8 minutes.

Sprinkle cheese over broccoli. Cook (micro) on HI, 30 seconds or until cheese begins to melt. Serve hot.

2 servings

CAULIFLOWER GRATINEED NOREEN

Cooking Time: 6½ to 8½ minutes

> 1 **large head cauliflower**
> 3 **tablespoons melted butter, margarine, or water**
> ½ **teaspoon garlic salt**
> ⅛ **teaspoon freshly ground pepper**
> ¼ **cup grated Parmesan cheese, divided**
> 2 **firm tomatoes, cut into wedges**
> ¼ **cup Italian seasoned bread crumbs**
> ¾ **cup (3 ounces) shredded Swiss or Cheddar cheese**

Remove large stem from cauliflower; cut or break off florets. Arrange in 2-quart microproof casserole.

Place butter in 1-cup glass measure. Cook (micro) on HI, 30 seconds. Pour melted butter over cauliflower. Sprinkle with garlic salt and pepper.

Cover and cook (micro) on HI, 5 to 6 minutes. Stir florets to coat with butter. Sprinkle with half of the Parmesan.

Arrange tomatoes over cauliflower and sprinkle with remaining Parmesan. Sprinkle bread crumbs and Swiss cheese over top.

Cover and cook (micro) on HI, 1 to 2 minutes or until cheese is melted. Serve immediately.

4 to 6 servings

BRUSSELS SPROUTS WITH GARLIC

Cooking Time: 8 minutes

> 1 **pound fresh brussels sprouts**
> ¼ **cup water**
> 2 **tablespoons butter or margarine**
> 1 **clove garlic, minced**
> **Salt and freshly ground pepper to taste**
> ¼ **cup grated Parmesan cheese**

Remove any dry or discolored outer leaves from sprouts. Trim stems. Using small sharp knife, cut a shallow "X" in stem end of each sprout. Combine sprouts and water in 1-quart microproof casserole.

Cover with casserole lid and cook (micro) on HI, 7 minutes. Set aside, still covered.

Combine butter and garlic in 1-cup glass measure and cook (micro) on HI, 1 minute.

Drain water from sprouts. Add butter mixture, salt, and pepper, tossing lightly to coat. Add cheese and toss again. Serve hot.

6 to 8 servings

EASY COUNTRY FRIES

Cooking Time: 36 minutes

> ¼ **cup instant minced onion**
> ½ **teaspoon salt**
> ½ **teaspoon freshly ground pepper**
> ½ **teaspoon paprika**
> 8 **medium potatoes**
> ½ **cup butter or margarine, divided**

Place wire rack in upper position of oven and preheat to 350°F.

Combine onion, salt, pepper, and paprika in small bowl; set aside.

Rinse potatoes and pat dry with paper towel (do not peel). Cut evenly into ¼-inch slices. Arrange ⅓ of the potatoes in 2-quart oval microproof and heatproof casserole. Sprinkle with ⅓ of the onion mixture. Dot with ⅓ of the butter. Repeat layering, ending with butter and onion mixture.

Cook (micro/convec) at 350°F, 21 minutes. Rotate casserole and continue to cook (micro/convec) at 350°F, 15 minutes or until crisp. Serve hot.

4 to 6 servings

TWICE-BAKED POTATOES

Cooking Time: 20 to 24 minutes

- **4 baking potatoes**
- **½ cup butter or margarine, softened**
- **½ cup dairy sour cream**
- **½ teaspoon salt**
- **⅛ teaspoon freshly ground pepper**
- **4 teaspoons crumbled cooked bacon (optional)**

Wash potatoes; pat dry with paper towel and pierce with fork in several places. Arrange in circle on paper towel on ceramic tray, spacing about 1 inch apart. Cook (micro) on HI, 12 to 14 minutes or until outside of potatoes begins to feel soft. Let stand several minutes.

Remove ceramic tray. Place wire rack in lower position of oven and preheat to 400°F.

Remove ¼-inch horizontal slice from top of each potato. Carefully scoop out pulp into medium bowl, keeping shells intact. Add butter, sour cream, salt, and pepper to pulp; beat with electric mixer until smooth.

Divide mixture evenly among shells, mounding slightly in center (or pipe in with pastry bag).

Place on heatproof platter. Cook (convec) at 400°F, 8 to 10 minutes or until edges begin to brown.

Sprinkle with bacon and serve immediately. Pass extra sour cream if desired.

4 servings

DELIGHTFUL YAMS

Cooking Time: 18 to 19 minutes

- **3 cans (16 ounces each) yams, well drained**
- **¼ cup fresh orange juice**
- **1 tablespoon cornstarch**
- **½ cup firmly-packed brown sugar**
- **¼ cup melted butter or margarine**
- **1 orange, peeled and cubed**
- **½ cup coarsely chopped walnuts**
- **1 tablespoon grated orange peel**
- **1½ cups miniature marshmallows**

Remove ceramic tray. Place wire rack in lower position of oven and preheat to 450°F.

Arrange yams in 1½-quart round microproof and heatproof baking dish or quiche dish. Combine orange juice and cornstarch in medium bowl; stir until cornstarch is completely dissolved. Blend in brown sugar and butter. Add orange, walnuts, and peel. Pour over yams.

Cook (micro/convec) at 450°F, 15 minutes. Arrange 1¼ cups marshmallows around rim. Mound remaining marshmallows in center.

Cook (convec) at 450°F, 3 to 4 minutes or until marshmallows are brown. Serve hot.

6 servings

**A Host of Potatoes
(Twice Baked Potatoes and
Delightful Yams, left)**

POTATO KUGEL

Cooking Time: 50 minutes

- 2 **medium onions, cut into eighths**
- 3 **eggs**
- 1½ **teaspoons salt**
- ½ **teaspoon baking powder**
- ¼ **teaspoon freshly ground pepper**
- 6 **medium potatoes, peeled and shredded**
- ½ **cup matzo meal**
- 2 **tablespoons vegetable oil, divided**

Combine onions, eggs, salt, baking powder, and pepper in 2-quart bowl. Add potatoes to onion mixture; mix well. Add matzo meal and blend. Stir in 1 tablespoon oil.

Remove ceramic tray. Place wire rack in lower position of oven and preheat to 350°F.

Coat 8-inch square baking dish with remaining oil. Pour in potato mixture. Cook (convec) at 350°F, 50 minutes or until crisp. Serve immediately.

6 servings

If you prefer, all-purpose flour can be substituted for matzo meal.

PARMESAN POTATOES

Cooking Time: 8 to 9 minutes

- 1 **pound potatoes**
- ¼ **cup butter or margarine**
- 8 **buttery crackers**
- ¼ **cup grated Parmesan cheese**
- 1 **teaspoon garlic powder**
- ¼ **teaspoon salt**
- ½ **teaspoon paprika**
- ⅛ **teaspoon freshly ground pepper**
- 1 **tablespoon grated Parmesan cheese**
- 3 **tablespoons chopped fresh parsley for garnish**

Peel potatoes and cut into 1-inch squares. Place butter in 1-quart microproof casserole or 8-inch round microproof baking dish. Cook (micro) on HI, 1 minute.

Add potatoes and coat well. Drain off any remaining butter; set aside.

Combine crackers, ¼ cup Parmesan, garlic powder, salt, paprika, and pepper in food processor or blender. Blend to make fine crumbs. Transfer cracker mixture to plastic bag. Add potatoes in batches and shake to coat evenly. Arrange potatoes in single layer in shallow microproof dish or pie plate just large enough to accommodate.

Cover with plastic wrap and cook (micro) on HI, 5 minutes. Remove cover and add reserved butter; stir well. Cook (micro), uncovered, on HI, 2 to 3 minutes or until potatoes are fork tender.

Sprinkle with remaining Parmesan and garnish with parsley. Serve hot.

4 servings

Add a pinch of dill, oregano, tarragon, or any other herb to cracker mixture for an interesting variation.

SCALLOPED POTATOES

Cooking Time: 19 to 22 minutes

- 4 **medium potatoes (about 1 pound), peeled and cut into ⅛-inch slices**
- 3 **tablespoons all-purpose flour**
- ½ **teaspoon salt**
- ½ **teaspoon garlic powder**
- ⅛ **teaspoon freshly ground pepper**
- 1 **cup milk**
- 2 **tablespoons butter or margarine Paprika**

Arrange half of the potatoes in 1½-quart microproof casserole. Combine flour, salt, garlic powder, and pepper. Sprinkle half of the mixture over potatoes. Repeat layering.

Pour milk over potatoes. Dot with butter and sprinkle with paprika. Cover and cook (micro) on HI, 12 minutes.

Remove cover and cook (micro/convec) at 350°F, 7 to 10 minutes or until potatoes are tender.

4 servings

For Scalloped Potatoes Au Gratin, follow above recipe and sprinkle ¾ cup shredded Cheddar cheese over each layer of potatoes.

Spaghetti Squash Primavera (right)

SPAGHETTI SQUASH PRIMAVERA

Cooking Time: 30 to 32 minutes

- 1 **spaghetti squash
  (1½ to 2 pounds)**
- 1 **large zucchini (about 8 ounces)
  cut into ½-inch slices**
- 1 **large green pepper, cut into
  1-inch pieces**
- 1 **stalk celery, sliced**
- ½ **teaspoon dill**
- ½ **teaspoon basil**
- ½ **teaspoon Italian herb seasoning**
- ¼ **cup butter or margarine**
- 2 **large tomatoes, coarsely chopped**
- ¼ **cup grated Parmesan cheese
  Chopped fresh parsley for garnish**

Pierce squash deeply in several places with long-tined fork. Place on microwave roasting rack. Cook (micro) on HI, 7 minutes.

Turn squash over and continue to cook (micro) on HI, 3 to 5 minutes or until soft.

Combine zucchini, green pepper, celery, dill, basil, and Italian seasoning in 1½-quart microproof and heatproof casserole. Dot vegetables with butter. Cover with casserole lid. Cook (micro/convec) at 350°F, 10 minutes.

Stir in tomatoes. Cover and cook (micro/convec) at 350°F, 10 minutes.

Cut squash in half and remove seeds. With two forks, carefully transfer squash strands to serving platter. Spoon vegetables over top. Sprinkle with Parmesan cheese. Garnish with parsley. Serve immediately.

4 servings

Basic White Sauce (page 113) can be the base for dozens of creative sauces. Use your ingenuity — add cheese, herbs, or a bit of onion, etc., to develop your own variations.

A glass measure and a whisk are all the utensils needed to make sauces with the microwave method of your micro/convection oven. Look what a sauce does here for an attractive vegetable platter.

There are a host of reasons why the microwave method of your micro/convection oven will make troublesome sauce preparation a thing of the past. Sauces do not stick or scorch as they do when not watched carefully during preparation by the stove-top method. Moreover, sauces heat evenly and require less stirring and cooking time than when prepared conventionally. An occasional stirring is all that is required to prevent lumping. After cooking, a quick whisking can be added to make a sauce velvety-smooth. And finally, in most cases sauce preparation using the microwave method can all be done in a single glass measure, cooking included. Preparation is quick. Clean up is fast. For these reasons we're sure you'll find yourself using this convenient feature of your oven frequently to add variety to host of dishes.

ADAPTING RECIPES

When looking for a sauce recipe similar to the conventional one you want to convert, find a recipe with a similar quantity of liquid and similar main thickening ingredient such as cornstarch, flour, egg, cheese, or jelly. Read the directions carefully to determine procedure, timing, and micro control setting. Then,

when you stir, notice the progress of the sauce, and remove when the right consistency or doneness is reached. Keep notes for future reference and follow these useful guidelines.

- You will notice that more flour or cornstarch is required in microwave cooking than in conventional cooking to thicken sauces and gravies, as they will not be reduced by evaporation.

- Stirring quickly two or three times during cooking is sufficient to assure even cooking. Too many stirrings may slow cooking.

- When sauces require time to develop flavor or if they contain eggs, which might curdle, they should be cooked slowly. Cook (micro) on 50 or even 30. Don't allow delicate egg yolk sauces to boil.

- Sauces and salad dressings with ingredients not sensitive to rapid heating should be cooked (micro) on HI. Basic White Sauce is an example.

- Use a microproof container about twice the volume of ingredients to safeguard against the sauce boiling over — so easy with milk and cream-based sauces.

- Bring cornstarch-thickened mixtures to a boil and remove as soon as thickened. Remember, overcooking will destroy the thickening agent.

BASIC WHITE SAUCE

Cooking Time: 3 to 4 minutes

> 2 **tablespoons butter or margarine**
> 2 **tablespoons all-purpose flour**
> ¼ **teaspoon salt**
> ⅛ **teaspoon white pepper**
> 1 **cup milk**

Place butter in 1-quart glass measure and cook (micro) on HI, 1 minute.

Add flour, salt, and pepper. Blend until smooth.

Whisk in milk and blend thoroughly. Cook (micro) on HI, 2 to 3 minutes, stirring halfway through cooking time.

Stir through several times. If thicker sauce is desired, continue to cook (micro) on HI, 20 seconds, repeating as needed and stirring through after each 20 seconds.

about 1 cup

BASIC CHEESE SAUCE

Cooking Time: 3 to 4 minutes

> 4½ **tablespoons butter or margarine**
> 3 **tablespoons all-purpose flour**
> 1¼ **cups milk**
> ¼ **teaspoon salt**
> ⅛ **teaspoon white pepper**
> ½ **cup (2 ounces) shredded sharp Cheddar cheese**

Place butter in 1-quart glass measure and cook (micro) on HI, 1 minute.

Add flour, salt, and pepper. Blend until smooth.

Whisk in milk and blend thoroughly. Cook (micro) on HI, 2 to 3 minutes, stirring halfway through cooking time.

Add cheese and beat until smooth. If cheese has not melted completely, cook (micro) on HI, 30 seconds.

1½ cups

TARRAGON SAUCE

Cooking Time: 3 to 4 minutes

> ½ **cup butter, melted**
> ⅓ **cup dry white wine**
> 1 **tablespoon tarragon vinegar**
> 2 **teaspoons tarragon**
> 1 **tablespoon chopped chives**
> ¼ **teaspoon salt**
> ¼ **teaspoon freshly ground pepper**
> ⅛ **teaspoon hot pepper sauce**
> 3 **egg yolks**

Combine all ingredients except egg yolks in 2-cup glass measure and blend well. Cook (micro) on HI, 1 to 2 minutes.

Beat egg yolks in small bowl. Stir small amount of butter mixture into egg yolks, then stir yolk mixture back into remaining sauce. Cook (micro) on 50, 2 minutes, stirring once during cooking time.

Beat until smooth and serve immediately.

1 cup

This sauce is excellent over poached eggs, broiled meat or poultry, or steamed vegetables.

HOLLANDAISE SAUCE

Cooking Time: 2 minutes

> ¼ **cup butter or margarine**
> 2 **teaspoons lemon juice**
> 2 **egg yolks, well beaten**
> 2 **tablespoons half and half**
> ⅛ **teaspoon salt**
> ½ **teaspoon dry mustard**

Place butter in 2-cup glass measure and cook (micro) on HI, 1 minute.

Stir in lemon juice. Add remaining ingredients and blend well. Cook (micro) on HI, 1 minute or until mixture begins to thicken, stirring twice during cooking time.

Beat until smooth. Serve immediately.

about ½ cup

HOISIN SAUCE

Cooking Time: 4 to 5 minutes

>   1 cup beef broth
> ¼ cup soy sauce
> ¼ cup dry sherry
>   2 tablespoons arrowroot or cornstarch
>   2 tablespoons molasses
>   2 tablespoons tomato paste
>   2 cloves garlic, minced
> ½ teaspoon ground ginger
> ⅛ teaspoon freshly ground pepper

Combine all ingredients in 4-cup glass measure and blend well. Cover with plastic wrap and cook (micro) on HI, 4 to 5 minutes or until thickened.

about 1¾ cups

This sauce goes well with stir-fried vegetables, meat, poultry, or seafood. Also try it with rice and with Western-style dishes.

BARBECUE SAUCE

Cooking Time: 8 minutes

>   1 small onion, chopped
>   1 clove garlic, minced
>   1 tablespoon butter or margarine
>   1 can (8 ounces) tomato sauce
>   2 tablespoons dark brown sugar
>   2 tablespoons lemon juice
>   1 teaspoon Worcestershire sauce
> ½ teaspoon salt
> ¼ teaspoon paprika
> ¼ teaspoon dry mustard
> ¼ teaspoon freshly ground pepper
> ⅛ teaspoon turmeric (optional)

Combine onion, garlic, and butter in 2-quart glass measure. Cook (micro) on HI, 3 minutes.

Add remaining ingredients and blend well. Cover with waxed paper and cook (micro) on HI, 5 minutes, stirring halfway through cooking time.

1½ cups

HOMEMADE SPAGHETTI SAUCE

Cooking Time: 24½ minutes

>   1 medium onion, chopped
> ½ stalk celery, sliced
>   6 mushrooms (about ¼ pound), sliced
> ½ green pepper, sliced into thin strips
>   2 cloves garlic, minced
> 1½ tablespoons vegetable oil
> ½ pound lean ground beef
>   1 can (14 ounces) tomatoes, chopped, liquid reserved
>   1 can (6 ounces) tomato paste
>   1 tablespoon chopped fresh parsley
> ½ teaspoon oregano

Combine onion, celery, mushrooms, green pepper, garlic, and oil in 2-quart microproof and heatproof casserole. Cook (micro) on HI, 6 minutes.

Stir in beef. Continue to cook (micro) on HI, 3½ minutes.

Stir through several times. Blend in tomatoes with liquid, tomato paste, parsley, and oregano.

Cover with casserole lid and cook (micro/convec) at 350°F, 15 minutes or until sauce is slightly thickened.

about 4 cups

CREAMY DIJON SAUCE

Cooking Time: 2 to 3 minutes

> ¼ cup dry white wine
>   2 tablespoons whipping cream
>   2 tablespoons butter or margarine
>   2 teaspoons Dijon-style mustard
> ¼ teaspoon tarragon

Combine all ingredients in 1-cup glass measure. Cover with plastic wrap and cook (micro) on 50, 2 to 3 minutes.

about 1 cup

Serve with meat, spread on sandwiches, or stir into your favorite casserole.

BEARNAISE SAUCE

Cooking Time: 1 to 2 minutes

    ½ cup butter or margarine
    4 egg yolks
    2 teaspoons tarragon vinegar
    1 teaspoon minced onion
    ½ teaspoon chervil
    ⅛ teaspoon white pepper
    1 teaspoon chopped fresh parsley

Place butter in 1-cup glass measure and cook (micro) on HI, 1 to 2 minutes or until butter bubbles.

Combine egg yolks, vinegar, onion, chervil, and pepper in blender. With blender at high speed, gradually add butter through cover opening and mix until sauce is thick and creamy. Stir in parsley. Serve warm.

½ cup

Serve over broiled steak, green vegetables, poached eggs, or fish.

BEEF GRAVY

Cooking Time: 5 to 6 minutes

    ½ cup beef drippings
    ½ cup all-purpose flour
    4 cups beef broth, heated
      Salt and freshly ground pepper
        to taste
      Bottled brown sauce (optional)

Combine drippings and flour in 4-quart microproof casserole and blend well. Cook (micro) on HI, 1 minute, stirring once during cooking time.

Stir in broth. Cook (micro) on HI, 4 to 5 minutes or until thickened, stirring halfway through cooking time.

Season with salt and pepper. Add several drops of brown sauce to deepen color, if desired.

1 quart

ORANGE SAUCE

Cooking Time: 2 to 3 minutes

    ⅔ cup orange juice
    3 tablespoons poultry drippings
    2 tablespoons brown sugar
    1 tablespoon cornstarch
    2 teaspoons grated orange peel
    2 tablespoons orange-flavored
        liqueur

Combine all ingredients except liqueur in 2-cup glass measure; stir well to dissolve cornstarch. Cook (micro) on HI, 2 to 3 minutes or until mixture thickens. Stir in liqueur.

about 1¾ cups

When poultry drippings are not available, increase orange juice by 3 tablespoons. Orange Sauce makes a nice dessert sauce as well as poultry sauce.

LEMON BUTTER SAUCE

Cooking Time: 1½ to 2½ minutes

    ½ cup butter or margarine
    2 tablespoons lemon juice
    ⅛ teaspoon salt
    ⅛ teaspoon white pepper

Combine butter, lemon juice, salt, and pepper in 2-cup glass measure. Cook (micro) on HI, 1½ to 2½ minutes or until butter melts. Stir through.

⅔ cup

Serve hot over seafood or green vegetables.

CITRUS GLAZE

Cooking Time: 1½ to 2½ minutes

    ½ cup sugar
    1 egg, lightly beaten
      Juice of 1 lemon

Combine sugar, egg, and lemon juice in 2-cup glass measure; stir until well blended. Cook (micro) on 50, 1½ to 2½ minutes or until sauce thickens.

about ½ cup

Use to glaze Cornish hen, chicken, or duck.

Hot Bacon Sauce (right) with Salad

VERMONT SAUCE

Cooking Time: 1½ to 2 minutes

- ½ cup dark corn syrup
- 2 tablespoons brown sugar
- 1 tablespoon honey
- 1 tablespoon water
- ¼ teaspoon maple extract

Combine all ingredients in 2-cup glass measure; stir until blended. Cook (micro) on HI, 1½ to 2 minutes or until syrup boils.

about ¾ cup

HOT BACON SAUCE

Cooking Time: 3½ to 4½ minutes

- 3 tablespoons sugar
- 3 teaspoons cornstarch
- 6 tablespoons vinegar
- ¼ cup water
- 8 slices bacon, cooked, crumbled, fat reserved
- 2 green onions, chopped

Combine sugar, cornstarch, vinegar, water, and bacon fat in 1-cup glass measure. Cook (micro) on HI, 3½ to 4½ minutes or until sauce boils. Stir in bacon and green onions.

about 1½ cups

This is the classic dressing used in making hot spinach salads and potato salad. The salad pictured is a special one with purple kale and mandarin oranges added to the spinach. Let your imagination go in creating your own great salad ideas.

CLARIFIED BUTTER

Cooking Time: 3 minutes

- 1 cup butter

Place butter in 2-cup glass measure. Cook (micro) on 40, 3 minutes or until butter is completely melted and solids sink to bottom, leaving clear liquid at top.
   Skim off any foam and discard. Carefully pour liquid into jar through cheesecloth-lined strainer.

about ¼ cup

TART CRANBERRY SAUCE

Cooking Time: 6 to 7 minutes

- 3 cups fresh cranberries
- ⅓ cup water
- ½ cup sugar

Combine all ingredients in 2-quart microproof bowl. Cover with plastic wrap and cook (micro) on HI, 6 to 7 minutes or until berries pop. Let cool. Cover and refrigerate until ready to serve.

2 cups

STRAWBERRY SAUCE

Cooking Time: 4 to 6 minutes

> 1 **pint fresh strawberries, hulled**
> **and cut in half**
> ½ **cup sugar**
> 2 **tablespoons cornstarch**
> ½ **cup water**
> 1 **tablespoon lemon juice**

Combine strawberries, sugar, cornstarch, water, and lemon juice in 4-cup glass measure; stir. Cook (micro) on HI, 4 to 6 minutes or until mixture boils and is thick and clear, stirring twice during cooking time.

Chill. Serve over pound cake, vanilla pudding, custard, or in parfaits.

2½ cups

You may substitute 1 package (1 pound 4 ounces) frozen strawberries, thawed, for fresh strawberries. Replace water with ½ cup juice from drained berries.

LEMON SAUCE

Cooking Time: 3 minutes

> ⅔ **cup water**
> ⅓ **cup sugar**
> 2 **tablespoons cornstarch**
> 3 **tablespoons lemon juice**
> 1 **egg yolk**
> 1 **tablespoon butter or margarine**
> 1 **teaspoon grated lemon peel**
> ⅛ **teaspoon salt**
> **Yellow food coloring (optional)**

Combine all ingredients in 1-quart glass measure and blend well. Cook (micro) on HI, 3 minutes, stirring halfway through cooking time.

Stir briskly until thick and smooth. Serve over pound cake.

about 1 cup

Strawberry Sauce (left) with Cake

RUM CUSTARD SAUCE

Cooking Time: 9 to 11 minutes

- 1½ **cups milk**
- ½ **cup light cream**
- ⅓ **cup sugar**
- ⅛ **teaspoon salt**
- 3 **eggs, lightly beaten**
- 3 **tablespoons rum**

Combine milk, cream, sugar, and salt in 4-cup glass measure; stir. Cook (micro) on 70, 3 to 4 minutes or just until mixture boils.

Stir ½ cup milk mixture slowly into eggs, then add to remaining milk mixture and stir until blended. Cook (micro) on 50, 2 minutes. Stir.

Cook (micro) on 30, 4 to 5 minutes, stirring once every minute, until thickened.

Cool to room temperature. Stir in rum.

2½ cups

Serve with bread pudding, banana pudding, poached peaches, or poached pears.

CHOCO-PEANUT BUTTER SAUCE

Cooking Time: 2½ to 4 minutes

- 1 **square (1 ounce) unsweetened baking chocolate**
- ¼ **cup milk**
- 1 **cup sugar**
- ⅓ **cup peanut butter**
- ¼ **teaspoon vanilla**

Combine chocolate and milk in 4-cup glass measure. Cook (micro) on HI, 1½ to 2 minutes. Stir until mixture is smooth. Add sugar, and stir again.

Cook (micro) on HI, 1 to 2 minutes, or until mixture boils. Add peanut butter and vanilla; stir until blended.

1 cup

Serve hot or cold over ice cream, cake, or sliced bananas.

HOT FUDGE SAUCE

Cooking Time: 4 to 5 minutes

- 1 **cup sugar**
- 2 **squares (1 ounce each) unsweetened baking chocolate**
- ⅓ **cup milk**
- 3 **tablespoons light corn syrup**
- 1 **egg, beaten**
- 1 **teaspoon vanilla**

Combine all ingredients except vanilla in 4-cup glass measure. Cook (micro) on HI, 2 minutes or until chocolate just turns glossy. Stir.

Cook (micro) on 60, 2 to 3 minutes, stirring halfway through cooking time.

Blend in vanilla.

Let stand to cool slightly before serving.

1 cup

Serve over ice cream, chocolate cake, fresh fruit, or use as a fondue for dipping pound cake or fresh berries.

RASPBERRY SAUCE

Cooking Time: 5 minutes

- 1 **package (10 ounces) frozen raspberries**
- 1 **teaspoon cornstarch**
- 1 **tablespoon water**

Place raspberries in 1½-quart microproof bowl. Cook (micro) on HI, 3 minutes.

Break up slightly with wooden spoon. Dissolve cornstarch in water. Stir in berries. Cook (micro) on HI, 2 minutes or until mixture thickens and becomes clear.

Stir through several times before serving.

about 1½ cups

Basic Pie Crust (page 128) bakes by the convection method. The microwave method can also be used to prepare a variety of crumb crusts.

Quick breads, sweet rolls, muffins, coffeecakes, pies, and cookies are easy to prepare when you take advantage of the convection method. In addition, microwave speed can be teamed with convection browning and crisping to help you prepare a wide array of home-baked treats.

Selection of *microproof* and *heatproof* muffin rings, ring molds, cake dishes, cookie sheets, pie plates, and bundt pans is important when you bake with the micro/convection method. You may find you have the equipment you need — a glass pie plate, or other glass baking dishes. All of your heatproof conventional bakeware is ideal for the convection method.

ADAPTING RECIPES

The convection method is the starting point for conversion of your own bread, coffeecake, or muffin recipes. Remember that except for the increased efficiency of the fan-circulated hot air, this method is identical to your conventional oven. There are, however, occasions when the micro/convection method is appropriate. See for example our recipe for Chocolate Cake for Two (page 126). Use this and the many other fine recipes in this chapter as starting points for converting your own recipes for baking in your micro/convection oven. Also follow these guidelines for best baking results.

- To raise yeast dough, half fill a 2-cup glass measure with water. Place it in the oven and bring to a boil on (micro) HI, 3 to 3½ minutes. Place dough in oven next to water. Set Micro Power at "1" (lowest possible setting other than zero) and timer at 10 minutes. When timer beeps, leave dough in oven another 20 minutes, or until double in bulk.

- Fill paper-lined muffin cups only half full to allow for muffins rising higher than they do when baked in a conventional oven.

- When preparing yeast dough, use a glass measure and the temperature probe set at 120°F to heat liquids to the exact temperature needed to activate the yeast.

- If a baked item appears done to you, open door and check with tester or toothpick, just as you do in conventional cooking. Interrupting the cooking does not erase the remaining cooking time. Touch START to resume cooking.

- During cooking, some baked goods may begin to rise unevenly with the microwave method. When you notice this, open door and rotate dish about one-quarter turn. Uneven rising is seldom significant because many items are inverted onto a serving dish and the variation in rising disappears.

For baking with the microwave method, cake pans and muffin cups are filled only halfway, as microwave baking causes more rising than conventional baking.

GUIDE TO CONVENIENCE BREADS*

Food	Programming Method	Setting	First Cook Time	Second Cook Time	Special Notes
Buttermilk biscuits, refrigerated, 8 oz.	convec	follow package directions			Remove ceramic tray. Place wire rack in lower position. Preheat. Use cookie sheet or foil tray.
Caramel rolls, refrigerated, 11 oz.	convec	follow package directions			Remove ceramic tray. Place wire rack in upper position. Preheat. Use cookie sheet or foil tray.
Cinnamon rolls, refrigerated, 9½ oz.	convec	follow package directions			Remove ceramic tray. Place wire rack in upper position. Preheat. Use cookie sheet or foil tray.
Cornbread mix, 15 oz.	convec	follow package directions			Remove ceramic tray. Place wire rack in upper position. Preheat. Use 8-inch square heatproof baking dish. Rotate halfway through cooking time.
English muffins, waffles, frozen, (2)	micro	HI	½ - 1 min.		Place on paper towels.
Hamburger buns, hot dog buns, frozen, 1 lb.	micro	30	1 - 2 min.	1 - 2 min.	Place on paper plate or towels.
Muffin mix	micro or convec	follow package directions			Remove ceramic tray for convec. Place wire rack in upper position. Preheat.
Refrigerated crescent, butterflake, other rolls, 8 oz.	convec	380°	10 - 13 min.		Remove ceramic tray. Place wire rack in lower position. Preheat. Use cookie sheet or foil tray.
Sweet rolls, muffins, (4)	micro	80	35 - 45 sec.		Place on paper plate or towels. Add 15 seconds of cooking time if frozen.

*Due to the tremendous variety in convenience food products available, times given here should be used only as guidelines. We suggest you cook food for the shortest recommended time and then check for doneness. Be sure to check the package for microwave and oven (convec) instructions.

QUICK CRESCENT ROLLS

Cooking Time: 15 minutes

- **1 loaf (1 pound) frozen bread dough**
- **1 egg, lightly beaten**

Thaw and proof dough as directed for Bread From The Freezer (page 122).

Roll out dough in shape of round pie crust ¼-inch thick. Cut into 12, equal-sized wedges. Roll up wedges from wide end toward tip. Seal ends firmly. Place on greased baking sheet. Bend to form crescents. Cover with towel. Let stand in warm, draft-free area until doubled. Gently brush tops with egg.

Remove ceramic tray. Place wire rack in lower position of oven and preheat to 350°F.

Cook (convec) at 350°F, 15 minutes or until golden. Serve warm.

12 rolls

For cloverleaf rolls: Divide dough into 36 pieces and form each piece into equal-size balls. Place 3 balls in each cup of muffin pan. Cover with towel. Let stand in warm draft-free area until doubled. Gently brush tops with egg. Sprinkle with poppy seeds, if desired. Place wire rack in lower position of oven and preheat to 350°F. Cook (convec) at 350°F, 9 minutes or until golden.

For cinnamon rolls: Roll dough to form 8x12-inch rectangle. Brush dough with 2 tablespoons melted butter. Combine 2 teaspoons cinnamon, ½ cup sugar, and ¼ cup raisins. Sprinkle mixture over dough, reserving 2 tablespoons. Beginning with 12-inch side, roll tightly jelly-roll fashion. Cut dough into 12 slices. Place in lightly buttered 9-inch pie plate. Brush dough with 1 tablespoon melted butter and sprinkle with remaining cinnamon mixture. Cover with towel. Let stand in warm draft-free area until doubled. Place wire rack in lower position of oven and preheat to 350°F. Cook (convec) at 350°F, 15 minutes or until golden.

GUIDE TO CONVENIENCE CAKES AND PIES*

Food	Programming Method	Setting	Time	Special Notes
Bar cookies, brownie mix	convec	follow package directions		Remove ceramic tray. Place wire rack in upper position. Preheat. Use 8-inch baking pan. Rotate halfway through cooking time.
Cake, frozen 2- or 3-layer	micro	30	2½ - 3 min.	Remove from foil pan to plate. Watch carefully; frosting melts fast. Let stand 5 minutes.
Cake mix	convec	350°	30 min.	Remove ceramic tray. Place wire rack in upper position. Preheat. Use 8-inch round baking pan. Rotate halfway through cooking time.
Cheesecake, 17 - 19 oz.	micro	30	4 - 5 min.	Remove from foil pan to plate. Let stand 1 minute.
Coffeecake, whole frozen, 10 - 13 oz.	micro	80	1½ - 2 min.	Place on paper plate or towel.
Cookies, 16 oz.	convec	350°	10 - 12 min.	Remove ceramic tray. Place wire rack in upper position. Preheat. Use cookie sheet or foil tray.
Cupcakes, crumb cakes, (1 or 2)	micro	30	½ - 1 min.	Place on shallow microproof plate.
Doughnuts, (4)	micro	80	35 - 40 sec.	Place on paper plate or towel. Add 15 seconds if frozen.
Fruit pie, 2-crust, 9″, 2½ - 3 lbs.	convec	follow package directions		Remove ceramic tray. Place wire rack in upper position. Preheat. Rotate halfway through cooking time.
Pastry shell, frozen	convec	follow package directions		Remove ceramic tray. Place wire rack in lower position. Preheat. Rotate halfway through cooking time.
Pound cake, frozen, 10¾ oz.	micro	30	2 min.	Remove from foil pan to plate. Rotate once. Let stand 5 minutes.
Danish Pastry, refrigerated, 11 oz.	convec	follow package directions		Remove ceramic tray. Place wire rack in upper position. Preheat.

*Due to the tremendous variety of convenience food products available, times given here should be used only as guidelines. We suggest you cook food for the shortest recommended time and then check for doneness. Be sure to check the package for microwave and oven (convec) instructions.

BREAD FROM THE FREEZER

Cooking Time: 53 to 58 minutes

> 1 loaf (1 pound) frozen bread
>   dough
> 1 cup water
> 1 egg, lightly beaten
>   Poppy seeds, sesame seeds,
>   uncooked oatmeal

Place frozen dough in 8x5-inch greased microproof loaf pan or on microproof dish. Half fill 2-cup glass measure with water and cook (micro) on HI, 3 minutes or until boiling. Leaving cup of water in oven, place loaf pan in oven.

Cook (micro) on 1, 10 minutes (this is the lowest energy setting available).

Turn dough over and cook (micro) on 1, 10 minutes. Let dough stand in pan 45 to 60 minutes or until at least doubled in size. Dough may now be worked, if desired, and shaped into rolls or fitted into pizza pan.

To bake loaf, generously grease 8x5-inch metal loaf pan. Turn dough into pan. Cover with towel. Let stand in warm draft-free area until doubled.

Remove ceramic tray. Place wire rack in upper position of oven and preheat to 350°F.

Brush top of loaf with egg. Sprinkle with topping, if desired.

Cook (convec) at 350°F, 30 to 35 minutes, turning halfway through cooking time if loaf seems to be cooking unevenly. Place on cooling rack and cool before slicing.

1 loaf

You'll have especially good results if the dough has been stored properly before use. Watch for signs of freezer burn or partial thawing before purchasing frozen bread.

BRAIDED BREAD

Cooking Time: 35 minutes

> Dough for Homemade White Bread
>   (right)
> 1 egg yolk, beaten
>   Poppy seeds, sesame seeds, or
>   uncooked oatmeal

Prepare and proof dough as directed. Generously grease metal baking sheet. Divide dough equally into thirds. Roll each into cylinder about 9 inches long. Braid cylinders together. Transfer to prepared sheet Cover with towel. Let stand in warm draft-free area until doubled.

Remove ceramic tray. Place wire rack in upper position of oven and preheat to 350°F.

Brush top of loaf with egg yolk and sprinkle with topping. Cook (convec) at 350°F, 35 minutes, rotating dish halfway through cooking time. Let cool on wire rack before slicing.

1 loaf

HOMEMADE WHITE BREAD

Cooking Time: 1 hour 12 minutes

> 4 to 5 cups all-purpose flour,
>   divided
> 2 tablespoons sugar
> 1 package active dry yeast
> 1 teaspoon salt
> 1 cup water
> ¾ cup milk
> 2 tablespoons butter or margarine
> 1 egg, room temperature

Combine 2 cups of the flour, sugar, yeast, and salt in large mixing bowl; set aside.

Place water, milk, and butter in 1-quart glass measure. Cook (micro) on HI, 2 minutes.

Add milk mixture to dry ingredients and beat with electric mixer on low speed for 30 seconds. Add egg and beat on high speed 3 minutes. Stir in enough of the remaining flour to make a soft dough.

Turn out onto lightly floured board and knead 7 minutes or until smooth and elastic. Cover dough and let stand 20 minutes.

Grease and flour four 3¼x5½x2¼-inch pans. Divide dough into 4 pieces, shape into small loaves, and place in pans. Cover with greased waxed paper. Let rise in warm, draft-free area 30 to 45 minutes, or until doubled in bulk.

Remove ceramic tray. Place wire rack in upper position of oven and preheat to 350°F.

Place 2 loaves in oven. Cook (convec), 35 minutes, rotating pans halfway through cooking time. Repeat with remaining loaves.

4 loaves

GARLIC BREAD

Cooking Time: 5 to 6 minutes

- 1 **loaf (1 pound) French or sourdough bread**
- ½ **cup mayonnaise**
- ¼ **cup grated Parmesan cheese**
- 3 **cloves garlic, minced or 1 teaspoon garlic powder Paprika**

Remove ceramic tray. Place wire rack in lower position of oven and preheat to 450°F.

Set foil or aluminum pan underneath rack to catch drippings. Slice bread in half lengthwise. Set halves cut side up on work surface.

Combine mayonnaise, cheese, and garlic in small bowl; blend well. Spread mixture generously over each half of loaf. Sprinkle lightly with paprika. Set bread directly on wire rack.

Cook (convec) at 450°F, 5 to 6 minutes or until topping is hot and bubbly.

8 servings

For variation, sprinkle with shredded mozzarella cheese before cooking.

BUTTERMILK CORN BREAD

Cooking Time: 20 to 25 minutes

- 1½ **cups cornmeal**
- 1½ **cups all-purpose flour**
- ½ **cup sugar**
- 1 **tablespoon baking powder**
- ⅛ **teaspoon salt**
- 1 **cup buttermilk**
- 2 **eggs, lightly beaten**
- ½ **cup vegetable oil**
- 1 **can (7 ounces) kernel corn with green peppers and pimiento, drained**

Remove ceramic tray. Place wire rack in upper position of oven and preheat to 350°F.

Lightly grease 9-inch square metal baking pan. Set aside.

Combine cornmeal, flour, sugar, baking powder, and salt; stir well. Mix buttermilk, eggs, and oil in separate bowl until well blended. Gradually add dry ingredients, stirring just until moistened. Stir in corn. Pour into prepared pan.

Cook (convec) at 350°F, 20 to 25 minutes, rotating halfway through cooking time.

Remove from oven and cool in pan 5 minutes. Cut into 3-inch squares and serve warm or at room temperature.

9 squares

ONION-CHEESE LOAF

Cooking Time: 35 minutes

- **Dough for Homemade White Bread (page 122)**
- ½ **cup instant minced onion**
- ½ **cup warm water**
- 1 **cup (4 ounces) shredded Cheddar cheese**
- 2 **tablespoons poppy seed, divided**
- 1 **tablespoon melted butter or margarine**

Prepare and proof dough through first step, as directed. Generously grease 9x5-inch loaf pan. Combine onion and warm water in 1-cup measure. Let stand 5 minutes to soften; drain well. Set aside 1½ tablespoons onion. Mix remaining onion with cheese and 1 tablespoon poppy seed in small bowl. Roll dough to form 6x12-inch rectangle. Sprinkle with cheese mixture and roll up. Shape into loaf and seal edge. Transfer to prepared pan. Cover with towel. Let stand in warm draft-free area until doubled.

Remove ceramic tray. Place wire rack in upper position of oven and preheat to 350°F.

Brush top of loaf with melted butter. Sprinkle with remaining onion and poppy seed.

Cook (convec) at 350°F, 35 minutes, rotating pan halfway through cooking time. Let cool on rack before slicing.

1 loaf

CINNAMON LOAF

Cooking Time: 30 minutes

> **Dough for Homemade White Bread (page 122)**
> ¼ **cup melted butter or margarine, divided**
> ½ **cup firmly-packed light brown sugar**
> ¼ **cup cinnamon**

Prepare and proof dough as directed. Grease 8x5-inch metal loaf pan; set aside.

Roll dough out into 8x12-inch rectangle. Brush with all but 2 teaspoons melted butter. Sprinkle brown sugar and cinnamon evenly over top. Carefully roll up into cylinder; shape into loaf. Transfer to prepared pan. Cover with greased waxed paper and let stand in warm draft-free area until doubled.

Remove ceramic tray. Place wire rack in upper position of oven and preheat to 350°F.

Brush top of loaf with remaining melted butter.

Cook (convec) at 350°F, 30 minutes, rotating halfway through cooking time if loaf seems to be cooking unevenly. Turn loaf out onto rack to cool. Serve warm.

1 loaf

PUMPKIN NUT RING

Cooking Time: 14 to 16 minutes

> 1 **cup canned pumpkin**
> 1 **cup sugar**
> ½ **cup buttermilk**
> ⅓ **cup vegetable oil**
> 2 **eggs, well beaten**
> 1⅔ **cups all-purpose flour**
> 1 **cup chopped walnuts**
> 2 **teaspoons pumpkin pie spice**
> 1 **teaspoon baking soda**
> ½ **teaspoon salt**

Place wire rack in lower position of oven and preheat to 350°F.

Generously grease 8-cup microproof and heat-proof ring mold. Combine pumpkin, sugar, buttermilk, oil, and eggs in large bowl and blend well. In another bowl, combine flour, nuts, spice, baking soda, and salt; mix thoroughly. Add to pumpkin mixture and beat well. Pour into prepared mold.

Cook (micro/convec) at 350°F, 14 to 16 minutes, or until bread appears set and begins to shrink away from sides of mold. Let cool slightly before removing from mold.

8 to 10 servings

CARROT CAKE

Cooking Time: 22 to 25 minutes

> 1½ **cups all-purpose flour**
> 2 **teaspoons cinnamon**
> 1½ **teaspoons baking soda**
> 1 **teaspoon nutmeg**
> ½ **teaspoon salt**
> 3 **cups grated carrots**
> 1½ **cups sugar**
> 1 **cup vegetable oil**
> 1 **cup chopped walnuts**
> 3 **eggs, beaten**

Frosting:
> 1 **package (8 ounces) cream cheese, softened**
> ½ **cup butter or margarine, softened**
> 2 **teaspoons vanilla**
> 3 **cups confectioners sugar, sifted**
> ¼ **cup chopped walnuts**

Place rack in upper position of oven and preheat to 350°F. Generously grease 12-cup microproof and heatproof bundt pan.

Sift together flour, cinnamon, baking soda, nutmeg, and salt in medium bowl. In large bowl, combine carrots, sugar, oil, nuts, and eggs. Add dry ingredients to carrot mixture and mix thoroughly. Turn into prepared pan.

Cook (micro/convec) at 350°F, 22 to 25 minutes, rotating pan halfway through cooking time. Let stand in oven 5 minutes. Turn out of pan onto serving platter.

Beat cheese and butter in large bowl. Add vanilla; mix well. Gradually beat in sugar. Fold in nuts. Frost cake. Sprinkle with additional chopped walnuts, if desired.

8 to 10 servings

BUTTERMILK BRAN MUFFINS

Cooking Time: 7 to 8 minutes

     2 cups whole wheat flour
    1½ cups whole unprocessed bran
         or bran bud cereal
     2 tablespoons sugar
    1½ teaspoons baking soda
     ¼ teaspoon salt
     2 cups buttermilk
     ½ cup molasses
     1 egg, lightly beaten
     3 tablespoons butter or margarine,
         melted
     1 cup chopped nuts

Remove ceramic tray. Place wire rack in upper position of oven and preheat to 370°F.

Prepare microproof and heatproof muffin pan with paper liners. Combine flour, cereal, sugar, baking soda, and salt in medium bowl. In large bowl, combine buttermilk, molasses, egg, and butter. Add dry ingredients and mix thoroughly. Fold in nuts. Fill liners ¾ full.

Cook (micro/convec) at 370°F, 3½ to 4 minutes per batch or until muffins test done.

12 muffins

ANGEL FOOD CAKE

Cooking Time: 35 to 40 minutes

     1 package (16 ounces) Angel
         Food Cake mix
         Raspberry Sauce (page 118)

Remove ceramic tray. Preheat oven to 350°F.

Prepare cake according to package directions. Pour batter into ungreased 10-inch metal tube pan. Place pan on oven bottom.

Cook (convec) at 350°F, 35 to 40 minutes, rotating pan halfway through cooking time. Invert pan onto cooling rack.

Let cake cool completely before removing from pan. Serve with Raspberry Sauce.

10 servings

PARTY CAKE

Cooking Time: 31 minutes

     2 cups all-purpose flour
    1¼ cups sugar
    3½ teaspoons baking powder
     1 teaspoon salt
     ¼ cup butter or margarine,
         softened
     ¼ cup vegetable shortening
     1 cup milk
    1½ teaspoons vanilla
     3 eggs
Frosting:
     ⅓ cup butter or margarine,
         softened
     3 cups confectioners sugar
     2 tablespoons milk
     1 tablespoon maraschino cherry
         juice
     1 teaspoon vanilla
     5 drops red food color
     8 maraschino cherries, drained
         and chopped

Remove ceramic tray. Place wire rack in lower position of oven and preheat to 350°F.

Grease and flour 13x9-inch microproof and heatproof baking dish, shaking out excess flour. Combine flour, sugar, baking powder, and salt in large bowl. Add all remaining ingredients except frosting and beat well. Pour into prepared dish.

Cook (convec) at 350°F, 25 minutes, rotating dish halfway through cooking time.

Cook (micro/convec) at 350°F, 6 minutes. Let stand in oven 5 minutes. Remove from oven and let cool.

Combine butter and sugar, blending thoroughly. Add milk, cherry juice, vanilla, and food color; mix until smooth. Stir in chopped cherries. Spread frosting over top. Cut into squares and serve.

16 to 20 servings

If you want to make a two-layer frosted cake, a browned appearance may not be important to you. You can prepare this cake by using microwave only. Pour batter in two 8-inch round microproof cake dishes. Cook each layer separately as follows: cook (micro) on 50, 8 minutes. Rotate pan ¼ turn and cook (micro) on HI, 1 to 2 minutes or until done. Turn out onto cooling rack. Cook second layer.

CHOCOLATE CAKE FOR TWO

Cooking Time: 8 to 10 minutes

- ¾ cup all-purpose flour
- ¼ cup cocoa
- ½ teaspoon baking soda
- ⅛ teaspoon salt
- ¼ cup butter or margarine
- ½ cup sugar
- 1 egg
- ⅓ cup milk
- ½ teaspoon vanilla
- ¼ cup chopped nuts

Place wire rack in upper position of oven and preheat to 350°F.

Grease 1-quart shallow microproof and heatproof casserole.

Combine flour, cocoa, baking soda, and salt in small bowl; mix well. Set aside.

Combine butter and sugar, blending thoroughly. Add egg and beat until smooth. Add milk to butter and egg mixture alternately with dry ingredients. Blend vanilla into batter. Fold in nuts. Spoon into prepared casserole.

Cook (micro/convec) at 350°F, 4 minutes. Rotate casserole and continue to cook (micro/convec) at 350°F, 4 to 6 minutes or until cake tests done.

Serve with ice cream and hot fudge sauce.

2 servings

PINEAPPLE PRALINE UPSIDE-DOWN CAKE

Cooking Time: 31 minutes

- ¼ cup butter or margarine
- ½ cup firmly-packed brown sugar
- 6 slices canned pineapple, well drained
- ¼ cup pecan halves
- 6 maraschino cherries
- 1¼ cups all-purpose flour
- 1 cup sugar
- 1 teaspoon baking powder
- ¾ cup milk
- ⅓ cup melted butter or margarine
- 1 egg, lightly beaten
- 1 teaspoon vanilla

Place ¼ cup butter in 9-inch round microproof and heatproof dish. Cook (micro) on HI, 1 minute.

Remove ceramic tray. Place wire rack in lower position of oven and preheat to 350°F.

Spread brown sugar evenly over bottom of dish. Place 1 pineapple slice in center. Surround with remaining slices. Arrange pecans around pineapple, rounded side down. Put cherry in center of each pineapple slice. Set aside.

Combine flour, sugar, and baking powder in large bowl. In another bowl, combine milk, ⅓ cup melted butter, egg, and vanilla. Add to flour mixture and blend thoroughly. Carefully pour batter into dish.

Cook (convec) at 350°F, 20 minutes, rotating dish halfway through cooking time.

Continue to cook (micro/convec) at 350°F, 10 minutes.

Remove from oven and let cool. Invert onto platter. Cut into wedges and serve.

8 servings

LEMON CHIFFON CAKE

Cooking Time: 35 to 40 minutes

- 2 cups all-purpose flour
- 1½ cups sugar
- 1 tablespoon baking powder
- ½ teaspoon salt
- ½ cup vegetable oil
- ½ cup cold water
- ¼ cup fresh lemon juice
- 6 egg yolks
- 2 tablespoons grated lemon peel
- 9 egg whites
- ½ teaspoon cream of tartar

Remove ceramic tray. Preheat oven to 350°F.

Combine flour, sugar, baking powder, and salt in large bowl. Make indentation in center. Add oil, water, lemon juice, egg yolks, and lemon peel, and stir until smooth.

In another large bowl, beat egg whites until foamy. Add cream of tartar and continue beating until stiff peaks form. Stir ¼ of egg yolk mixture into whites. Gently fold in remaining egg yolk mixture and blend thoroughly. Turn into ungreased 10-inch metal tube pan. Place pan on oven bottom.

Cook (convec) at 350°F, 35 to 40 minutes, rotating pan halfway through cooking time. If additional browning is desired, let stand in the oven an additional 5 minutes.

Invert onto rack and let cool completely.

8 servings

Frost with your favorite glaze.

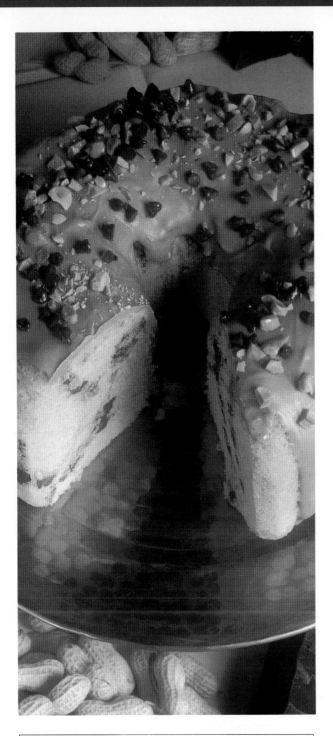

Peanutty Chocolate Cake (right)

PEANUTTY CHOCOLATE CAKE

Cooking Time: 15 minutes

  1 **package (18 ounces) yellow cake mix**
  ½ **cup creamy peanut butter**
  4 **large eggs**
  ¾ **cup water**
  ⅓ **cup vegetable oil**
  1 **cup chopped unsalted peanuts, divided**
  1 **cup semisweet chocolate morsels, divided**
    Caramel Glaze (below)

Place wire rack in lower position of oven and preheat to 350°F.

Combine cake mix, peanut butter, eggs, water, and oil in large bowl. Beat on medium speed for 3 minutes. Pour one-third of the batter into 12-cup microproof and heatproof bundt pan. Sprinkle one-third cup each of the peanuts and chocolate morsels over the batter. Pour another one-third of the batter carefully over peanuts and chocolate morsels. Sprinkle one-third cup each of the peanuts and chocolate morsels over batter. Repeat with remaining batter, peanuts, and chocolate morsels.

Cook (micro/convec) at 350°F, 15 minutes, rotating pan halfway through cooking time.

Let stand 15 minutes. Turn out of pan onto serving platter. Spoon warm Caramel Glaze over cake and let cool completely.

8 to 10 servings

CARAMEL GLAZE

Cooking Time: 3½ minutes

  2 **tablespoons butter or margarine**
  ¾ **cup firmly packed brown sugar**
  1 **tablespoon cornstarch**
  ⅛ **teaspoon salt**
  ¼ **cup milk or whipping cream**
  1 **teaspoon vanilla extract**

Place butter in 2-quart microproof bowl. Cook (micro) on HI, 1 minute.

Stir in brown sugar, cornstarch, and salt. Gradually add milk, stirring to blend. Cook (micro) on HI, 2½ minutes. Stir in vanilla.

about 1¼ cups

PECAN PIE

Cooking Time: 13 minutes

- ¼ **cup butter or margarine**
- 3 **eggs, well beaten**
- 1 **cup sugar**
- ¾ **cup light corn syrup**
- 2 **cups pecan halves**
- 1 **teaspoon vanilla**
- 1 **prebaked Basic Pie Crust (right)**

Place butter in 1-quart microproof bowl. Cook (micro) on HI, 1 minute.

Place wire rack in lower position of oven and preheat to 350°F.

Combine eggs, sugar, corn syrup, pecans, and vanilla in medium bowl; blend well. Turn mixture into crust. Cook (micro/convec) at 350°F, 12 minutes.

Let stand in oven 5 to 10 minutes. Cool on rack 15 to 20 minutes before serving.

8 servings

DEEP DISH CRANAPPLE PIE

Cooking Time: 50 minutes

- 1¼ **cups sugar**
- ½ **cup all-purpose flour**
- 8 **to 9 tart green apples, peeled,**
  cored, and sliced (about 4 cups)
- 2 **cups fresh or frozen cranberries**
- 2 **tablespoons butter or margarine**
  Pastry for Basic Pie Crust (right)
- 1 **egg white mixed with 1 teaspoon**
  water (optional)

Remove ceramic tray. Place wire rack in lower position of oven and preheat to 400°F.

Combine sugar and flour in small bowl; blend well. Alternate layers of apples, cranberries, and sugar mixture in 8-inch square heatproof baking dish, beginning and ending with apples. Dot with butter.

On lightly floured surface, roll dough out into 9-inch square. Fold dough in half, set over fruit and unfold. Press against edge of dish. Cut slits in top to allow steam to escape. Brush crust with egg mixture.

Cook (convec) at 400°F, 50 minutes. Serve warm.

8 to 10 servings

Whenever you have pastry dough left over, remember Grandma's trick. Roll out dough; brush with egg white mixture; sprinkle with sugar and cinnamon. Arrange on cookie sheet. Set on wire rack. Cook (convec) at 420°F or until cookie-crisp. Break into pieces as quick-energy finger food.

BASIC PIE CRUST

Cooking Time: 12 minutes

- 1 **cup all-purpose flour**
- ½ **teaspoon salt**
- ⅓ **cup shortening**
- 2 **to 3 tablespoons cold water**
- 1 **egg, lightly beaten**

Remove ceramic tray. Place wire rack in lower position of oven and preheat to 420°F.

Mix flour and salt in medium bowl. Cut in shortening, using pastry blender or 2 knives, until mixture resembles coarse meal. Stir in water, 1 tablespoon at a time, until flour is moistened. Shape dough into ball, then flatten on lightly floured surface. Roll dough into circle about ¼-inch thick and 2 inches larger in diameter than 9-inch microproof and heatproof pie plate or quiche dish. Fit into pie plate and trim, leaving ½-inch overlap. Turn excess dough under to form rolled rim. Flute edges. Pierce crust with fork and brush crust with beaten egg.

Cook (convec) at 420°F, 12 minutes, rotating plate halfway through cooking time. Let cool.

One 9-inch pie crust

For two-crust pie or 2 one-crust pie shells: Double each ingredient except egg white. Mix as directed. Divide dough in half. For two shells, prepare and cook separately as directed above. For two-crust pie, roll out one half and cook as directed above. Fill as directed in specific recipe. Roll out second half of dough and finish according to recipe directions.

If you are preparing a pie shell for a pie that is cooked by convection only, or for a pie requiring no cooking once the filling is added, you may use a metal pie plate.

APPLE PIE

Cooking Time: 45 minutes

    **Pastry for Basic Pie Crust
        two-crust pie (page 128)**
¾　**cup sugar**
¼　**cup all-purpose flour**
¾　**teaspoon cinnamon**
¼　**teaspoon nutmeg**
⅛　**teaspoon salt**
8　**medium-size tart green apples,
        peeled, cored, and thinly sliced**
2　**tablespoons butter or margarine**
1　**egg white, lightly beaten**

Remove ceramic tray. Place wire rack in lower position of oven and preheat to 400°F. Bake bottom pie crust according to directions on page 128.

Combine sugar, flour, cinnamon, nutmeg, and salt in large bowl; mix well. Add apples and toss until coated. Spoon apples into prebaked crust. Dot with butter. Brush rim of crust with egg white. Roll out uncooked dough to thickness of ⅛ inch and drape over fruit. Press edges of pastry together with fork to seal. Cut slits in top crust to allow steam to escape. Brush top with remaining egg white.

Cook (convec) at 400°F, 45 minutes. Let cool 5 to 10 minutes before serving.

8 servings

PUMPKIN PIE

Cooking Time: 40 minutes

1½　**cups canned or cooked
        pumpkin**
1　**cup half and half**
½　**cup firmly-packed brown sugar**
2　**eggs, beaten**
1　**tablespoon all-purpose flour**
1　**teaspoon cinnamon**
¼　**teaspoon ginger**
¼　**teaspoon nutmeg**
¼　**teaspoon salt**
⅛　**teaspoon ground cloves**
1　**prebaked Basic Pie Crust
        (page 128)**

Remove ceramic tray. Place wire rack in lower position of oven and preheat to 350°F.

In large bowl, combine all ingredients except pie crust; blend thoroughly. Pour into pie crust.

Cook (convec) at 350°F, 40 minutes. Let stand in oven 5 minutes before serving.

8 servings

BLACK BOTTOM PIE

Cooking Time: 7 to 7¾ minutes

¼　**cup water**
2　**squares (1 ounce each) unsweetened
        baking chocolate**
2　**cups half and half**
4　**eggs, separated**
¾　**cup sugar, divided**
3　**tablespoons cornstarch**
2　**teaspoons vanilla**
1　**prebaked Basic Pie Crust
        (page 128)**
2　**tablespoons milk**
1　**envelope unflavored gelatin**
2　**teaspoons dark rum or 1 teaspoon
        rum extract**
¼　**teaspoon cream of tartar**
    Shaved chocolate

Combine water and chocolate in small microproof bowl. Cook (micro) on HI, 1 minute or until chocolate is shiny. Stir through until chocolate is completely melted. Set aside to cool.

Place half and half in 2-cup glass measure. Cook (micro) on HI, 1½ minutes. In small bowl, beat egg yolks until pale yellow. Stir into half and half. Mix ½ cup of the sugar with cornstarch and blend into half and half.

Cook (micro) on HI, 2 minutes. Stir through several times and continue to cook (micro) on HI, 2 to 2½ minutes or until mixture has thickened, stirring every 30 seconds. Blend in vanilla. Add 1 cup custard to melted chocolate and blend well. Pour chocolate mixture into pie crust and refrigerate.

Combine milk and gelatin in 1-cup glass measure. Cook (micro) on HI, 30 to 45 seconds. Stir through several times until dissolved. Blend into remaining custard. Stir in rum. In large bowl, beat egg whites with cream of tartar until foamy. Gradually add remaining sugar, beating constantly until stiff peaks form. Stir one-fourth of the custard into egg whites. Gently fold in remaining custard. Spoon into crust. Sprinkle with shaved chocolate. Refrigerate until serving time.

8 to 10 servings

Apple Pie (page 129),
Strawberry Rhubarb Pie (below),
Perfect Lemon Meringue Pie (right)

STRAWBERRY RHUBARB PIE

Cooking Time: 60 minutes

⅔ **cup sugar**
3 **tablespoons cornstarch**
2 **cups unpeeled rhubarb, diced**
2 **cups fresh strawberries, hulled**
Pastry for Basic Pie Crust,
2-crust pie (page 128)

Remove ceramic tray. Place wire rack in upper position of oven and preheat to 450°F.

Combine sugar and cornstarch in large bowl; stir until well mixed. Add rhubarb and strawberries; stir until fruit is coated with sugar mixture.

Divide pastry dough in half. Roll out one of the halves into 12-inch circle. Gently fit dough into 9-inch pie plate. Roll out remaining dough into 12-inch circle and cut into ½-inch lattice strips. Pour fruit filling into pie shell. Weave lattice strips over top, pressing ends of strips to bottom crust to seal. Flute edges.

Cook (convec) 450°F, 10 minutes. Rotate pie.

Cook (convec) 350°F, 45 minutes. Let stand in oven 5 minutes. Let cool 10 to 20 minutes before serving.

6 to 8 servings

PERFECT LEMON MERINGUE PIE

Cooking Time: 10 to 13 minutes

⅓ **cup cornstarch**
½ **cup cold water**
1¾ **cups sugar, divided**
1 **cup hot water**
¼ **teaspoon salt**
5 **eggs, separated**
2 **tablespoons butter or margarine**
½ **cup fresh lemon juice**
2 **tablespoons finely grated**
lemon peel
1 **prebaked Basic Pie Crust**
(page 128)
¼ **teaspoon cream of tartar**
½ **teaspoon vanilla**

In 2-quart microproof bowl, dissolve cornstarch in cold water. Add 1¼ cups sugar, hot water, and salt; blend well. Cover and cook (micro) on HI, 6 to 7 minutes or until mixture is thick and clear, stirring occasionally.

In another bowl, beat egg yolks until thick. Beat gradually into cornstarch mixture. Cook (micro) on HI, 2 minutes. Add butter; stir until melted. Blend in lemon juice and peel. Pour into crust. Set aside to cool slightly.

Remove ceramic tray. Place wire rack in lower position of oven and preheat to 450°F.

In large bowl, beat egg whites and cream of tartar until foamy. Gradually beat in remaining sugar until whites are stiff and glossy. Blend in vanilla. Spread over cooled filling, sealing to edges.

Cook (convec) at 450°F, 2 to 4 minutes or until meringue is lightly brown. Let cool to room temperature before serving.

6 to 8 servings

CHOCOLATE CHIP COOKIES

Cooking Time: 40 to 48 minutes

- 1 **cup butter or margarine,
    room temperature**
- ¾ **cup sugar**
- ¾ **cup firmly-packed brown sugar**
- 2 **eggs**
- 1½ **teaspoons vanilla**
- 2½ **cups all-purpose flour**
- 2 **cups semisweet chocolate morsels**
- 1 **cup chopped walnuts**
- 1 **teaspoon baking soda**
- 1 **teaspoon salt**

Remove ceramic tray. Place wire rack in upper position of oven and preheat to 330°F.

Combine butter, sugars, eggs, and vanilla in large bowl and beat until smooth. Stir in remaining ingredients, and blend well. Drop dough by rounded tablespoonfuls onto ungreased baking sheet, spacing for 24 cookies.

Cook (convec) at 330°F, 10 to 12 minutes. Let cool on wire rack. Repeat with remaining dough.

Store in airtight container.

about 4 dozen

PEANUT BUTTER COOKIES

Cooking Time: 24 to 26 minutes

- 1 **cup natural-style crunchy
    peanut butter**
- ½ **cup butter or margarine,
    softened**
- ½ **cup firmly-packed
    brown sugar**
- ½ **cup sugar**
- 1 **egg, lightly beaten**
- 1 **teaspoon vanilla**
- 1½ **cups all-purpose flour**
- ¾ **teaspoon baking soda**
- ¼ **teaspoon salt**

Remove ceramic tray. Place wire rack in upper position of oven and preheat to 350°F.

Lightly grease aluminum or metal baking sheet. Combine peanut butter, butter, sugars, egg, and vanilla in large bowl and beat until smooth. Blend in flour, baking soda, and salt. Shape dough into 30 one-inch balls.

Arrange 15 balls on prepared sheet, spacing 3 inches apart. Flatten into 2-inch rounds using fork in a criss-cross pattern.

Cook (convec) at 350°F, 12 to 13 minutes or until cookies are lightly browned and appear done.

Repeat with remaining dough.

30 cookies

CHOCOLATE NUT BROWNIES

Cooking Time: 7 to 8 minutes

- 2 **squares (1 ounce each) unsweetened
    baking chocolate**
- ½ **cup unsalted butter**
- 2 **eggs, lightly beaten**
- ¾ **cup sugar**
- ½ **cup all-purpose flour**
- 1 **tablespoon vanilla**
- 1 **teaspoon baking powder**
- ¼ **teaspoon salt**
- 1 **cup coarsely chopped walnuts**
- 1 **cup semisweet chocolate morsels**
    Confectioners sugar

Combine chocolate and butter in 2-quart glass measure. Cook (micro) on HI, 1 to 2 minutes or until butter is melted. Stir to blend and finish melting chocolate.

Add eggs, sugar, flour, vanilla, baking powder, and salt to chocolate mixture; blend well. Stir in nuts and chocolate morsels.

Turn into 9-inch deep dish microproof pie plate or quiche dish. Cook (micro) on HI, 6 minutes. Sprinkle with confectioners sugar. Brownies will firm as they cool.

Let cool completely before cutting into wedges.

about 10 brownies

Use a conventional candy thermometer outside the oven or the traditional cold water test when making candy with the microwave method of your oven. Microwave thermometers for use inside the oven are also available.

Making candy is easy and fun with the microwave method of your micro/convection oven. No troublesome double boiler is needed. Scorching is virtually obsolete. And you need no special utensils, except perhaps a conventional candy thermometer for use outside the oven. Microwave thermometers that can be used right in the oven are also available, if you find yourself unable to resist the allure of cooking candies frequently in your oven. The temperature probe, incidentally, cannot be used, as cooking temperatures for making candy are beyond its range.

If you're looking for something light and refreshing, you'll find fruit prepared in your micro/convection oven a true delight. Not only does it hold its color, but its texture and flavor are exceptional, as virtually no moisture is lost when the microwave method is used.

All in all, your micro/convection oven is an outstanding cooking appliance for preparing a host of candy, fruit, and pudding recipes. In this chapter, we hope you will find the sampling sweet enough to whet your appetite.

Chocolate tends to hold its shape when melted by the microwave method. Don't overcook. It will lose its shape as soon as it is stirred.

ADAPTING RECIPES

The best procedure for adapting your own candy, pudding, and fruit recipes is to find a recipe in this chapter that is similar to the one you want to try.

■ Also be aware that it's important to compare the amount of any water, milk, or fruit juice called for in the conventional recipe to the amount called for by a recipe in this chapter. You may need to reduce such liquids a bit because evaporation is so minimal when the microwave method is used.

■ You can substitute fruits rather freely for those in the following recipes. You will get better results if you select fruit of uniform size when cooking whole fruit.

■ One final note: Baked custards should be removed from the oven when centers are just about firm. They will set as they cool.

GUIDE TO CONVENIENCE DESSERTS*

Food	Programming Method	Setting	Time	Special Notes
Fruit, frozen, 10 oz.	micro	HI	5 to 5½ min.	Slit pouch. Place on microproof plate. Flex pouch halfway through cooking time to mix.
Fruit turnover, 12½ oz.	convec	follow package directions		Remove ceramic tray. Place wire rack in lower position. Preheat. Use metal baking sheet.
Pudding and pie filling mix, 3¼ oz.	micro	HI	6½ to 7 min.	Follow package directions. Stir every 3 minutes.

*Due to the tremendous variety in convenience food products available, times given here should be used only as guidelines. We suggest you cook food for the shortest recommended time and then check for doneness. Be sure to check the package for microwave and oven (convec) instructions.

SUGAR-GLAZED WALNUTS

Cooking Time: 8 to 8½ minutes

> **2 cups walnut halves**
> **¾ cup sugar**
> **¼ cup water**

Grease baking sheet.

Combine all ingredients in 1-quart glass measure. Cook (micro) on HI, 8 to 8½ minutes or until sugar has caramelized.

Stir through several times. Pour out onto prepared sheet. Let cool completely. Store in airtight container.

2 cups

ALMOND BARK

Cooking Time: 6½ to 8½ minutes

> **1 cup whole blanched almonds**
> **1 teaspoon butter or margarine**
> **1 pound white chocolate**

Place almonds and butter in 9-inch glass pie plate. Cook (micro) on HI, 4 to 5½ minutes or until almonds are toasted, stirring twice during cooking time. Set aside.

Place chocolate in large microproof mixing bowl. Cook (micro) on HI, 2½ to 3 minutes or until softened.

Stir in almonds and pour onto waxed paper-lined baking sheet. Spread to desired thickness and refrigerate until set. Break into pieces.

1½ pounds

CREME CARAMEL

Cooking Time: 17 to 19 minutes

> **⅔ cup sugar, divided**
> **2 tablespoons water**
> **2 cups milk**
> **3 eggs**
> **3 egg yolks**
> **1 teaspoon vanilla**

Combine ⅓ cup of the sugar and water in 1½-quart microproof and heatproof brioche dish or fluted dish; blend well. Cook (micro) on HI, 4 minutes or just until mixture turns brown. Carefully tilt dish to coat bottom and sides evenly. Set aside.

Place milk in 1-quart glass measure. Cook (micro) on HI, 3 to 4 minutes or until scalded, watching closely so milk does not boil.

Place wire rack in lower position of oven and preheat to 350°F.

Combine eggs, egg yolks, remaining sugar, and vanilla in 2-quart bowl; beat until well blended. Slowly add hot milk, beating constantly until smooth. Pour into caramelized dish.

Cook (micro/convec) at 350°F, 10 to 11 minutes or until custard begins to shrink away from sides of dish.

Let cool completely. Run knife along edge of custard before turning out of mold onto smaller platter.

6 to 8 servings

PEANUT BRITTLE

Cooking Time: 10 to 11 minutes

- 1 cup sugar
- ½ cup corn syrup
- 1¾ to 2 cups raw peanuts
- 1 teaspoon butter or margarine
- 1 teaspoon vanilla
- 1 teaspoon baking soda

Generously grease baking sheet.

Combine sugar and corn syrup in 2-quart glass measure. Cook (micro) on HI, 4 minutes.

Stir in peanuts using wooden spoon. Continue to cook (micro) on HI, 4 minutes.

Stir in butter and vanilla. Cook (micro) on HI, 2 to 3 minutes or until microwave candy thermometer registers 300°F (or until small amount of mixture separates into hard and brittle threads when dropped into very cold water).

Blend in baking soda and stir until mixture is light and foamy. Pour onto prepared sheet, spreading quickly to edges using back of wooden spoon. As candy cools, stretch into thin sheet using palms of hands.

Let cool completely. Break into pieces. Store in airtight container in cool place.

about 1 pound

FRESH FRUIT COMPOTE

Cooking Time: 10 minutes

- 2 peaches, quartered and pitted
- 4 apricots, halved and pitted
- 10 cherries, halved and pitted
- 1 small bunch seedless grapes

Combine all ingredients in 1-quart microproof bowl.

Cook (micro) on HI 10 minutes or until juices bubble. Gently stir through several times.

4 servings

RICE PUDDING

Cooking Time: 42 to 43 minutes

- ½ cup long grain rice
- 1 cup water
- ½ cup sugar
- 1 tablespoon cornstarch
- ⅛ teaspoon salt
- 3 egg yolks, lightly beaten
- 2½ cups milk
- ½ cup raisins

Topping:
- ¼ cup sugar
- 1 teaspoon cinnamon
- 3 egg whites
- ½ teaspoon cream of tartar

Combine rice and water in 1-quart microproof bowl. Cover with plastic wrap and cook (micro) on HI, 8 minutes. Cover and set aside.

Remove ceramic tray. Place wire rack in lower position of oven and preheat to 350°F.

Combine sugar, cornstarch, and salt in medium bowl. Add egg yolks and milk to cornstarch mixture. Beat with rotary beater until smooth. Stir in rice and raisins. Pour into ungreased 2-quart casserole. Cook (micro/convec) at 350°F, 30 minutes. Remove from oven. Set aside.

Preheat oven to 400°F. Combine sugar and cinnamon in small bowl. Combine egg whites and cream of tartar; beat until foamy. Add cinnamon mixture, 1 tablespoon at a time, beating until stiff peaks form. Spread evenly over pudding, sealing edges. Cook (convec) at 400°F, 4 to 5 minutes or until meringue is lightly golden. Serve warm.

6 to 8 servings

CHOCOLATE-DIPPED FRUIT AND NUTS

Cooking Time: 2 to 3 minutes

- ½ **pound dark chocolate**
- ½ **pound white chocolate**
- ½ **pound milk chocolate**
  Assorted fruit and nuts

Place dark chocolate in 4-cup glass measure. Cook (micro) on HI, 2 to 3 minutes or just until chocolate appears shiny. (Chocolate will hold its shape.) Stir until smooth.

Dip fruit and nuts into chocolate, one at a time, leaving part of fruit uncovered. Place in candy cups or on waxed paper while chocolate sets.

Repeat with remaining white chocolate, milk chocolate, fruit, and nuts.

about 70

FLUFFY TAPIOCA

Cooking Time: 11 minutes

- 2 **cups milk**
- 3 **tablespoons quick-cooking tapioca**
- 5 **tablespoons sugar, divided**
- 1 **egg, separated**
- ⅛ **teaspoon salt**
- 1 **teaspoon vanilla**

Combine milk, tapioca, 3 tablespoons of the sugar, egg yolk, and salt in 2-quart glass measure; mix well. Let stand 5 minutes. Cook (micro) on HI, 6 minutes or until boiling.

Beat with wire whisk until well blended. Cook (micro) on 70, 5 minutes.

Stir in vanilla. Beat egg white in small bowl until foamy. Gradually add remaining sugar and continue to beat until soft peaks form. Gradually stir egg white into cooked tapioca. Stir until just blended.

5 servings

Top with your favorite sauce.

Chocolate-Dipped Fruit and Nuts (left)

BAKED APPLES

Cooking Time: 4½ to 5½ minutes

- 2 **large baking apples**
- 2 **teaspoons butter or margarine**
- ¼ **cup firmly packed brown sugar**
- ¼ **teaspoon cinnamon**
- 2 **teaspoons golden raisins**

Core apples and slit skin around middle of each apple to prevent skin from bursting. Place apples in small individual microproof baking dishes.

Place butter in 1-cup glass measure. Cook (micro) on 50, 30 seconds. Stir sugar, cinnamon, and raisins into melted butter. Fill each apple with sugar mixture. Cover each dish with plastic wrap. Cook (micro) on HI, 4 to 5 minutes or until tender.

2 servings

Jumbo Meatballs (page 63), Cauliflower Gratinéed Noreen (page 108), and Fresh Fruit Compote (page 134) are illustrated in correct whole meal cooking positions.

A Barbecued Chicken whole meal features the micro/convection method as a special technique.

The capability for cooking entire meals in your micro/convection oven is a true convenience. For those times when speed is of the essence, special techniques have been developed which allow you to cook two or three dishes simultaneously. Because speed is so important, these "whole meal" cooking techniques use the microwave method on HI, although you can also choose the micro/convection or convection methods when appropriate. For example, you can return food, cooked whole-meal on microwave, to the oven for top browning by the convection method.

For the most successful whole meal, it is important to consider the placement of dishes in the oven, the size and shape of microproof containers, the kinds of food you select, the timing, and other factors. This chapter presents step-by-step instructions that will enable you to plan your own whole meals. These basic tips will assist you in achieving whole meal success.

- Since microwaves enter from the top of the oven, they are primarily absorbed by food placed on the wire rack; a smaller amount reaches the ceramic tray. Place quick-cooking food on the ceramic tray; longer cooking food on the wire rack.

- An ideal procedure for whole meal cooking is to place two foods with similar cooking times on the wire rack and one food with a shorter cooking time on the ceramic tray. Similarly, one dense food with a long cooking time is placed on the wire rack while one or two short cooking dishes are placed on the ceramic tray.

- If all foods require the same cooking time, reverse the location of dishes in the oven halfway through cooking period.

IMPORTANT GUIDELINES FOR TIMING
(Applicable to microwave-only whole meal technique.)

☐ If all foods take 15 minutes or less individually, add cooking times together and program the menu for the total time.

☐ If all foods take 16 to 35 minutes individually, add cooking times together and subtract about 5 minutes.

☐ If any one food takes over 35 minutes, all the food can be cooked in the time suggested for food taking the longest time.

- While the wire rack can be used in either the lower or upper position, the upper position is generally best. Use the lower position whenever greater capacity is needed on the top, or when using micro/convection or convection if the height or thickness of the food places it too close to the heat source.

- The chart on this page presents six main dishes appearing in the recipe chapters and 12 complementary dishes. There's no need to keep with the particular combinations we've provided. Simply choose any dish from column "A" and complete the menu with any from "B" and "C".

- Follow this step-by-step procedure when cooking "whole meal":

  1. Choose your menu.

  2. Review the individual recipe. You may find that an ingredient should be prepared ahead. (Onion is often sautéed as a separate step, for example.)

  3. Check the dishes to be sure they fit in the oven together. Change the size and type of dish as required. Be sure you are always thinking microproof.

  4. Place dishes in oven with densest or most slowly cooking food on the wire rack and less dense or more quickly cooking food on the ceramic tray.

  5. Apply the rules from Important Guidelines for Timing (page 136). The approximate cooking time for each recipe follows the recipe title in the menu chart.

  6. Most recipes in whole meal cooking are best stirred or rearranged halfway through cooking time.

Now let's take a step-by-step look at the Jumbo Meatballs menu as a demonstration:

(A) Jumbo Meatballs
     (page 63) . . . . 15 minutes
(B) Cauliflower Gratinéed Noreen
     (page 108) . . . . 8½ minutes
(C) Fresh Fruit Compote
     (page 134) . . . . 10 minutes

Applying the first rule from Important Guidelines for Timing, as all three foods require 15 minutes of cooking time or less, we find that this meal will cook in 33½ minutes.

1. Prepare the Jumbo Meatballs according to the recipe; omit the cornstarch and water at this time. Cover and set aside.

2. Prepare Cauliflower Gratinéed Noreen according to the recipe, omitting tomatoes, Parmesan cheese, Swiss cheese, and bread crumbs at this time. Cover.

3. Prepare Fresh Fruit Compote.

MICROWAVE WHOLE MEAL MENUS

A	B	C
One-Step Lasagna (37) (page 100)	Brussels Sprouts with garlic (8) (page 108)	Parmesan Potatoes (9) (page 110)
Oriental Beef (15) (page 65)	Green Beans Amandine (9) (page 107)	Chocolate Nut Brownies (8) (page 131)
Jumbo Meatballs (15) (page 63)	Cauliflower Gratinéed Noreen (8½) (page 108)	Fresh Fruit Compote (10) (page 134)
Chicken Marengo (50) (page 77)	Stuffed Tomatoes (16) (page 107)	Simple Herbed Rice (14) (page 98)
Scallops au Vin (8½) (page 85)	Cheese Broccoli (8½) (page 108)	Baked Apples (5½) (page 135)
Shrimp Veracruz (13) (page 86)	Carrots, 10 oz., Frozen (9) (page 102)	Fluffy Tapioca (11) (page 135)

4. Place wire rack in upper position of oven. Place meatballs on rack. Place cauliflower dish and fruit dish on ceramic tray. Cook (micro) on HI, 33½ minutes. After 10 minutes, stir cornstarch and water into meatballs and cover. Add tomatoes, bread crumbs, and cheeses to cauliflower.

5. Remove dishes from oven and let stand, covered, on heat-resistant surface for 5 minutes.

SPECIAL TECHNIQUES

This special method cooks (micro) on HI, for approximately half of the cooking time and micro/convection for the remainder. Microwave speed gets it started; micro/convection provides texture and browning. The menu:

Barbecued Chicken
  (page 76) .... 30 minutes
Baked Potatoes, 4 medium,
  (Guide, page 103) ....,...... 14 minutes
Broccoli, 1 pound,
  (Guide, page 102) .... 9 minutes

1. Timing and method for this menu has been tested for you.

2. Note dish selection and placement in the photograph.

3. Prepare chicken according to directions in the recipe.

4. Scrub and pierce potatoes. Set aside. Clean broccoli, split stems, arrange in 1½-quart microproof casserole. Cover with plastic wrap.

5. Place chicken, potatoes, and broccoli in oven. Cook (micro) on HI, 25 minutes.

6. Remove chicken and broccoli from oven. Let broccoli stand, covered. Remove wire rack. Rearrange potatoes, placing two at extreme left and two at extreme right. Preheat oven to 330°F.

7. Turn chicken over (skin side up). Brush liberally with Barbecue Sauce. Return to preheated 330°F oven, place chicken dish between potatoes. Cook, (micro/convec) at 330°F, 20 to 25 minutes or until chicken is done.

8. Remove chicken from oven; let stand. Check potatoes for doneness; they may need a few additional minutes of cooking (micro) on HI.

9. Discard plastic wrap from broccoli. Return to oven and cook (micro) on HI, 1 to 1½ minutes or until hot. Serve.

As you continue to enjoy micro/convection cooking, you'll discover many time-saving whole meal techniques on your own. Simply remember that the convection method is similar to your conventional oven, that the microwave method uses the "Guidelines" on page 136; and that the micro/convection method gives convection benefits with microwave energy.

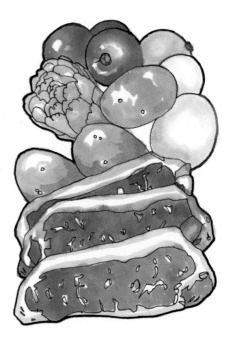